THEIR OTHER SIDE

BY THE SAME AUTHOR

A Circular Journey
Rome Burning, poetry
Umbertina, a novel
*The Dream Book: An Anthology of Writings by Italian American
    Women*
Love in the Middle Ages, a novel
More Italian Hours, short fiction
Festa: Recipes & Recollections of Italian Holidays
Aldus and His Dream Book
Chiaroscuro: Essays of Identity

THEIR OTHER SIDE

Six American Women and the Lure of Italy

Helen Barolini

Fordham University Press NEW YORK 2006

Copyright © 2006 Fordham University Press

Library of Congress Cataloging-in-Publication Data

Barolini, Helen, 1925–
    Their other side : six American women and the lure of Italy / Helen Barolini.—1st ed.
        p. cm.
    Includes bibliographical references and index.
    ISBN-13: 978-0-8232-2629-0 (cloth : alk. paper)
    ISBN-10: 0-8232-2629-8 (cloth : alk. paper)
    1. American literature—Women authors—Italian influences.
2. Italy—In literature.   3. Women authors, American—Homes and haunts—Italy.   4. Women authors, American—19th century—Biography.
5. Women authors, American—20th century—Biography.   I. Title.
PS159.I8B37   2006
820.9'3245—dc22   2006029458

Printed in the United States of America
08 07 06   5 4 3 2 1
First edition

CONTENTS

ACKNOWLEDGMENTS

Excerpts from this work appeared in shortened versions in these publications: "The American Discovery of Italy" in *Americans in Modern Italy*, a special issue of *The Cesare Barbieri Courier* (n.d.); "The Italian Side of Emily Dickinson," *The Virginia Quarterly Review*, Summer 1994; "The Shadowy Lady of the Street of Dark Shops," *The Virginia Quarterly Review*, Spring 1998; and "Mabel Dodge Luhan: In Search of a Personal South," *Southwest Review*, Summer 1998.

In gathering material for this book, I had access to the resources of various libraries and historical societies either through personal visits or correspondence, as well as encounters with many interested and helpful people along the way. It is a pleasure to thank the staff of my nearest and most-used libraries at Sarah Lawrence College and Mercy College—they provided unfailing and friendly assistance. I gratefully record the personal attention of Prof. Maria Xenia Wells and the Harry Ranson Humanities Research Center at the University of Texas at Austin, and the Fondazione Caetani in Rome which gave permission to examine the correspondence of Marguerite Caetani. I also would like to personally thank the Rare Book and Manuscript Collection Library at Columbia University, the Fitzwilliam Museum in Cambridge, England, the Houghton Library at Harvard University, the Massachusetts Historical Society in Boston, the Special Collections at Georgetown University Library, the Special Collections at the Syracuse University Library, the University of Washington Libraries, the Public Library of New London, Connecticut, the manuscript collection of Beinecke Library at Yale University, and the Centro Studi Americani in Rome. While in Rome during a residency at the American Academy, I benefited both from access to its fine library and from its central location on the Janiculum Hill, so close to landmarks associated with the 1848–49 Rome Revolution in which Margaret Fuller participated.

I am indebted to the following persons for providing me with texts, introductions, information, or illuminating insights that helped in the development of my work: Walter Arnold, Cristina Anzilotti, Michael Biddle, Frances Biddle, Schuyler Chapin, Bell Gale Chevigny, Tea Codignola, Spencer Evans, Sally Fitzgerald, Denis Greenan, Mary Greenly, Lu Hamlin, Shirley Herbert, Esme Howard, James Laughlin, Suzanna Lengyel, Lauro Marchetti, Ben Morreale, Becca Mudge, Frank Nigro, Benedetta Origo, Florence Phillips, Giuliano Prezzolini, Laurance and Isabel Roberts, Eugene Walter, Maria Xenia Wells, and Sheila Wertheimer. And a special word of appreciation to Kenneth Maddox, Art Historian at the Cropsey-Newington Foundation, Hastings-on-Hudson, New York, for directing me to Maria Cropsey's correspondence. And, most of all, my gratitude to Robert Oppedisano for his belief in, and support of, my work. Thank you, all!

Acknowledgments of illustrative material:

Cover illustration: *Venetian Scene* by James McNeill Whistler, from New Britain Museum of Art, New Britain, Connecticut.

Daguerreotype of Margaret Fuller, the Schlesinger Library, Radcliffe Institute, Harvard University.

Daguerreotype of Emily Dickinson, Amherst College Archives and Special Collections, by permission of Trustees of Amherst College.

Photograph of Constance Fenimore Woolson, call no. pfMS Am 1094, Box 1, by permission of the Houghton Library, Harvard University.

Photograph of Mabel Dodge Luhan, Yale Collection of American Literature, Beinecke Rare Book and Manuscript Library.

Photographs of Marguerite Caetani, Harry Ransom Humanities Research Center, the University of Texas at Austin.

Drawing of Iris Origo by Augustus John, by permission of Benedetta Origo.

PROLOGUE

"Write me a Prologue," Bottom instructs his fellow players in *A Midsummer's Night Dream* to center the audience's attention on what was coming. And so, by way of prologue, let me establish how I connected to Italy and why I set about to probe its legendary appeal to other women who came, saw, and were conquered.

For me, as a girl in upstate New York, there was always the notion of the "otherness" of Italy. My imagination was easily and early fed through a favorite book, *A Child's History of the World*, with its accounts of ancient Rome and classical mythology, the Church and saints, and the glories of the Renaissance; then there were the sounds of Italian opera from Texaco's Saturday afternoon broadcasts from the Met; and, once, when I was ten or so, the mysterious appearance of a grave, mannerly, older Italian relative visiting from Rome who hinted at a different, somehow more distinguished life from what I knew in Syracuse, New York.

My Italian American family had conflicted feelings toward Italy. Given the prejudicial attitudes toward Italian Americans prevalent in the 1930s, when film gangsters with Italian names became an accepted stereotype, when the buffoon figure of Il Duce ruled a fascist Italy, and when the Second World War made that country an enemy of the United States, my parents' leeriness was understandable. Still, I clung to my feeling that there had to be something more, something wonderful to be discovered in the land my grandparents had left. Although I had no language with which to speak to them, I knew that they had come from Calabria and

Sicily—the area my *Child's History of the World* called Magna Graecia, seat of a once-rich and flourishing ancient civilization. I felt connected to that place and to that history.

In high-school Latin class I read as prophecy the line that Virgil gives Aeneas to send him on his way from Dido: *Italiam non sponte sequor* (I am pushed toward Italy and it is beyond my control).[1] Italy as destination was lodged in my imagination and in my future. In addition to its familiar tourist lures and that which inspired past centuries of Anglo-American travelers to Italy—that is, the sense of arriving at the archetypal motherland from which Western civilization flowed—the Italy I sought would be a homecoming to my own heritage.

I was a twenty-two year old post-graduate student at the University of London assigned by my hometown Syracuse newspaper to write about the first postwar Olympics then being held in England. I knew that having gotten that far, I would soon cross my own Rubicon and find my way to Rome. In the fall of 1948, I arrived in the austerity of a bombed-out, defeated and depleted Italy. My arrival coincided with a new era: Italy was about to be rediscovered by Americans. Italian-American ex-GIs were returning to Italy to study, to write, to experience for the first time an Italy that was something more than the backward, impoverished place their fathers or grandfathers had fled from, or the ridiculed regime lampooned in Charlie Chaplin's 1940 film *The Great Dictator*. Alfred Kazin describes in his autobiography that when he got a Guggenheim Fellowship just after the war, he headed for Italy and the "ship to Genoa was full of Italian Americans carrying over radios, electric appliances, cigarettes by the trunkful. There were also anti-Fascist intellectuals returning from their long American exile."[2] Despite the ravages of war apparent throughout the country, in a chapter entitled "Never Had It So Good," Kazin asserts that to "an American writer seeing it for the first time, Italy was heaven." I, too, was there to experience Italy's renewal and resurgence. All the pent-up creativity suppressed in two decades of dictatorship burgeoned in political reformation, social programs, innovative architecture, cinema, painting, and literature.

I lived with Italian families while learning the language and continued to send off my "Letters from Abroad" to the *Syracuse Herald-Journal.* But what really happened was the birth of my creative life: plunged into a different culture and language, I found myself all the more reconnected to my origins and I wrote my first poetry in an intense rediscovery of my mother tongue. In a sonnet called "Umbria," which would give the title to my first collection, I extolled the experience of simply being there.

Only now have I learned that my early sojourn in Italy had much in common with that of another American a century earlier: in 1860, twenty-two year old Henry Adams, scion of the illustrious family of presidents and scholars, was also in Europe for the first time, sending dispatches to the *Boston Courier.* It seems we both used the same stratagem of writing a newspaper column to justify to a skeptical family that staying on in Italy was worthwhile, that something was being produced. Adams's words about being in Rome could have been mine: "gradually after . . . [the] first few days I became drunken with excitement. . . . [the happiest days] known ever to have existed."[3] A little less than a decade later, another New England Henry, of the distinguished James family, would arrive in Italy on his own passionate pilgrimage.

For me, Italy was even more than what it was for Adams and James since it was part of who I was. Yet I have often wondered at the flood of literature about Italy written by Americans of every background except Italian. So much of the writing on Italy is not from that long-lost or strayed child of the motherland, the Italian American, but from those who have adopted Italy as a generous foster mother. In fact, until the mid-twentieth century it was not Italian Americans but the Anglo-descended elite and intellectuals

of American society who went to Italy, who formed Dante societies at home, who learned Italian and translated the *Divine Com-
edy*. It was the fashion to love Italy as Henry Adams recorded in
his autobiography when he noted that his sister Louisa, "like all
good Americans and English, was hotly Italian."[4]

In Italy I studied; I began to speak the language; I met and
married Antonio Barolini, an Italian journalist and poet, and with
him started a home and a family. I translated his work and began
to write my own. I wrote of D. H. Lawrence in Sicily, James Joyce
in Trieste, and of the contrast between the views of Mrs. John
Ruskin and Margaret Fuller conceiving a unified Italian nation.
I began to think of other women whose imagination had succumbed to the lure of Italy.

Who has not dreamed of going forth to meet the unknown in
some new land, and thus in oneself? It is a timeless way of finding oneself. Long before it was my dream, it was that of English
gentlemen: Roger Ascham's 1570 *The Scholemaster* compares the
English gentlemen's trip to Italy to Ulysses' voyage, saying that in
addition to the wit and wisdom to be gained, travelers must be-
ware the temptress Circe, who could make a "plaine English man,
a right Italian." The danger of the Italianizing influence perdured
into the Victorian age where it was personified in Anthony Trol-
lope's *Barchester Towers* in the character Madeleine Stanhope,
called "the Italian woman," since in marriage she had become
Signora Neroni and thus "an Italianized charmer" with "an easy,
free, voluptuous manner" that put the Englishmen who called on
her into a tailspin.

Still, Italy was assumed to be a man's dream. "Italia! O Italia!
Thou who hast / the fatal gift of beauty" declaimed Lord Byron
on his romantic pilgrimage. And Robert Browning's words are
engraved in the Venetian palazzo where he died: "Open my heart,
and you will see / Graved inside of it, Italy."

"Life is very pleasant in Italy if you are a man," E. M. Forster noted in his novel, *Where Angels Fear to Tread*, emphasizing its restrictions on the English woman Lilia, who, enamored of Italy and a much younger Italian, finds marriage to him and life there a dreadful mistake. Lilia is depicted as the typical English lady tourist, a "privileged maniac, on solitary walks" in the lushness of Italy; having sunk into remorse over her foolish marriage she finally dies in childbirth, the Victorian fate of choice for erring women. Recently I read a description of a college course entitled "A Literary Journey to Italy," which offered Italy through the fiction and journals of male travelers and writers only. Yet women wrote of Italy as well, and they describe an Italy that was not for men only. The Italian experience opened also for women a freedom of creative expression and lifestyle they had not enjoyed at home.

On this point the 1807 publication of French intellectual and writer Germaine de Staël's novel *Corinne, ou l'Italie* is especially significant; it was the first work to fix Italy as the land where the imaginative woman "of genius" could come into her own. Mme. de Staël's feminist novel swept through Europe and reached across the Atlantic. *Corinne*, the story of an Anglo-Italian woman who favors her Italian side in order to realize her poetic nature and is acclaimed in triumph in Italy, introduced nineteenth-century women like Margaret Fuller, Emily Dickinson, and Elizabeth Barrett Browning to the notion that "Italy" and its gifts were as equally accessible to them as to any man.

In different ways and to different degrees, to many thinking women Italy came to signify release from some control, a transforming catalyst (liberating or dooming, but always powerfully shaping) from what Dickinson called the Swissness of lives—so clockwork, orderly, and bland as the national cheese. In fact it was Dickinson who, though never having got to Italy, provided the springboard for this present work through her prescient poem

#80 which begins: "Our lives are Swiss," then declaims that over the Alps "Italy stands the other side." Therin lies, for me, the impetus to uncover what Italy meant in the lives of certain gifted women. Italy held all the lures to tempt American women: pageantry; natural beauties; the presence of history, art, and the humanities; a pleasing climate and a tolerant people plus reprieve from the habits and restrictions of home.

My representative women are the nineteenth-century authors Margaret Fuller, Emily Dickinson, and Constance Fenimore Woolson; and, in the twentieth century, Mabel Dodge Luhan, Marguerite Caetani, and Iris Origo. There is range to the six women's lives: from Emily Dickinson's Amherst cloister and the tragedies of Margaret Fuller and Constance Woolson through the glittering, kaleidoscopic existence of Mabel Dodge Luhan, to the contemplative and productive lives of the two titled women, Principessa Caetani and Marchesa Origo. From backgrounds of wealth, family position, and advantage came Luhan, Origo, and Caetani; Fuller and Woolson worked at their writing to support themselves. Some women were prophetic, revolutionary, or even shocking in their views; others were traditionalists. Luhan married four times, Dickinson and Woolson, never. Three married Italian noblemen and had children in Italy. Two made their homes in Italy, two returned to the States, one never decided, and Emily Dickinson stayed put at home, traveling Italy in imaginative verse. And their total production of books (dozens) far exceeds the total among them for children (seven). All the women were remarkable, and their lives encompass many aspects of the human condition: struggle, ease, repression, fulfillment, glory, failure, heartbreak, heroism, scandalous marriage, blessed singleness, tragic death, suicide, ordinariness, notoriety, sexual adventuring, solitary reclusiveness, child-bearing out of wedlock, and revolutionary activism. Their lives crossed with many prominent artists, writers, statesmen, revolutionaries, and travelers.

In her memoir, *Images and Shadows*, Iris Origo wrote, "every life is not only a string of events: it is also a myth."[5] And, in fact, these women have the mythic about them. Several became fictional characters in other writers' works: Margaret Fuller as the doomed Zenobia in Hawthorne's *Blithedale Romance*; Constance Woolson is very much the May Bartram of Henry James's *cri de coeur, The Beast in the Jungle* and, all too bitterly ironic, the partial model for Milly Theale who, in *Wings of the Dove*, goes to Venice to die; Mabel Dodge Luhan is Edith Dale in Carl Van Vechten's *Peter Whiffle*; and Emily Dickinson's legend created the play "The Belle of Amherst."

Italy was *incantesimo*—an enchantment—that had long drawn travelers to a dream of Arcadia. Italy proved the ideal locus for Ovid's tales of metamorphosis, and for personal metamorphoses, as shown in Henry James's early novel *Roderick Hudson*, wherein, by the very shock of contrast, Italy provided the American the tools of self-transformation. Italy was a goal and a magnet precisely because it was so much the Other, so much the place against which those of the New World could weigh and measure a personal idea of Self.

As a married resident of Rome, I lived just around the corner from 60 Piazza Barberini where Margaret Fuller had taken lodgings in 1848; I often frequented the British Council library, located just up the street in the same Palazzo Malduro where an American writer, Anne Brewster, had resided from 1868 to 1889. Brewster was a single woman from Philadelphia who, after a first trip to Italy in 1857, returned to spend the rest of her life writing accounts of Italy for American publications. Part of Italy's appeal for Americans was how well and how cheaply they could live there; for a pittance agreeable servants and enormous *palazzi* were available in Rome, Florence, or Venice. Anne Brewster, hard-pressed to earn a living in the states, had fourteen rooms in the center of Rome for $35.00 a month and could travel about, live well, accumulate antiquities and a first-rate library (bequeathed to the Library Company of Philadelphia), and have the services of a cook, manservant, and maid on her minimal income.[6]

Living in Rome, I became more and more aware of the shades of the illustrious who had walked the same streets, seen the same sights, been filled with the same wonder. The terrace of our apartment overlooked the gardens of Palazzo Barberini where Milton, a guest of Cardinal Barberini, had strolled during his visit to Rome in 1639. Each day, while walking my youngest child to her convent school at Trinità del Monte, I glimpsed the corner room overlooking the Spanish Steps in the area known in Roman dialect as *er Ghetto der gli Ingresi*—the English ghetto—where Keats spent the last month of his pitifully short life flinging from the window the wretched food sent up to him before finally crying out to his companion Joseph Severn, the most magnanimous of friends, "Severn . . . I am dying."[7] Always I was aware of those earlier visitors in the same streets and among the same sights—the "ghosts" who haunted Henry James's reevocation of expatriate life in Rome. Even fictional characters like Daisy Miller or Hawthorne's faun-like Donatello seemed real and very present in my Roman life.

In marginal ways, my path crossed with some of the women of this study when my husband became a contributor to Marguerite Caetani's *Botteghe Oscure* and I met Iris Origo in the home of Roman friends. Those like Constance Woolson I came to know of later, in the wake of the feminist movement when so many women notable in their own times, then forgotten, were restored to us. And I met others, as when Antonio was the U.S. correspondent for the Italian paper *La Stampa* and we lived for a period in

Croton-on-Hudson outside New York City where Mabel Dodge once resided and was still a talked-about presence.

I began to wonder about the difference between an Anglo-American sensibility to Italy and my own; is there, in fact, a difference? Henry James made a distinction between native Italian writers and those not native to Italy who wrote about it. He maintained that the Italian fiction of non-Italian writers would inevitably be "second-rate and imperfect." He referred pointedly to the Roman setting of Hawthorne's *A Marble Faun* and judged that a writer cannot project himself into an atmosphere which has not been transmitted to him through inheritance. James could not, at that time, consider Italian American writers because there were none. Of course, he then went on to contradict himself completely by writing his own Italian-based novels—*Portrait of a Lady, Princess Casamassima,* and *Daisy Miller.*

The earliest American visitors to Italy were looking to the past for the lessons of history and institutions in the very stones and ruins of ancient Rome. Blended with their awe were feelings of moral uplift through the positive comparison of their new republic to the monarchies of Europe. They enjoyed a certainty of divine guidance for their new enterprise for, fine as it was, Italy was sunk under the burden of its past while America was the land of the bright future. Though some stayed, most Americans returned home with their patriotism and pride reinforced.

Italy became a mindset, an abstraction of notions, a way of being—at its best the beloved Mother of Western civilization, but otherwise a torment, an enigma, a problem to the conscience of those reared with a rigorous "Northern" temperament, as opposed to a relaxed "Southern" one. "Oh, for a beaker full of the warm South," declaimed Keats in his "Ode to a Nightingale" and he meant not only Southern clime but also the more sensual and genial attitudes toward life associated with the Mediterranean people. It is clear in references from American and other Grand Tour travelers, from the poets and seekers, that Italy stood for the artistic freedom, creativity, and humanistic values they felt lacking at home. Italy was still the land where the natural virtues had not been completely overlaid with the materialistic ones of industrialized and mechanized societies. What Americans got from two centuries of Italian visits was often written up by the travelers themselves.

In 1933 appeared a pioneering work, *Come gli Americani scoprirono l'Italia* (*How Americans Discovered Italy*), by Giuseppe Prezzolini, Italian critic and author, curmudgeon supreme, and dear friend. Prezzolini, a professor emeritus when Antonio and I first met him in his aerie above Columbia University, died in 1982 in Switzerland, a centenarian still actively writing his column for an Italian paper. His innovative, sometimes querulous work on Americans in Italy defended Italy's honor against the harsher criticisms of some of those he documented and whom he, in turn, decried as puritan zealots. To them he proudly countered that Italy's most precious gift was to teach the art of living, what Henry James called the "sweetest impression of life."

Prezzolini's book was forerunner to Van Wyck Brooks's extremely popular 1958 *Dream of Arcadia: American Writers and Artists in Italy, 1760–1915,* which he dedicated to art connoisseur Bernard Berenson. The two books cover much of the same ground but are quite different in tone. Prezzolini documented all types of Americans abroad from 1750 to 1850, citing diaries, letters, and the memoirs of travelers who were honeymooners, consular officials, merchants, historians, the rich and leisured on tour, physicians and lawyers, commodores and sailors, clergymen and scientists as well as artists. Brooks instead limited himself to the impact Italy made on American artists and writers up to World War I. Characteristically, in the 1971 reissue of his book, Prezzolini mentioned *Dream of Arcadia* with praise but redefined the dream: for the majority of the earliest American travelers, he contended, the country was a huge museum, a kind of attic to rummage in to discover the past; for closet hedonists it was the invitation to explore sin. As Henry James had once noted, "the whip in the sky" of Puritan conscience was delightfully absent in Italy.

Yet Brooks's title is apt; it echoes Thomas Cole's *Dream of Arcadia,* a well-known painting of an idealized Italian landscape which had the effect of at once directing and summarizing the earliest American travelers' expectation of Italy. Cole's 1838 canvas captured the vision that Italy represented romantically: in the foreground a bucolic grove with rustic people redolent of long-ago sturdy virtues and pastoral simplicity while the requisite homage to antiquity is captured in the background by a light-bathed classic temple sited on a distant hill. For those with a romantic imagination and the wherewithal to travel, Italy was indeed mythologized as Arcadia in painting and in prose and, *pace* Prezzolini, Brooks's title is remarkably apt in identifying the nineteenth-century American view of Italy as a dreamland of classical resonance. Hawthorne, among others, was haunted by the idea of Arcadia/Eden and the loss of innocence that marked mankind's Fall. The well-traveled Julia Ward Howe, who was in Italy in 1843 on her honeymoon, extended it long enough to give birth to her first child in Rome, naming her Julia Romana. Howe, a reformer, writer, and lecturer at home, remained an enthusiastic visitor to Italy and could write home contentedly from Rome in 1877, "*Et ego in Arcadia vixi,*" claiming even then, with no hint of irony, to have lived in Arcadia.[8] But that was true not only for Americans—when Goethe visited Rome he fantasized his burial in the Protestant Cemetery as a "*sepolchro* in Arcadia."

Arcadia persists as durable archetypal memory even now. On a visit to contemporary American artist Cy Twombly's studio in a venerable *palazzo* in the historic center of old Rome, I noted a photo of him in an exhibition brochure where he appeared as "artist in Arcadia." Sitting braced against one of a few low, leafy trees among which sheep grazed in the rolling countryside outside Rome, a pensive Twombly idles in the dappled shade and looks out to a distant horizon as if to the romantic expanse of the Roman *campagna* which so shaped the imagination of nineteenth-century American artists; consciously or not, the photo has all the attributes of the artistic picturesqueness for which Americans flocked (a sheepish pun) to Italy. One of the works of Twombly's long career in Rome, where he is noted for his fine calligraphic evocation of Roman myth and memory in elegant contemporary graffiti, is called *Arcadia*. Some myths do not so much die as become recast. Or, can we also read into the American travelers' enthusiasm for the scenes of shepherds and goatherds and picturesque peasant girls in costume an underlying condescension toward the backward bumpkin? For many nineteenth-century American travelers, including the fastidious Henry James and the well-heeled Edith Wharton, the notion seems to have been: let them be picturesque for our amusement as long as we have our conveniences. More recently, William Vance's magisterial two-volume work, *America's Rome*, has taken up the story of the eternal city and the Americans who there sought, as if from the Cumaean Sibyl, the questions and answers of life. The lure of Italy goes on apace.

It is almost a litany of "Let me count the ways . . ." to run through the attractions Italy once had for the American visitor. New World citizens could both honor the spiritual birthplace of their government and also learn valuable lessons from the visible remains of fallen Rome. For artists, Italy was the great teacher, the source of both material and inspiration; for idealists, it was a place layered by millennia of history and of people's experience and therefore made tolerant of the human condition and human foibles. As Mme. de Staël's fictional character Corinne observed of the Italians, "they are used to others coming to their land to see and to observe. And whether out of pride or indifference, they do not try to impress their opinions on anyone."[9] For all travelers, if the voyage of discovery took at all, it was one of self-discovery. The great lessons of travel, Laurence Sterne had declared some centuries earlier, were *savoir vivre* and to know oneself. From the testimony left in diaries, travel journals, and letters from abroad it becomes apparent that Italy was uniquely equipped to be the enabler, the catalyst, the opportunity to reach into the soul of the traveler from the New World and to discover the hidden self. Italy's "otherness" represented another side not only geographically, but almost as if one could pass through the looking glass into some other reality.

My interest in feminist issues drew me to the women I profile in this book, for each seemed to ask: How, as a woman, do I live my fullest? How do I make my own life significant? Fuller was adamant and courageous about a woman's right to decide her own destiny; Dickinson chose her art above everything else; Woolson's is the familiar story of a conflicted woman of talent who feels her qualities as woman and artist are glossed over, never fully recognized, and who literally dies of it. Mabel Dodge (later Luhan) is an entertainment—a frankly bizarre and intriguing personality who avidly aspired to embody her times. Iris Origo, born to privilege, overcame the conventions associated with it to become a writer-scholar and countrywoman, partnering an experimental farm with her husband. Princess Caetani exemplifies that rare American woman who married into European nobility without becoming a mere society fixture, but, on the contrary, emerged as an important catalyst in contemporary literature. This is a telling of their individual stories wherein the lives of all were enriched by the double cultural legacy they enjoyed. The commonality in background that connects them is their American parentage. Together they provide multiple perspectives on the question of Italy as creative catalyst.

Henry James, whose novels so earnestly delve into the matter of Europeanized Americans, would never agree that one could accommodate two sides and his characters often experienced the split between their American self and their affinity for Europe. For him, the matter was not merely the momentary dilemma between the pull of the Old and New World, it was, as he discussed with his friend Daisy Chanler (herself the Rome-born daughter of expatriate Americans), a case of conscience. James disapproved of a divided allegiance and felt that one had a duty to make (as he did) a deliberate and irrevocable choice between America and Europe. To which another friend of Chanler observed: "Dear Henry, he forgets how easy it has become to cross the ocean; the issue that so worries him does not exist."[10]

As I read the travelers' accounts, I began to hear the patriarchal refrain in some of the scolding about the conditions in Italy a century and a half ago: repeatedly Italy was called to task like a wayward child who defied law and order (with the great exception, of course, of Stendhal who had his lightening-strike of Italy as an adolescent of seventeen and who remained love-struck by Italy the rest of his life). Italy seemed to challenge male attitudes of rational conduct, logic, and regularity. Italy was not tidy. There was a discernible hedonism and looseness in the very air, somnolent and enervating, that defied patriarchal structure. Italy abounds in quandaries. Despite their apparently formal and traditional core of society, Italians resist predictable patterns, slip from the grasp of authoritarianism, and defy rigid ordering. It was felt that the Italians were much too individualistic, imaginative, and fantasy-laden and their country too beautiful for its own good. Like a woman, perhaps. Could that be why the judgments of women travelers are often less harsh, less startled, even less threatened by their experience of Italy?

Nineteenth-century American women proved more politically progressive in many instances than their conservative expatriate countrymen, artists such as Luther Terry and authors such as Nathaniel Hawthorne and Henry James who, despite their dislike of Roman Catholicism, supported foreign-backed papal dominion against the Italian independence movement. Margaret Fuller, instead, participated wholeheartedly in the resurgent movement for Roman liberation and a united Italy; and so, less actively, did Elizabeth Barrett Browning, writing from Casa Guidi in Florence. Later, Julia Ward Howe (founder of a *Circolo Italiano* in Boston and author of our *Battle Hymn of the Republic* as well as a biography of Margaret Fuller) was a passionate supporter of Italian independence even as others declared that Italians were not fit for self-government.[11] Harriet Beecher Stowe was as deeply sympathetic to the Italian nationalist cause as Hawthorne, in Italy at the same period, was indifferent or even hostile. About the French occupying troops in Rome, he wrote in his journal, "I have no quarrel with the French soldiers . . . it seems as if they were nearer akin to me than these dingy and dusky Romans."[12] Hawthorne had longed to return home to Concord after his stint as consul in Liverpool, but had been coaxed to Italy by his wife Sophia who, from her youth, had dreamed of reaching that country of art and beauty: "Oh why not live in Rome," Sophia Peabody, age twenty-three, wrote to her sister in 1832, "Pack up—Betty—& let us be off—& live in Rome—the eternal—imperial 'Mother of dead empires'—the city of the soul—the retreat of the arts & graces—the garden of Nature!"[13] Sophia's exhortation quite summarized the lures that brought Americans of her time to Italy.

While nineteenth-century American men tended to condemn Italy's prevailing stagnant political and social conditions, women instead searched for some understanding of the country's plight; Mark Twain sermonized relentlessly against the superstition and ills of the Catholic Church, but Harriet Beecher Stowe felt the human attraction of its rituals and ceremonies as a welcome contrast to Puritan severity. In her novel *Agnes of Sorrento,* she attempted to understand the Church historically, both the good and the bad. Anne Hampton Brewster became a convert to Roman Catholicism as did, in her later life, Hawthorne's own daughter, Rose, who founded the Dominican Congregation of St. Rose of Lima and located her community of nuns outside New York City in the town named for her, Hawthorne. That same community, by saving $15,000 out of their living expenses, financed in 2006 the reinterment of Sophia, who had been buried in England, alongside Nathaniel in Concord, Massachusetts.

There is further testimony in Julia Ward Howe's *Reminiscences* of how at ease women felt in Italy. And William Vance astutely noted in *America's Rome* that Queen Margherita, the first queen of a unified Italy, was the central, adored, unifying figure for Rome as capital of the new nation; she was "in effect a female and secular pope" once the former Papal States were integrated into Italy and the papacy was confined to Vatican City.[14] "Italy receives me as a long-lost child," Margaret Fuller wrote to her New England family, "and I feel myself at home here." She let herself go into a "trance of repose" among a "people . . . indolently joyous." Constance Woolson wrote home in her own ecstasy of discovery: "Florence! I foresee that I am going to be quite roused up here. Florence is all that I have dreamed of and more." Emily Dickinson called Italy: "My Blue Peninsula of delight." Each of the women in this study, with her American background, set out at a different stage in her life to find a new direction. Was the quest, perhaps, to find the spirit's home? Metaphorically, they left home to refind it.

Remembering Prezzolini's disgust at a nineteenth-century Protestant minister named George Cheever whom he characterized as turbulent and violent and full of intransigent attacks on Catholic Italy, it is fascinating to speculate on whether that early fire and brimstone Cheever was ancestor to the contemporary author and our former neighbor, John Cheever, who spent a year in

Rome in the 1950s as recipient of a Guggenheim grant and enjoyed exercising his Italian with my husband. Cheever's journals reveal an uncanny replica of many of the same reactions recorded by earlier New England travelers who failed to burrow below surface judgments to some deeper understanding of Italy. On his first night in Rome, John Cheever walks to the Spanish Steps and is a little disappointed . . . it rains in Rome, the weather is not classical; he has been short-changed everywhere; he notes, dispiritedly, the dash and sexuality of Roman men. Later he records lying sleepless in strange beds and wondering why he ever left his cozy home. In the kitchen of the Palazzo Doria where he and his family will spend the year, the gas stove leaks . . . the drains are clogged. He notices the Americans in Rome, at cafes, and "they are not pretty" . . . "the flowers on Raphael's tomb are straw." He reminds himself that he, too, has a past—houses and people and an old name—and the Mediterranean is not a part of it. "And yet," he writes, "I have dreamed of the Mediterranean for ten years; it is in some way a part of our dreams."[15] But was it still for him the Arcadian dream? That dream which so fatally involved paradox?

John Cheever's spleenish reaction seems that of his Puritan forebears as he echoes the crabbed misanthropy of Nathaniel Hawthorne, who compiled a veritable litany of laments on his arrival in Rome in January 1858: "Cold, nastiness, evil smells, narrow lanes between tall, ugly, mean-looking, white-washed houses, sour bread, pavement most uncomfortable to the feet, enormous prices for poor living, beggars, pickpockets, ancient temples and broken monuments with filth at the base, and clothes hanging to dry about them, French soldiers, monks and priests of every degree, a shabby population smoking bad cigars."[16] Yet John Cheever had withal a growing awareness of some deeper human truth to be found in Italy's ancient stores. It would be, perforce, a truth as profoundly different to his view of the world as it was in the previous two centuries to the Americans who preceded him. "This is not," he notes, "a difference of language, race, climate, or custom; it is a vastly different approach to the wellsprings of humanity." And in a museum, shabby and unclean, and so bone-chilled his very marrow is frozen, some truth comes through despite the surroundings: he gets, despite the bad lighting, an honest insight into human nature. Still, the civilization on a whole strikes him, the writer, as it did the long-ago parson: licentious.

A century after Thomas Cole's painting of Italy as Arcadia and just at the onset of World War II, a remnant of the old dream was still playing in the American imagination. Elizabeth Madox Roberts, then a popular American novelist, wrote a poem called "Ellen Chesser's Dream of Italy" based on a character from her novel *The Time of Man* in which Italy stood for something desired beyond the dreariness of ordinary life. For Ellen Chesser, daughter and wife of poor American tenant farmers always on the move, always in search of "some better country," Italy meant a golden paradise of sun and light in contrast to the stark grey reality evoked through the image of rain beating down on drab boards "where the window pane was gone."

The mythic appeal of Italy continues today: witness Susan Sontag's postmodern *The Volcano Lover*, a novel subtitled *A Romance* and set in eighteenth-century Italy. It is an unexpected about-face from Sontag's posture as activist, rational avant-garde critic. One does not associate Sontag with romanticism, but given her love for Italy and frequent journeys there, can it be that in this novel her "other side," too, surfaced? The novel is based on the historic persons of Sir William Hamilton, his wife Emma, and Lord Nelson and the historic events occurring in late eighteenth-century Naples. It is also an extraordinary reevocation of Italy as Arcadia. The subconscious, interior love of Arcadia, of romanticism, and of collecting as a way of holding onto the past which manifests in Sir William (known as the Cavaliere throughout the novel), the volcano lover, is reflected in Sontag's evident sympathy for that character. Yet, in the end, her romantic infatuation cannot hold; the book's final pages are the monologue of an imprisoned revolutionary woman who predicts the eventual triumph of the liberal cause. Such an ending reads as if Sontag forced herself to concur with William James as he chides brother Henry: Yes, Italy is pleasant, but it's child-play; it's time to grow up; there's real work to be done, and that's best done home in America, not over there.

So many works on Italy abound that I had to ask myself, why another? In this case, I wanted to discover whether the women of this study could find the particular nourishment that Mme. de Staël insisted Italy granted women. And further, any study of the lives of others heightens awareness of one's own. Henry James had this perception concerning American artist Jasper Cropsey and his family resident in Rome in the late 1840s (who, for James, stood for all Americans of that time in Italy); thus James asked and answered, "what the Cropseys can have been doing by the bare banks of the Tiber."[17] And he came to the conclusion that the questions are in themselves "thrilling" because they require us, in living "over people's lives," to "live over their perceptions, live over the growth, the change, the varying intensity of the same." In other lives, we find something of our own. In defining others, we come to self-definition.

The stories of these six American women and their connection to Italy enriched my own connection to my ancestral homeland. Why had they come? What had they found? What was given to them by their exposure to an old world land and culture? What had changed in their lives? I found in my questions of them answers to the same questions in my own life. And so I start with the one who was in Italy the earliest, Margaret Fuller, whose trail I always seemed to be following when I lived in Rome. She was a towering woman whose story is a dramatic revelation of intellectual achievement, romance, adventure, and tragedy.

Margaret Fuller, 1810–1850

1. *Ardor and Apocalypse: The Timeless Trajectory of Margaret Fuller*

On a glorious, clear, cool, and sun-lit October afternoon, I was present at the outdoor dedication of the Newington-Cropsey Foundation Gallery of Art in Hastings-on-Hudson, New York. The gallery was conceived and built by Barbara Newington to honor her great-grandfather Jasper Cropsey, an eminent nineteenth-century artist of the Hudson River School. Fronted by a duck pond and set in a hollow east of the river and below the slope where Cropsey's home, Ever Rest, is visible, the edifice rises like a version of the Taj Mahal or Alhambra, something exotic in any case for a small river town. Within is housed a permanent collection of Cropsey's luminous paintings as well as exhibits of contemporary artists of the representational persuasion, an ongoing Hudson River School.

The dedication ceremony featured a brass band, speakers, and a perfect day; the white ducks on the pond were joined that afternoon by mallards stopping off on their journey south. A light wind came off the river; sun glinted through leaves of orange, russet, yellow, bronze, and crimson. It was the kind of fall day and view of which Cropsey had been the master artist. And as much as an American autumn, views of the Roman forum or the aqueduct stretching across the Campagna or the moonlit temples of Paestum were also Cropsey's signature. As with his mentor Thomas Cole, and so many other American artists, Cropsey, too, had paid his visit and homage to Italy and painted its views.

The day was redolent of the gentle melancholy of autumn and of things past, leading me to recall not only Cropsey in Rome from 1847 to 1849, but also Margaret Fuller who was among his American friends there. New England-born Margaret Fuller (1810–50) was a well-respected author at home when she was appointed by the *New York Tribune* to Europe as the first American woman overseas correspondent. In Rome she wrote of the 1848 uprising that ushered in the unification of Italy, even as she participated in it with Giovanni Ossoli, the young Italian nobleman whose child she bore and whom she was then to marry. Escaping to Florence when Rome was retaken by French and papal forces, they eventually sailed for Fuller's homeland only to perish with their child, shipwrecked, off Fire Island, so close to New York harbor.

Jasper and Maria Cropsey were among those who gathered in Margaret's small quarters on the Via del Corso on Monday evenings when she received friends (giving no refreshment, she wrote her mother in New England, but rather keeping plenty of inexpensive fresh flowers around). Margaret loved social occasions, but lived frugally, always short of money despite her hard work. Maria Cropsey, in a letter home, described being in Margaret's company for a concert and then at a "festa" when, in honor of a Roman delegation, the American residents turned out to see the banners (including an American flag) and flower-strewn streets. As Maria said, and Margaret would have concurred at that moment in her life, "It is all a 'festa' here."[1] Just a year later when the Cropseys were already back in New York City, they were shocked by the news of the shipwreck, though Jasper made no note of their Rome friend's tragic end in his journal.

Had Cropsey been a portraitist, he, too, might have painted Margaret in Rome. But it was fellow American artist Thomas Hicks who painted her posed against a backdrop of Venice where they had first met. Hicks gave her a softened, wearied expression which is explained by her secret, troubling pregnancy and general state of dejection at the time. Following Margaret's death, Hicks wrote a condolence note to her mother referring to the difficult period when Margaret sat for him: "In the winter of 1848 in Rome in many of her hours of loneliness, I stood in the relationship to her of a brother."[2]

The daguerreotype that Margaret Fuller posed for to give to her family and friends in July 1846 before she left for Europe is her true likeness. Taken at the New York studio of John Plumbe and referred to by Margaret in letters to her brother Richard, that early photograph is a character pose: one hand against her wide brow, Margaret gazes down thoughtfully at an open book; her nose is Roman, her mouth firm, her chin ample, and her hair looped around her ears into a braided bun above the nape of her neck. She has a purposeful look about her that accentuates her strengths and combines with the appeal of a woman who shows both intelligence and an air of femininity in her attire.

But it was not from that likeness that Alonzo Chappel, a nine-teenth-century mass producer of engraved historical scenes and personages for American journals, schoolbooks, and histories, based his own prettified-for-the-popular-press version of Margaret Fuller. Chappel had never met Fuller but pictured her as a round-faced ingénue with curls to her shoulder and a simpering look signifying little character and less mind, an image quite inter-changeable with his similar versions of Charlotte Brontë or Eliza-beth Barrett Browning. Unfortunately, it is Chappel's image that the Fuller descendants have conserved and that has been unac-countably reproduced in several biographies—unaccountable be-cause anyone writing of Fuller should be acquainted with Margaret's daguerreotype and realize how far removed that image is from Chappel's version. The touch-up done to Fuller's looks was also done to her life by Ralph Waldo Emerson, James Free-man Clarke, and William H. Channing, her friends and then the editors of her *Memoirs*. As Katherine Anthony noted in her psychological biography, "Margaret Fuller was a modern woman who died in 1850. . . . Her legend was created mainly by unemancipated men . . . who, through Puritanism and Chivalry, distorted her picture."

Never completely banished, but languishing and lampooned on the sidelines of American literature through the uses made of her by so many notable male authors, Margaret Fuller continued to be the butt of a literary ridicule meant, by extension, for all intellectually ambitious women who didn't know their place. Fuller's self-confidence was often caricatured by those like James Russell Lowell who satirized her "I-turn-the-crank-of-the-Universe-air" in his long poem "Fable for Critics." (A later member of the famed Lowell clan, poet Amy Lowell, responded with her own "Critical Fable" that included these lines: "My dear Sir . . . if you'd not been afraid / Of Margaret Fuller's success, you'd have stayed / Your hand in her case and more justly have rated her.") But even Virginia Woolf considered her a Bluestocking curiosity when she made this entry in her diary: "I think one day I shall write a book of 'Eccentrics.' Mr. Grote shall be one. Lady Hester Stanhope. Margaret Fuller. Duchess of Newcastle. Aunt Julia?"[3]

I have been captivated, instructed, moved, and tracked by Margaret Fuller ever since I lived just around the corner from her final Rome lodging at Piazza Barberini. I, too, was a young woman journalist on my own in Rome and had come to value Fuller's venturing spirit, her mental agility to grow from one experience to another, and her ability to appreciate Italy from more than a tourist's viewpoint. When I lived in Rome she became my subject as an American heroine of the Italian Risorgimento for an Italian radio-drama. And still her life continues to expand for me.

The Margaret Fuller I know was a socially enlightened and original thinker, loyal, generous, and heroic. I was more interested in her commitment "to live a life of significant action" and her place as a dominant figure in nineteenth-century American cultural history than in the gossipy details of her rejections by men, whether she was really married or not to Ossoli, or the descriptions that misrepresent her as ugly, preposterous, or ridiculous. She was demanding and high-strung, and doubtless had her less attractive qualities. "Her regal self-importance, her extravagant claims for her powers, her insensitivity toward persons who she judged did not share her appetite for freedom . . . her obsession with being understood, often on her own terms even though she could not define the terms"[4]—these are aspects of her arrogance (or awkwardness) that Fuller's biographers have often described. But in the end she lived a life authentic to herself, something rarely achieved by anyone including her detractors.

Having first known Margaret Fuller in Rome, I again evoked her in Hastings-on-Hudson. One hundred fifty years earlier Margaret made several trips "up the river"—as a sightseer, as a journalist to interview women prisoners at Sing Sing for the *Herald-Tribune*, and then as an author wanting to isolate herself at Fishkill Landing while working on a book. At the dedication of the gallery to Margaret's friend Jasper Cropsey, her story came back to me as charged as ever.

That story is an outsize one. It was, and remains, a powerful chapter in an American woman's development beyond the barriers of time and place. Italy became the place of Margaret's transformation not only in the human terms of motherhood, but in terms of heroic stature as well. Fuller's life illustrates a woman's striving to act out her own character, to achieve fulfillment both intellectually and emotionally. It is documented not only in her writings for publication, but also in surviving correspondence and in her *Journals*. As I continue to know Fuller, deeper grows the imprint of the strength of her character and the originality of her thought. She does not recede, but grows with time.

Still, the keepers of culture like to pigeon-hole and so her place is problematic: is she a writer, a literary critic of her times on par with Edgar Allan Poe, a thinker, a lecturer, a social reformer, or a revolutionary? Since she is all of those she has no settled niche in American writing and is not as well known as she should be. She does not rank as a great writer, her work does not immediately command as does Emily Dickinson's, nor did she ever have the popularity accorded Harriet Beecher Stowe for her *Uncle Tom's Cabin*. Commanding a complex personality combining many gifts, Fuller attained a position in American cultural history without, paradoxically, ever becoming widely known, much less read.

And yet, she endures. Legendary in her lifetime, Poe noted: "Humanity is divided into Men, Women, and Margaret Fuller."[5] She burrowed into the consciousness of her better-known male contemporaries who used her as the model of the overreaching woman and then provided the needed moral by showing how such women come to a bad end. Yet Emerson considered her his best audience; and for Horace Greeley, the *Herald-Tribune* publisher who, after reading her, hired her as the first woman critic ever employed by a major paper, she was "the loftiest, bravest soul that has yet irradiated the form of an American woman."[6]

Who was the woman who elicited both great vilification and veneration? Sarah Margaret Fuller was born in 1810 in Cambridgeport near Boston. She came of vigorous New England stock—independent, out-spoken, opinionated, contrary—as in the case of her Fuller grandfather who, driven out of town for preaching against the Revolution to his congregation of Minutemen, returned as a farmer to fight his way back into favor, and then represented the town at a constitutional convention where he voted against the document because it recognized slavery. In a family known for its independent-minded members, the most recent notable descendant to carry these genes was the late inventive genius

R. Buckminster Fuller, Margaret's great-nephew. Another descendant, John P. Marquand, the son of her great-niece Margaret Fuller Marquand, was also to write for the *New York Herald-Tribune* before becoming a noted novelist of manners of upper-class life in Boston.

Sarah Margaret, the eldest of seven surviving children borne by Margarett [sic] Fuller, was educated by her father, Timothy, according to the strict regime given to prepare Fuller boys for Harvard. He not only laid out the rigor of her training in classical texts, but influenced the very formation of her mind as demonstrated very clearly from the language that was permitted her: she was never to frame her thoughts in what, still today, would be considered a female style—deferential, self-negating. In an age when women were taught to appropriate a special language of politeness and complaisance, Mr. Fuller forbade Margaret the use of phrases like "I am mistaken" and "It may be so." He gave her a strong sense of self-respect and self-reliance, the "masculine" strengths of concreteness, a historical consciousness, a belief in life over literature, and Thomas Jefferson as an American ideal. From Margaret's sketch of her youth, written in 1840 as an introductory chapter to an intended but uncompleted autobiographical romance, it was the history of ancient Rome that was the supreme influence: "In vain for me are men more, if they are less, than Romans."

She, as her father, admired books which exalted a life of action. And in this allegiance was ground for future difficulty: how to reconcile her historical consciousness and belief in action with the constrictions of being female? Timothy Fuller's way was not that of *The Young Lady's Book*, a popular manual which, no doubt, thoroughly confused the well brought-up American young women of the time with the impasse that "the female mind is acknowledged to possess all the faculties, and to be capable of like improvements, with that of a man," while at the same time urging obedience to men as a virtue of religious duty: "in whatever situation of life a woman is placed, from her cradle to her grave, a spirit of obedience and submission, pliability of temper, and humility of mind, are required from her."[7] Such double-talk was guaranteed to put educated women in an untenable position and, despite the advantages of Margaret's early training, she, too, felt the bind of this paradox even as she neutralized it through deft argument in her *Woman in the Nineteenth Century.*

In letters she wrote when she was seven or eight, Margaret reported dutifully of her studies in music, writing, Latin, math, and Valpy's *Chronology of Ancient and English History* to her father when he served in Washington as a congressman. From childhood on, her letters reveal a genuine interest in people, a great capacity for understanding and affection, an enjoyment of social activities, and a great liking of rambles in natural surroundings. She had both a social and a serious bent.

At age ten she wrote to a friend: "I wish you would write me a note today and tell to me what events have diversified your journey through life since our roads parted and what reflections, if any, such events have suggested to your youthful mind. *Dites Moi ses nouvelles aussi.*" Among her father's papers was found an eerily prophetic note in Margaret's handwriting at the same age: "On the 23rd of May, 1810, was born one foredoomed to sorrow and pain, and like others to have misfortunes. She had feeling which few have, which is the SOURCE of sorrow." In fact, she saw keenly into her nature and felt always the pull of destiny upon her despite a youth filled with the real pleasures of outings, balls, and social occasions.

At thirteen, Margaret had been, according to a male intellectual companion, "so precocious in her mental and physical developments . . . [that] she had her place in society, as a lady full-grown."[8] In 1825, on the occasion of Marquis LaFayette's visit to America, Margaret, then fifteen, was invited to a reception to meet him.

She wrote him in advance expressing both the ardency of her feelings and the thoughtfulness of her reflections: "Sir, I cannot resist the desire of saying, 'LaFayette I love I admire you' . . . the contemplation of a character such as yours fills the soul with a noble ambition. Should we both live, and it is possible to a female, to whom the avenues of glory are seldom accessible, I will recall my name to your recollection." She was, as she told a teacher, determined on distinction.

Yet as an adult, Margaret looked back in judgment on the mistakes and pressures of her rearing. "With me," she wrote, "much of life was devoured in the bud. . . . Certainly I do not wish that instead of masters I had read baby books, written down to children, and with such ignorant dullness that they blunt the senses and corrupt the tastes of the still plastic human being. But I do wish I had read no books at all till later—that I had lived with toys and played in the open air." She attributed to her rigorous early education the misfortunes of her health. She refers to over stimulation that resulted in sleep-walking and nightmares filled with classical backgrounds absorbed from her reading of Virgil. She was prescient in dream recording that predates Freud. By age twelve she suffered from what would be a lifetime of headaches and nervous complaints. This is her description of a girlhood day:

> I rise a little before five, walk an hour, and then practice on the piano, till seven, when we breakfast. Next I read French—Sismondi's *Literature of the South of Europe*—till eight, then two or three lectures in Brown's *Philosophy*. About half-past nine I go to Mr. Perkins' school and study Greek till twelve, when, the school being dismissed, I recite, go home, and practise again till dinner, at two. Sometimes, if the conversation is very agreeable, I lounge for half an hour over the dessert, though rarely so lavish of time. Then, when I can, I read two hours in Italian, but I am often interupted. At six, I walk,

or take a drive. Before going to bed, I play or sing, for half an hour or so, to make all sleepy, and, about eleven, retire to write a little while in my journal, exercises on what I have read.

If Margaret felt too much had been asked of her by her father, she also acknowledged that much had been given to her by his requiring beyond what was then asked of female children and that his instilling of discipline into her life was necessary to a nature like hers disposed to "infatuation and self-forgetfulness." It is a sound proposition that if more is required of one, more will be produced. Margaret's neurasthenia was probably due more to the effect of the barriers placed on women once they were educated beyond "their sphere" than to the intellectual demands on her individually. Her illnesses, headaches, and nervous prostration echo the afflictions commonly suffered by other women of her day (e.g., Alice James or even Elizabeth Barrett before she eloped and escaped to Italy). What Margaret lamented in her adult years was not so much what her father had demanded of her, as what had remained unexpressed and ungratified in her emotional need to find a man worthy of her gifts, and one who did not reject her affections.

As a teenager, Margaret read Germaine de Staël's *Corinne*. Written by Mme. Staël to vindicate her own lofty nature, it resonated with educated women everywhere who felt their gifts had not been recognized. Though denounced from the pulpit, generations of young women, thrilled by its heroine and its descriptions of Italy, yearned for the acclaim afforded Corinne against the backdrop of Rome. Corinne perfectly states the pull of competing choices and the division it causes in achieving women: whether to realize their gifts or their "natural" call to domesticity; a dilemma that, in the almost two hundred years since Mme. de Staël wrote of it, still abides, still wounds, still confounds. The novel is about dualism; the exotic heroine and her pale lover personify the tensions of nationalism (The North vs. The South), of temperament (reason vs. feeling), of art theory (classic restraint vs. spontaneity); and the great choice, love or career, is the crux of the problem. And it still is today.

In presenting this quandary, Staël sets up a duel between male and female in which both will lose, but Corinne will lose more since she must (in the accepted formula of the time) die, while Oswald is left with a passionless marriage to Lucile the homebody. Corinne, indeed, is a two-time loser, since she first sacrifices her artistic gift to love, and then loses her very life.

Fuller, *au contraire*, saw union as the only possible solution: "Yet the time will come, when, from the union of this tragic king (the man in me rushes forth) and queen (the woman in me kneels and weeps), shall be born a radiant sovereign self." It was Emerson who called Fuller an American Corinna; being compared to the brilliant improviser and declaimer of Staël's novel could only have gratified her. That Margaret Fuller stuck out as an anomaly in New England not only for her intellect, but for her enthusiasms and free thinking, was what Emerson had in mind when he characterized her as "an exotic . . . a foreigner from some more sultry and expansive climate."

It was not so much as literature or moral text that *Corinne* had a powerful influence on Margaret Fuller, but rather as the reinforcement of the Romantic myth of Italy. Margaret's early classical education had grounded her in the sturdy republican virtues of the ancient Rome she venerated; from childhood she had been ardent in her support of an America that embodied those virtues. The United States was the New Rome and to the United States would be entrusted a role analogous to that when *Pax Romana* dominated the then known world. But in *Corinne*, Italy stood also for the place of self-realization for the superior woman. Lord Nelvil (who, with Lucile, stands for Anglo-American values) foolishly hoped that Corinne would prefer "domestic happiness" to "the luster of . . . genius." For Corinne, as for Margaret Fuller, what choice could that have been?

When Margaret was twenty-three, Timothy Fuller retired from political life and moved his family to the relative isolation of Groton to become, as his father before him, a farmer. Margaret, who thrived on conversation and intellectual exchange, particularly suffered from being separated from her friends; she was now relegated to teaching her four youngest siblings at home. In this period she began her readings in German, attracted to the Romantic Movement and especially Goethe who became a powerful influence and whose work she was to introduce to the American public. She gathered material for a projected biography of Goethe—a work never realized as her interests grew in other directions. She went from being a literary scholar and translator (in effect, an accessory to another's life and work) to becoming her own spokesperson.

Margaret Fuller was plain; early in her teens she came to terms with her looks deciding with gallant bravado that she could be "bright and ugly." Yet, if not beauty, she had another allure. Frederic Henry Hedge, a fellow Transcendentalist, left this description: "her face was one that attracted, that awakened a lively interest . . . that fascinated. You saw the evidence of a mighty force." In Rome, in the rapture of her love affair with Ossoli, without ever alluding to her romance, she described the effect of it on her when she wrote home: "There is a Polish countess here, who likes me much. . . . This woman envies me; she says, 'How happy you are; so free, so serene, so attractive, so self-possessed!'" It was the dream of the Yankee Corinna come true—she was in Italy, she was loved.

Fuller was an emancipated woman before there was such a term, an equal in intellect to any of her male circle of friends, yet by her late twenties she was viewed as a spinster surcharged with an intensity, Emerson noted, "bewailing her virginity and languishing for a husband."[9] Her friend, Henry David Thoreau, also unmarried, never suffered such commentary for being a bachelor. It was years before William Henry Channing, who became a devoted friend, could even bring himself to be introduced to the formidable Miss Fuller. Margaret did nothing to diminish her intensity, rather accentuating it by the earnestness of her look with the strange, unremitting blinking of her eyelids and pecking movements of her head that were noted by all her contemporaries. Indeed, the term "ophidian," serpentine, was used to describe Margaret. Oliver Wendell Holmes, a childhood friend of Margaret's who was made to feel stupid as a boy when she spoke words he didn't know, went so far as to make the trait the basis for a novel, *Elsie Venner*, that conjectures whether the venom of a prenatal snake bite can affect the offspring (like original sin) and make it predisposed to evil and then responsible for future actions. Holmes explores this through the contrived story of poor Elsie, with "her inherited ophidian tastes and tendencies"[10] and "her strange eyes and the snake look in them" acquired through her mother's prenatal poisoning by a rattler. There is something marvelously comic, as well as bizarre, in this rattlesnake thriller with this pointed reference: "[Elsie] narrowed her lids slightly, as one often sees a sleepy cat narrow hers—somewhat as you may remember our famous Margaret used to, if you remember her at all."[11]

The men of her generation and acquaintance, like Holmes and Lowell, satirized Margaret but none quite with the perversity of Nathaniel Hawthorne, a friend for whom she said she felt affection as to a brother. Hawthorne, in his journal, seemed to have dumped his own obsessive sexual feelings from years of early "sublimation" onto Fuller. Strangely, he put off marriage until he was thirty-eight since he wanted to preserve all his powers for his art; Margaret was thirty-seven when she had her first sexual experience. Hawthorne's early repression and possible incestuous fantasies (made all the more real by his familiarity with Salem records documenting the conviction of three of his ancestors for crimes of incest) seem to have been conveniently displaced onto Margaret and her love for Ossoli. Hawthorne describes her union with Ossoli as that of a fallen woman, she no better than her sisters in shame and the man she chose who was so inferior as to be almost imbecilic. Hawthorne had never met Ossoli but was repeating gossip picked up in Rome in the late 1850s. Hawthorne's extreme censure of Fuller is very suspect; D. H. Lawrence sees through it in his *Studies in Classic American Literature*: "That blue-eyed darling Nathaniel knew disagreeable things in his inner soul. He was careful to send them out in disguise."[12] Possibly recasting his own obsession with sex as sin, he disguised his feelings of guilt and aimed them at his former friend Margaret.

Henry James, perhaps filled with the sense of inadequacy of one who could only note history, not participate in it as Fuller did, evoked her in his biography of William Wetmore Story as a "Margaret-ghost" hovering like a lost soul over the old passages rather than a vital presence in American thought.[13] She was not, as James was, an "Arcadian" who wanted a static Italy which would never evolve beyond its picturesqueness. Fuller went far beyond the sightseers and the lovers of papal pageantry: she compared the state of Italians with that of New World Indians, slaves, or even women as the victims of oppression both physical and psychic.

Long after Fuller's death, men still carped at her: why hadn't she written more, Percy Miller (who edited a collection of Fuller's writings in 1963) wondered querulously, just as Betty Friedan was launching *The Feminine Mystique* to answer that and other questions about women's silence. Despite the fact that Margaret's letters and journal entries constantly cite financial problems, Miller seems to have no idea how onerous it could be for a nineteenth-century woman to earn her living, nor the problem of a single person having to invest so much time in social arrangements just to keep up morale and keep the mind working. Yet Fuller refers constantly to the pressures this put on her and the effect it had on her health.

Nonetheless, she had a gallantry about her. She dressed with a certain unconventional dash—often with a flower in her hair and, because of her near-sightedness, used a lorgnette. She had grown up well-connected and in a certain refinement as the daughter of a congressman in the great house of Cambridgeport. When she visited the rugged Brook Farm community, she was given the one china cup and saucer they possessed while the others drank from mugs. Even when she struggled with penuriousness, she tried to present herself well dressed, always had flowers on hand, and someone to serve her. She was a presence and was immediately felt. Edgar Allan Poe (who was born just a year before Fuller and was to die, as she, at age forty) met her in New York literary circles, and writing in his *Broadway Journal*, August 1846, made the astute appraisal that her personal character and her printed book "are one and the same thing . . . her literary and her conversational manner are identical."[14] He then went on to describe her: "She is of medium height; nothing remarkable about the figure; a profusion of lustrous light hair; eyes a bluish gray, full of fire; capacious forehead; the mouth when in repose indicates a profound sensibility, capacity for affection, for love—when moved by a slight smile, it becomes even beautiful in the intensity of this expression; but the upper lip, as if impelled by the action of involuntary muscles, habitually uplifts itself, conveying the impression of a sneer."

Emerson, when he first met her, had written: "It is always a great refreshment to see a very intelligent person. It is like being set in a large place. You stretch your limbs and dilate to your utmost size."[15] Margaret would have liked to have excited a more passionate response to life and to her own gifts upon Emerson. She learned from him, but as her own tastes and interests broadened, she outgrew his New England narrowness, his airy idealism at the expense of present activism. She was more fiery-souled than the resident sage of Concord; she needed not bucolic concord, but the winds of discord, debate, and dissension to bring out her deepest convictions. Her letters attest to a passionate nature that preferred, as she put it, the poet's abandon to the pedant's thoroughness. She had admonished her mentor Emerson in one of their cold-warm, attractive-repelling conversations to "forego these tedious, tedious attempts to learn the universe by thought alone."

Her great desire was Europe. There she would have brought to completion her ongoing work on Goethe; there she would have been at the fount of her classical education and ideals; there she would meet the authors and social thinkers whose work she followed so intently. She was thwarted when she was twenty-five in her first travel plan by the early death of her father, which made her the head of the family with a pressing need to earn her own living thenceforth. This she did at first by teaching in several schools, including Bronson Alcott's Temple School. In 1839, her translation of Eckermann's *Conversations with Goethe* was published but neither that nor subsequent translations brought her any money. She managed to support herself, after she stopped teaching, by initiating a subscription series of conversations for women which she, born on a Wednesday ("Wednesday's child is full of woe . . ."), held for five years in Elizabeth Peabody's Boston bookstore on Wednesday at noon.

The first Conversation took place on November 6, 1839, with twenty-five women of the Boston elite present. Margaret shared with them her conviction that women were not really being taught anything, even if schooled in the same material as men. For the great difference forever dividing male from female was in the application of learning. "Men are called on, from a very early period, to reproduce all that they learn; their college exercises, political duties, professional studies and first actions of life in any direction call on them to put to use what they have learned. But women learn without any attempt to reproduce that learning." Margaret's Conversations were meant to remedy this defect—they were to be immediate exercises in self-expression. With her enormously successful Conversations, Margaret had created an early form of consciousness-raising as she showed women how to think themselves out of that male construct: "woman's sphere."

Margaret's acquaintance with Emerson and early association with the Transcendental Club led to her being named in 1840 the first editor of their magazine *The Dial*, another consuming task which paid her nothing but gave her exposure as a major American literary critic and cultural commentator. She was not yet a social activist; she was disinterested even in the Abolition movement. She declined to join the experimental Brook Farm though she visited and led Conversations there. She confided her doubts about the communal experience to her journal: "Community seems dwindling to a point, and I fancy the best use of the plan, as projected thus far, will prove the good talks it has caused here, upon principles. . . . We are not ripe to reconstruct society yet."

A few months later, overworked and yearning as she always was for some perfect soul-mate or for escape to her longed-for Europe, loneliness or despair made her pour out to her journal, "Once I was almost all intellect; now I am almost all feeling. Nature vindicates her rights, and I feel all Italy glowing beneath the Saxon crust. This cannot last long; I shall burn to ashes if all this smoulders here much longer. I must die if I do not burst forth in heroism or genius."

In 1843, Margaret resigned from *The Dial* and that summer, with James and Sarah Clarke, she traveled over the Great Lakes to what were then the Western states—an excursion that opened her mind to social conditions. This was concrete experience in a new territory, a valuable counterpoint to Transcendental theorizing in New England. In Michigan, Wisconsin, and Minnesota she observed a whole range of new places and people—native peoples, settlers, Chicago, immigrants, laborers, women in the West. Emerson encouraged her to expand her travel notes and letters into a book. To do so, Margaret had been given permission to use Harvard's library, the first woman ever to enter the all-male precincts. When *Summer on the Lakes, 1843* was published in 1844, its insights caught the attention of Horace Greeley, publisher of the *New York Tribune*, who offered her a job at his paper as literary critic and commentator on social conditions.

The move to the more stimulating center of New York to work on the *Tribune* in proximity to the activist Greeley was another transforming milestone. In her early thirties, another unrequited infatuation, this time with William Clarke, brother of her travel companions, had led her to record in her journal: "[I] have suffered on every side 'the pangs of despised love.' . . . Is it because, as a woman, I am bound by a physical law, which prevents the soul from manifesting itself? Sometimes the moon seems mockingly to say so—to say that I, too, shall not shine, unless I can find a sun. O cold and barren moon; tell a different tale, and give me a son of my own." O prophetic soul, one can only answer to those poignant words, knowing what in fact is in her future—both the centering sun of a man's love, and a son of her own.

Margaret's sojourn at Concord in the summer of 1844 among three married couples—the Hawthornes, the Emersons, and the

Channings—must have prepared her for the writing of *Woman in the Nineteenth Century*. Certainly she had already seen the lot of settlers' wives in the West, experienced her own delusion in the hope of a romance with William Clarke, and then found in Concord a study of an array of marriages from the idyll of the Hawthornes to the disaster of her sister Ellen's marriage to Ellery Channing. Margaret must have pondered the alternative for a woman to marriage at any cost.

In New York, working on the *Tribune*, Fuller turned to meaningful work: following the well-laid lines of her Boston Conversations, she was educating an audience through over two hundred widely read *Tribune* essays. Her interest encompassed literature, but broadened into social matters as well; her deep belief, from her classic education, in the active role of history-making over the more passive role of literary concerns was coming to the fore. Ann Douglas in her instructive study of nineteenth-century America, *The Feminization of American Culture*, advances the notion of a Henry James understandably troubled by the very idea of Fuller: she stood for the masculine surge of history, he for the feminine stasis of literature.

During the fall of 1844, Fuller was at Sing Sing Prison to meet with the female inmates, most of whom were prostitutes. She recorded, "These women were among the so-called worst but nothing could be more decorous than their conduct, and frank too. All passed much as in one of my Boston classes. I told them I was writing about Woman; and, as my path had been a favoured one, I wanted to gain information of those who had been tempted to pollution and sorrow. They seemed to reply in the same spirit in which I asked."[16] She returned to address them on Christmas Day. Those encounters with the prostitutes at Sing Sing and the comparisons Fuller drew between their state and that of so-called respectable married women, exposed her to the traditional hypocrisy and dishonesty in human relationships and became material for some of her arguments in her next book, *Woman in the Nineteenth Century*. In terms of her times, Fuller regarded the women as victims of an oppressive patriarchal society which punished them, the prey, rather than the male, the predator.

The book Margaret was writing was one Horace Greeley had suggested as an expansion of her earlier *Dial* essay on men and women's rights. He published *Woman in the Nineteenth Century* in 1845. As could only be expected, it met with jeers and derision and was denounced as depraved. It also sold out its first edition in a week. In the United States, that proto-feminist tract became the basis of the American women's movement; abroad it spread Fuller's name. Margaret herself felt that with its publication, "the measure of my footprint would be left on the earth."

The book is a somewhat unwieldy compendium: her prevalent classical allusions and literary asides are juxtaposed with original thinking and sharp psychological insights as in her intimation of Jung's theory of the anima/animus nature. She reiterated her convictions: she knew of the ageless cycle of woman deriving her self-image from men, but in the transcendental lesson of self-reliance, Margaret wanted a woman to form her own inner standards and consciousness of self; she recognized women's sexuality and also the perniciousness of the double standard in society; she rejected the destructive flattery implied in saying of a woman "she has a masculine mind" or "she has surpassed her sex," for women do not wish to be men but only to be themselves; she advocated vocational freedom asking only that men remove the arbitrary barriers they had put in place to hinder women, for though women's domestic arts are not to be despised, they are not the only attribute of a woman's life. "It is," she concluded, "a vulgar error that love, *a* love, to woman is her whole existence." As Fuller could well see, "now there is no woman, only an overgrown child"; what she wanted for herself is what any woman would aspire to: "that my life be beautiful, powerful, in a word, a complete life." Though she had planted the seed, it would take another seventy-five years before the nineteenth amendment to the Constitution gave American women the right to vote and almost another half century before the women's movement advanced Fuller's agenda.

It was not only the subject of women that Margaret Fuller addressed but the over-all condition of America in her time. "Since the Revolution," she wrote in one of her *Tribune* pieces, "there has been little, in the circumstances of this country, to call out the higher sentiments. The effect of continued prosperity is the same on nations as on individuals—it leaves the nobler faculties undeveloped. . . . In a word, the tendency of circumstances has been to make our people superficial, irreverent and more anxious to get a living than to live mentally and morally."[17] This statement seems made for today. America had disillusioned Fuller with its growing materialism and faith in commercialism above all else, its unfettered expansion into Indian lands, the opprobrium of slavery, and finally the stain of the Mexican-American War with its covert territorial aims, as troubled a conflict in her time as the Vietnam War was in ours.

Even as she was gaining public recognition, Fuller's journal entries continue to document her inner conflicts. In New York she had been attracted to a German-Jewish businessman named James Nathan to whom, after an initial meeting she had written: "I have long a presentiment that I should meet one of your race . . . but I did not expect so gentle and civilized an apparition and with blue eyes!" Her correspondence to Nathan, on notepaper with delicate floral engravings in the left top corner, progress from invitations to further meetings to flirtatious incitements to declarations of emotional devotion and dependence: "I like to be quite still and have you the actor and voice" she wrote him, unwittingly emulating Corinne's fatal dependence on Oswald, a man unworthy of her. Perhaps the Nathan episode can be attributed to the inevitable deflation period that seems to hit an author following book publication and leaves one vulnerable to outlandish emotional situations. Or was it another instance of the dilemma of gifted women who, the more they cherish their independence, the more prone they are to become dependent in a relationship? Before things went too far, Nathan, using her for contacts, returned to Europe.

Fuller's *Papers on Literature & Art* (1846), consolidated her reputation; she had hoped her "Miscellanies," as she referred to her several hundred essays, would be published; if they had, they would have filled several volumes. However, Wiley & Putnam was unwilling to include material "likely to offend the religious public." Scornfully, Margaret wrote to editor Evert A. Duyckinck, "Now you well know that I write nothing which might not offend the so-called religious public" for, as she said, catering to such a public would be too foreign to her nature. As she explained to Duyckinck, "The attractive force of my mind consists in its energy, clearness, and I dare to say it, its catholic liberality and fearless honor. Where I make an impression it must be by being most myself."

She complained of the "thinness" of the resulting collection and the misrepresentation of her full range in the omission of all of her pieces on Continental literature, including the controversial material on Goethe and George Sand. Literature was not to be an asylum, she said, but a marketplace and a thoroughfare. In her words, literature should "be regarded as the great mutual system of interpretation between all kinds and classes of men. It is an epistolary correspondence between brethren of one family."[18] Still, in just three years, she had produced three books; her name would be known when she arrived in London, Paris, Rome.

In 1846, Greeley made Margaret's own long-delayed desire to travel in Europe come true by naming her the country's first female foreign correspondent, commissioned to send back dispatches to the *Tribune* on literary and social concerns, and evaluate Europe's long cultural traditions with the emerging ones of her own country. Just before sailing, Margaret sent her daguerreotype to friends and one, Caroline Healey Dall, remembered the likeness for its "majestic, Juno-like curve of the throat, which was more than beauty."[19]

Margaret arrived first in England with travel companions Marcus and Rebecca Spring and their young son Eddie, whom she was to tutor in exchange for her travel expenses. In London, Margaret met Italian patriot-in-exile Giuseppe Mazzini, the first of two men who would most profoundly affect the rest of her life. He became the immediate inspiration for her dedication to the cause of Italian freedom. Her early education made her immediately sympathetic to the realization of a new Rome republic free from papal and foreign dominion. In her last dispatch to the *Tribune* from England, Fuller wrote of the importance of Mazzini's work, reminding her fellow Americans that they should have an especial interest in Italy, the mother of our language and our laws, our greatest benefactress in the gift of genius. Mazzini had given her the urgency of here and now, of real action in the real world.

She traveled through England and France meeting all the greats through letters of introduction. She beheld the wonders of art; informed, and keenly aware, she also saw that much of Europe was on the verge of revolutionary change. She openly declared herself in a dispatch to the *Tribune* as one of those Americans "who take an interest in the cause of human freedom . . . who look with anxious interest on the suffering nations who are preparing for similar struggle" to that which her countrymen had not so long ago won in their own Revolution. She was to send back thirty-seven dispatches, the first dated August 23, 1846, from Westmoreland in England and the last on January 6, 1850, from

Italy. What began as travel letters with insights into social conditions gradually became an intense account of the political upheaval that was sweeping the Continent.

By then Fuller was disengaged from Emerson's influence and that of the transcendentalists, had relinquished her study on Goethe and, in a sense, literature itself, for immersion in contemporary life and issues. She had simplified and focused her aim, leaving one life behind for another. In her short life this was an outstanding trait, she could regroup after losses and go on to new achievement, she was always *in fieri*—becoming and developing. She continued to transform herself so that her achievement was, in large part, her life.

On the Continent, Margaret had desired above all to meet George Sand and when the occasion came in Paris, the French woman greeted her expansively: "*Ah, c'est vous!*" acquainted as she was with Fuller's name from *The Dial* and *Woman in the Nineteenth Century*. Margaret always revered George Sand for having the courage to live her life as she chose. But even without the material advantages of a Germaine de Staël or a George Sand, both of whom had wealth, a sympathetic milieu, and the support of devoted lovers, Fuller set herself to fight the same battles. Not as a recluse, like Emily Dickinson, sheltered in her father's fine house, nor as an aristocratic woman of privilege, but as a solitary, wage-earning woman did Margaret Fuller engage the reality of her times. Despite her formidable self-confidence and connections to the best minds in Europe, Fuller daily faced the struggle to survive. For her it was not a question of choosing a professional career over love and parenthood. She wanted both, as men do, without having to choose one over the other. Nor did she want to be the exception to the rule; she wanted to change the rule to benefit everyone of her sex.

In Paris Margaret also met Polish poet and patriot-in-exile Adam Mickiewicz, to whom she felt an immediate bond. For his sake she would almost have lingered in Paris, but she was committed to continue to Italy with the Springs. She left with Mickiewicz' admonition to liberate herself as well as the suppressed people of Europe. "You are a true person," he wrote her, "the only woman to whom it has been given to touch what is decisive in the present world and to have a presentiment of the world of the future."

In March 1847, Margaret Fuller—no longer young, never pretty, but of commanding intellect and passionate and noble conviction—fulfilled her lifetime dream by sailing into the bay of Naples to discover Italy. It was the very year that Maria Mitchell, another enterprising New England woman, discovered a new comet, a good omen if ever there was one, Margaret, a believer in signs, might have thought. In Paris, Margaret's French teacher had already told her she spoke and acted like an Italian, which only increased her feeling of destiny.[20]

On April 4, 1847, at evening vespers on Easter Sunday at St. Peter's in Rome, Margaret became separated from her companions and, appearing lost, attracted the attention of a young man, the Marquis Giovanni Angelo Ossoli, who came to her aid. He escorted her on the walk back to her lodgings. Margaret, in her long-ago learned Italian, was able to converse with him. He was of the so-called Black nobility from the family allegiance to the papacy; his eldest brother was secretary to the Pope's Privy Council and other brothers were officers in the papal Guard. Though a devout Catholic, Ossoli did not approve of the Pope's temporal power and hadn't entered the Guard. She learned that he, too, believed in a united Italy—a republic! Enthusiastically, as always to a like-minded person, Margaret told him of her friendship with Mazzini. Though Ossoli was ten years her junior and not at all as well-read or intellectually trained as she, his views coincided with hers.

Biographers tend to be astounded at the idea of the handsome young marquis being attracted to plain Miss Fuller, but they miss the essence: she had the gift of drawing out unsuspected qualities from those she befriended, she stimulated their interior growth, she gave them a higher self. For Ossoli, in his restricted provincial milieu, her attention must have been like life-blood finally coursing through his veins. That she was older could only have added to the attraction for him, replacing the maternal love he had lost at age six. And for Margaret, Ossoli offered a quiet steady devotion that more than compensated for the more eligible minds who had engaged, then fled her. Ever after, Margaret and Ossoli were to observe April 4th as their special day.

Still, to complicate matters, Margaret seemed to have pursued anyone in Rome she was attracted to. Shortly after her meeting with Ossoli, Margaret wrote a letter of enticement to the twenty-three year old artist Thomas Hicks, addressing him "Dear Youth" and chiding "I do not understand why you do not seek me more. . . . You are the only one whom I have seen here in whose eye I recognize one of my own kindred. I want to know and to love you and to have you love me. . . . How can you let me pass you by, without full and free communication?" To which Hicks replied in part: "It is you who are young for every pulse of your being is full and warm with Love. Why would you be endeared to me? . . . Do you not see that I cannot make you happy?"

Margaret's letter to Hicks was, previous to Bell Gale Chevigny's documentation in *The Woman and the Myth*, wrongly identified as one written to Ossoli, which reinforced the theory that Margaret had immediately enticed him into a relationship. But there is the obvious contradiction: Ossoli could not read English and that if Margaret had intended a letter for him she was able to write in Italian.

Hicks's negative reply did not lay her low. She overcame it by the excitement of being in Rome and, very likely, by Ossoli's flattering attendance on her. She might well have had in mind the letter from Mickiewicz which had awaited her arrival in Rome: "Seek the society of Italians," he had written her, "conversations with Italians, the music of Italians. . . . Now enjoy what surrounds you. Breath life through all your pores . . . learn to appreciate yourself as a beauty." Margaret wrote home to her friend William Henry Channing: "Art is not important to me now . . . I take interest in the state of the people, their manners, the state of the race in them. I see the future dawning."

When, by summer, it came time for the Springs and Fuller to leave Rome and travel north for the return trip to America, Margaret accompanied them only as far as Venice. As she would much later write her sister Ellen in explanation of why she had first left Ossoli and then returned: "I loved him and felt very unhappy to leave him; but the connection seemed so much in every way unfit, I did not hesitate a moment." In the north of Italy she made the acquaintance of Marchesa Costanza Arconati Visconti who was to become Margaret's closest Italian friend. As Margaret pondered whether to follow her heart or her reason she could well have imagined herself a Yankee Corinne in Italy. We know how she chose. In the fall she was once again in Rome and, in the veritable fall of her life, Margaret and Ossoli became lovers. It was for Fuller a beautiful season in which emotional and sexual fulfillment coincided with full intellectual commitment to the cause of a free Italy. How did she later explain what happened? Quite simply (in words echoing her written defense of George Sand), "I acted upon a strong impulse. . . . For good or for bad, I acted out my character."

Never did a couple more aptly describe their partnership than did Margaret and Ossoli: they called each other *caro/a consorte* which connotes not just consort in the marital sense but a sharer of fate, *la sorte*, for they were, indeed, inextricably bound together in the same destiny, linked forever to their common end. From childhood, Margaret had been obsessed by fate or destiny and refers to it over and over again. Ossoli, for his part, had had the kind of Catholic education that reinforced a resigned belief in *che sarà, sarà.*

That Margaret had some previous inkling of the difficulties ahead was already signaled by her letter to a friend at home in which she says she wishes she might have come abroad ten years earlier for "how true was the lure that always drew me towards Europe" but now her "strength has been wasted from not growing in the right soil." Strangely, those phrases were repeated a year later in a letter to Emerson from Rome which began "Italy has been glorious to me" but then voiced one of her ominous premonitions. Typical of her mood swings, she goes from elation to dejection only to end her letters with a switch to present affairs in which personal worries are subsumed in her political interests and her zeal in writing about them.

In Rome, she and Ossoli lived apart; her lodgings were on the Corso near the Caffè Belle Arti where she dropped in to pick up current news on unfolding events; he continued to live in the family palazzo with his ailing father. With Ossoli's help, Margaret began collecting books, papers, wall posters, and pamphlets as the idea of a history of Italy in its revolutionary period took shape in her mind—events were moving rapidly all over Europe and the fact of being in Rome in the midst of the ferment was thrilling to her. Ossoli himself enrolled in the Civic Guard which was formed following the demands upon clerical authorities by Angelo Brunetti, the people's leader.

Mary Russell Mitford, the English novelist and friend of Elizabeth Barrett Browning, would later give this tart, personal summary of Fuller: "A strange wild woman, who was, they say, insupportable at Boston but became better at New York where she was treated only as a lion, better still at Paris, where she knew little French; still softer in England where she was talked over by

Carlyle; and really good and interesting in Italy where the woman took completely the place of the sybil." Margaret had softened; and she found Italians sympathetic to her character: "They admire the ready eloquence of my nature and highly prize my intelligent sympathy . . . with their sufferings." On her part, her enthusiasm for the Italian people showed in her description of their faces: "so full of character, dignity, and what is so rare in an American face, the capacity for pure, exalting passion." She was far beyond the usual American travelers who sought an unchanging Rome, an Arcadian Italy. The American colony in Rome wanted things to stay as they were. They had always distinguished between Italy, the treasure trove of art, and Italians the unworthy custodians. Fuller decried those who defamed the Italians by thinking them unfit for freedom and unworthy of their past heritage.

Fuller's brief and beautiful season ended in despondency at the beginning of 1848. With the arrival of the winter rains, she found she was pregnant. It must have been the greatest trial of her life. Aside from her chronic bad health and debilitating headaches, she had the bleak, damp weather to depress her and, most probably, given her age and nervous constitution, the nausea and general malaise common to many women in the first months of pregnancy. She feared death. She thought she would not survive the ordeal of childbirth and her letters during the winter of 1848 are full of dejection along with railings against her constant money troubles. "Never forget," she writes her brother Richard, "how lonely my position is now and how desolate and suffering it might be made." She hoped for a legacy from her uncle, Abraham Fuller, who, recently deceased, had left an extensive estate. But the final reckoning was a humiliating sum, slightly more than $200.00. "My uncle died as he had lived," she would write to a friend who thought her an heiress, "hard-hearted against me . . . it makes me sad to think how easy it would have been for my uncle by a legacy of a few thousands to put an end to the embarrassments and cares of which I have had my share."

As it was, Margaret did have generous friends and immediate family members who helped from time to time; Richard, in fact, replied that he and the family wrote infrequently so as not to have her pay costly postage on their letters, as was the custom at the time. He provided some consolation to her morale and her money problems with the assurance that the family was prepared to give her $500.00: "It is due to you as the bright ornament of our family, it is due for your cares and attentions in many years past." Never was truer recognition given. But such small remedies never gave Margaret the solid base of security she longed for; she lived always on the edge of financial emergency and actual distress.

All that long, rainy Roman winter of 1848, while Margaret in her *Tribune* communiqués displayed a public, professional mien of engaged reporter on the scene of the momentous rebellions in Europe, in her private correspondence she wrote of poor health, loneliness, and forebodings of death. Writing to her closest friend, Caroline Sturgis Tappan, Margaret looks back at the interval of Italy in her life: "When I arrived in Rome, I was at first intoxicated to be here. The weather was beautiful, and many circumstances combined to place me in a kind of passive, childlike well-being. That is all over now, and with this year, I enter upon a sphere of my destiny so difficult, that I, at present, see no way out, except through the gate of death."

Destiny is omnipresent in her dark thoughts: "It does not seem to be my fault—this destiny: I do not court these things, they come. . . . *É il mio destino* say the Italians." To her brother she used her familiar simile of sea and ships when she wrote of family affairs: "We are never wholly sunk by storms, but no favorable wind ever helps our voyages to surprizing good results." To another correspondent she wrote, "The drama of my fate is very deep, and the ship plunges deeper as it rises higher." She could even jest at her forebodings, as she does in a brief note to Frederic Hedge, an old friend from home who passed through Rome asking her for letters of introduction: "If I never get back and in my sick moping moods I fancy I shall not; it seems so far off; you must write a good verse to put on my tomb-stone."

At times she seems to think that if she survives child-birth, she will return to live quietly in some country place with her brother Richard. What use has it been, after all, to use up her strength for nothing that seems of permanent value, to be ill paid, and to spend her health? In such spirit she uncharacteristically expresses an old cliché: "Amid the corrupt splendors of the old world [I] pine for the pure air of my native land." The old contrast between evil Europe and pure America that once she would have disdained now seems, in her low state, to be all too true.

But to another correspondent she speculates that a return to the U.S. would be a return to a life of fatigue to which she felt quite unequal . . . nor could she yet bear to leave behind scenes of greatness and beauty where she had been enabled to forget her woes. Her uncertain plans veer from staying to going: "If my affairs do not go better I shall return home next Spring." Yet, in response to Emerson's letter from Paris asking her to join him there to return to the states, she replied, "I would like to return with you, but I have much to do and learn in Europe yet. I am deeply interested in this public drama, and wish to see it played out. Methinks I have my part therein, either as actor or historian."

Yet she feels wearied even by her great passions for Italy and Ossoli: "The beautiful forms of art charm no more, and a love, in which there is all fondness, but no help, flatters in vain." Actually, Ossoli's situation was almost as dire as hers and eventually it would be only her meager resources that sustained them.

Throughout that winter of 1848 more than fifty uprisings had erupted in Europe, signaling the most widespread political upheaval in modern history. At issue, she informed her *Tribune* readers, was "the great controversy . . . between the despotic and the republican principle."[21] And yet she survives that dread winter, hopeful that, after conceding a constitution to Rome in March 1848, Pope Pius IX (Pio Nono) will maintain his promises of liberalization. She recovered her enthusiasm for public events even as her political acumen grew.

To William Henry Channing she exulted: "I have been engrossed, stunned almost, by the public events that have succeeded one another with rapidity and grandeur. It is a time such as I always dreamed of. . . . I rejoice to be in Europe at this time, and shall return possessed of a great history . . . it will take three months . . . to finish. It grows upon me." Did she subliminally use the terms of gestation—"engrossed," "grows upon me"— because of the approaching birth of her child as well as of her book? To us now there is a double meaning in the very words that she "shall return possessed of a great history," since the literal written history sank to the ocean floor while her own personal one (all the secret life in Italy of which no one in America yet knew anything) was to become notorious, diffused, and lasting.

By April, with a marked commitment to Mazzini's Republican cause, Margaret felt that "The Gods themselves walk on earth, here in the Italian Spring." Her spirits had revived and she wrote to an acquaintance, "These are great times, my dear Mr. Coleman. No piping times, but good loud swell of the trumpet . . . the men, women and children of Italy show a noble spirit and one that should lead to a solid peace, a real growth." She made some pleasant trips to the hill-towns ringing Rome, her spirits were buoyed by the political scene which increasingly seemed to favor the triumph of a Rome republic. Her hopes were raised: "Everything confirms me in my radicalism; and, without any desire to hasten matters, indeed with surprise to see them rush so like a torrent, I seem to see them all tending to realize my own hopes," she wrote to her friend Costanza Arconati Visconti on May 27, 1848, also advising her that it was her last day in Rome.

Margaret had, all along, been making plans for seclusion away from Rome during the last months of pregnancy by telling friends that she was going off to summer in the mountains at Aquila to work on her book. She prepared Thomas Hicks in Paris, to whom she had sent her papers, with her last wishes: "You would say to those I leave behind that I was willing to die. I have suffered in life far more than I enjoyed. . . . I have wished to be natural and true, but the world was not in harmony with me."

Once in the mountains, predictably, she suffered loneliness and the distance from Ossoli as well as from the events which so galvanized her. Yet her letters were duplicities: laments of her ailments to Ossoli ("*mi sento tutta sola, imprigionata, troppo infelice*"), paeans of praise for the beautiful countryside and the needed solitude to work on her history to her friends and family. The strain of maintaining the pretense about her whereabouts as well as the motive must have been the worst of burdens for someone like Fuller who valued sincerity above all else, who had declared, "Give me truth; cheat me by no illusion."

Finally, she moved from the remoteness of Aquila to Rieti, a town in the Sabine hills some forty miles from Rome, which made it easier for Ossoli to visit her more often. She lived for those visits: "*Mio amore,*" she wrote him, "Near here there is a beautiful place where we can go together if I am able to go out when you come. I will wait for you on Sunday morning and again I will have your coffee ready."

She tried to keep abreast of events through the newspapers which Ossoli sent, she improved her Italian through reading and speaking and had begun to think wholly in it; she engaged the interest of the simple people around her who, she wrote Emerson, find her *simpatica* but, passing her on her solitary walks, always

refer to her as *poveretta, sola soletta*—a poor thing, all alone (antici-
pating poor Lilia in *Where Angels Fear to Tread*). A series of misun-
derstandings resulting from her lack of clarity about her
whereabouts, the difficulties of foreign exchange, and problematic
mail service exasperated her grievous financial difficulties since
money that Greeley had remitted long before was never received.

Yet she kept up her pose: "The country continues most beautiful," she wrote her banker in Rome, "and they have been thresh-
ing the grain in a patriarchal manner very pretty to see. But the
heat is now excessive. What times in Rome! If it were not too far,
I would go there a few days to see for myself." To Ossoli, in Italian, she reported finding an apartment along the Velino river
which flows through Rieti with a nice view from a long loggia off
her bedroom overlooking the river with its banks of "whispering
willows" where she paces on "glorious moonlight nights." The
place suits her well—"I never in my life had a room I liked as I
do this," she wrote home. And, "I could not live without her," she
says of her servant who washed clothes on a large stone in the
river, cooked, sewed, and ironed for her.

Living is cheap: the three-room apartment costs nine dollars a
month, fruit for the day five or six cents, and she can get "the best
salad enough for two persons for one cent a day." Nevertheless,
she was in constant anxiety about money. Down-hearted from
worry about her future, she wrote her brother, "Sometimes it
seems to me I have no friend, or some one would divine how I
am placed and find the means to relieve me. . . . I feel that if any
one in America had been interested to enable me here to live and
learn on my own way, I could have made, at least, a rich intellectual compensation. But people rarely think one like me worth
serving or saving." She was right; only men received financial
support in recognition of their intellectual or artistic gifts; only
beautiful women were kept in comfort in return for their sexual
favors.

Her only solace was Ossoli. She wrote him in Rome to come, that from where she is she will be able to see his stagecoach passing over the bridge, the Ponte Romana. Toward the end of her pregnancy, uncertain whether she would survive the birth of her child, always pinched for money (lack of which prevented her having an excursion to see the nearby birthplace of Ovid), and worrying about remittances that never arrived, she tired easily and did not write much. She tried the patience of Horace Greeley when during her absence from Rome there was an unaccountable six-month hiatus in her dispatches to the *Tribune*. He himself was in financially troubled circumstances and had to sell a part interest in the *Tribune* to raise funds.

Margaret felt that the Italian sun had awakened in her a luxuriant growth that overtook her very mind—"This green may be all of weeds," she wrote, "I hardly care—weeds are beautiful in Italy." She longed to see Ossoli ("when I think that it is possible for me to die alone without touching a dear hand") but told him that given the precipitous political events and his role in the Civic Guard, he must do what duty and honor demand first. Still, "I think often of you . . . if we could be together it would be a consolation, but now everything is going badly. . . . It makes me unhappy that it is necessary to wait so many days before you come, so many so many. I am happy that now I have your little portrait, often I look at it. God keep you."

She must have also brooded incessantly on the question of marriage to Ossoli. Marriage was no haven to Margaret Fuller, who had fully endorsed the concept of women remaining single. Margaret was not averse to a relationship without marriage. She had seen at firsthand the ruined marriages of several of her acquaintances including that of her sister Ellen's with Ellery Channing. It was a constant reminder, as she wrote Richard: "Ellen has wed herself to difficulties from which only the death of her husband could free her."

Aside from her strong belief that a partnership between a man and woman need not be legalized by conventional marriage, there were particular reasons against it for her and Ossoli to ponder: she loved him without doubt and he had tenderly returned that love, but as Anna Karenina was to wonder, is love enough? There were the strictures of society to consider, and on the personal side the great gap between their intellectual compatibilities; further, Ossoli had no professional training which would enable him to support the family, and his youth made Margaret wonder candidly in a letter to William H. Channing if his affection for her would last. For Ossoli's part, marriage with a non-Catholic was not only impossible in the Papal States but would have absolutely disinherited him and severed him from his family and station in life as he had known it.

But she filled her love letters to Ossoli with yearning for him and basic instructions on practical matters during that summer of her seclusion. Writing in Italian gave her thoughts a simplicity of expression which is in marked contrast to the overwrought and abstract, almost hallucinatory, love letters she had penned a few years earlier to James Nathan, the imagined lover.

Rieti, where Margaret lived for the last part of her pregnancy, is on the old consular road, Via Salaria, which starts from Rome and crosses the central mountain range to the Adriatic. The area around Rieti was a site of the Sabine people until conquered by Rome, whose mark is left in the still intact ancient gateway, Porta Romana, and in remnants of the Roman bridge over the river Velino. I know the town, can locate where Margaret lived in lodgings over the river, and can retrace her steps where she strolled to pass her time between Ossoli's visits.

Rieti's municipal building, Il Comune, is located in the upper town on its principal square, Piazza Vittorio Emmanuele II, from which run the two main arteries, Via Garibaldi and Via Roma, names from the Risorgimento. In the commune's arched portico plaques and sculptures commemorate the illustrious heroes of Italy's unification alongside the names of the town's fallen patriots. Missing in that display, and from any history or description of the town, is any reference to Margaret Fuller, who gave birth to her son in Rieti before returning to Rome to play such an important part in the events of the 1848–49 revolution. She had walked Rieti's streets and taken the air and seen the views from the little park bordered with boxwood which is adjacent to the imposing Palazzo Vincentini at the high point of town; she had written parts of her *History* in Rieti; she had seen and described Garibaldi and his rowdy troops' ride through the piazza.

The air, just as she described it, is good; the small town still restful. And yet, I thought, how lonely and strange it must have been for her to be there. The birth of the baby occurred on September 5th. Though still embroiled in the political unrest in Rome, Ossoli managed to be with her. He returned immediately to the city and she wrote him on September 7th, surprised, elated, happy to be alive, and addressing him as her dearest consort: "I feel much better than I hoped. The child is doing well too . . . [and] very beautiful, everybody says so. . . . I hope he will be calmer when you come. . . . Embracing you and kissing you in this dear baby I have in my arms I am Your Affectionate Margaret."

Ossoli officially recognized his son, who was named Angelo Eugene Ossoli, and had a document drawn up in which he named the child heir to his title. There was only a month for Margaret to be with her child before she left him with a wet nurse and returned to Rome, taking up lodgings at Piazza Barberini, and resuming her dispatches to the *Tribune* as a desperately needed source of income. In Rome she was publicly immersed in the stirring events happening in Italy and honed her writing to its best expression as she revealed the progression of her social thought in her dispatches. The *Tribune* articles are full of immediacy, and a powerful prose imbued with the intensity of her engagement in the republican cause. They make riveting reading even today and in dispatch #25 she announced that she would chronicle the events she was witnessing in her book-in-progress.

She triumphantly announced the Pope's flight from Rome in November 1848. Yet in a journal entry for January 1, 1849, she is more contained about the Constituent Assembly's ability to steer the new Roman Republic: "There may be many breakers yet before that shore is reached." Still a romantic, she saw the drama unfolding before her as the triumph of good over evil. That was her heroic, public side.

In the United States, at the beginning of 1849 Elizabeth Blackwell graduated first in her class from Geneva Medical College and became the first qualified woman physician in the country, which, if the news reached her, must have gratified Margaret even though she had passed beyond her feminist concerns for the larger ones of Italy's liberation and America's renewal. Perhaps she had heard that the New York state legislature had enacted the Married Woman's Property Act—one of the first such pieces of legislation to insure a woman's rights in the country. And in the summer of 1848 the first women's rights convention had been held in Seneca Falls.

Privately and secretly she was an unwed-mother in anguish at being separated from her infant son and in constant worry over him. She was torn with remorse but found no other way to earn his keep than by her work in Rome. Her ambivalence was great and occasionally became displaced and was expressed as her view of the Italian people—publicly she praised their spirit, privately she sometimes found them "coarse, selfish and ignorant," and about Garibaldi and his "desperadoes" she also had qualms.

In February 1849, Rome was declared a Republic with universal suffrage. The revolution became a war of national liberation all documented in Margaret's dispatches.

James Russell Lowell, who was married to one of the women who had attended Margaret's Conversations in Boston, continued his barbed, sarcastic allusions to Margaret when he wrote to William Wetmore Story, their mutual friend in Rome: "My advice to you is to come directly home as soon as you receive this. I have it on good authority that the Austrian Government has its eye on Miss F. It would be a pity to have so much worth and genius shut up for life in Spielberg. Her beauty might perhaps save her. Pio Nono also regards her with a natural jealous eye, fearing that the College of Cardinals may make her the successor of Pope Joan." By March, Mickiewicz was in Rome and helped her shake off her melancholy. Then Mazzini arrived. They were the persons she most esteemed in Europe. Her energies revived even as she noted the departure from Rome of many Americans, including the Cropseys.

By April 1849, the French army, treacherously called in by the Pope against his own people, marched on Rome; at their first attack they were driven back by Garibaldi. At that time Margaret received a request from Princess Belgioioso asking her to direct the Fatebenefratelli hospital on the island in the Tiber. The fight to maintain the precarious freedom of the Republic found Ossoli on the battlements and Margaret nursing the wounded.

Her dispatches to the *Tribune* became terse, dramatic. On May 6th, "I write you from barricaded Rome." She vainly hopes that the United States will recognize Republican Rome and though she foresees the crushing of the patriot forces by the French army, she also foresees the future: "The result is sure . . . the work is done; nor can it stop til Italy becomes independent and united as a republic." Around her lies devastation: Villa Borghese in ruins as are the villas on the Janiculum; even the church of San Pietro in Montorio, flying the black flag to show it is a hospital of wounded, is bombed.

The state of siege is terrible and on the night of the June 30th bombardment, Margaret called Lewis Cass, the American chargé d'affaires, to her to give him papers for her family in event of her death as she left to join Ossoli, exposed on the Pincian Hill where he commanded a battery. It was her intention to remain with Ossoli and share his fate. They survived the French assault. Recalling those times, Margaret wrote to her sister: "During the siege of Rome I could not see my little boy. What I endured at the time in various ways not many would survive. In the burning sun I went every day to wait in the crowd for letters about him. Often they did not come. I saw blood that streamed on the wall where Ossoli was. I have a piece of bomb that burst close to him. I sought solace in tending the suffering men. But when I beheld the beautiful fair young men bleeding to death, or mutilated for life, I felt the woe of all the mothers."

Years after the events of 1848–49, Louisa May Alcott (who as a child remembered Fuller teaching at her father's school), met Mazzini in London and heard him recall Margaret's great courage in Rome. James Russell Lowell, who had earlier roasted her in his satire, now extolled Margaret's bravery and retorted angrily to the Catholic Bishop of New York who was soliciting aid for the Pope while inveighing against the Rome populace and "the female plenipotentiary" of the *Tribune*. Margaret herself would remark that were it "another century" she would ask for the post of American ambassador to Rome herself.

As George Eliot wrote, so others have concurred: "Every reader of Margaret Fuller's *Life* must have felt the superiority of the letters she wrote from Italy over her earlier journals and correspondence. A straining after some unattained effect had given way to calm vigour, and magniloquence to noble simplicity. It was clear that the blossoming time of her nature had come. Her affections had been drawn into their proper channel; her intellect had found its proper soil in the deep rich loam of European civilization, and her wide sympathies had found a grand definite object in the struggles of the Italian people." In Italy came the moment of Fuller's greatest achievement both in her work and in her life. Once having objected to the blind optimism of communal living at Brook Farm, eight years later she was affirming herself an associationist, "a believer that the next form society will take in remedy of the dreadful ills that now consume it will be voluntary association in small communities."

By the end of June the Republic had fallen. Walt Whitman, a fervent follower in America of Fuller's dispatches, commemorated with sorrow the demise of "That brief, tight, glorious grip / Upon the throats of kings." Defeat marked the closure of activism in Margaret's own life. After a last meeting with Mazzini on July 4th, Margaret and Ossoli fled Rome as the French occupied it.

More distress awaited Margaret and Ossoli when they reached Rieti and found their child almost dead of malnourishment. With the most strenuous efforts they nursed Angelino back to health, but in a letter to Lewis Cass, Margaret reported, "he is so weak it seems to me he can scarcely ever revive to health. If he cannot, I do not wish him to live; life is hard enough for the strong, it is too much for the feeble. Only, if he dies, I hope I shall, too. I was too fatigued before, and this last shipwreck of hopes would be more than I could bear."

The family left the Papal States, where Ossoli would have been hunted down as a traitor, for the relative security of Florence. There Margaret tried through Carlyle (an unlikely prospect, given his anti-republican views) to find an English publisher for her *History*, but was rejected. Had it been accepted perhaps Margaret and her little family would not have had to leave Italy. It was her evil star, as she had often noted, that decided crucial events of her life.

In Florence, the fugitives did find some tranquility and the brief sweetness of a life together. Their arrival in the fall of 1849 came as a shock to the Anglo-American community there. Elizabeth Barrett Browning reported Margaret Fuller's appearance "with a husband and a child above a year old. Nobody had even suspected a word of this underplot, and her American friends stood in mute astonishment before this apparition of them here."[22] Margaret Fuller had missed meeting Elizabeth Barrett in London in September 1846 when she called at Wimpole Street with a letter of introduction, for Miss Barrett had just eloped to Italy with Mr. Browning.

In Harvard's Houghton Library is a letter dated May 9, 1851, from Ossoli's sister, Marchesa Angela de Andreis, to Margaret's sister Ellen Channing, that relates the fugitives' story and tells of their marriage. Once routed from Rome, and with no prospects for Ossoli in Italy, their future seemed to lie in a return to Margaret's homeland. Practical considerations dictated the necessity of marriage and Margaret finally revealed her union with Ossoli and the fact of their child to her friends and family in America.[23] "As to marriage," she wrote her sister, "I think the intercourse of heart and mind may be fully enjoyed without entering this partnership of daily life, still I do not find it burdensome," thus ratifying her married state with circumspection.

Despite Mrs. Browning's initial coolness toward meeting Margaret, the two women, who had both had spectacular romances and had become middle-aged mothers within months of each other, grew close in Florence. Elizabeth Barrett Browning matched Margaret in erudition and in ardor for the cause of Italian unification. Margaret the revolutionary was soon borrowing patterns for baby's caps from Mrs. Browning.

Margaret now presented herself as Marchesa Ossoli and signed her letters Margaret Ossoli. She had always, in her communications with Ossoli, even as they fought for a republican Rome, addressed letters to him with his full-blown title: Il Nobil Uomo/ Signor Marchese Gio.Angiolo Ossoli. Writing to Marchesa Arconati, Margaret somewhat apologetically ridiculed the notion of a title for a republican like herself, but it was, she said, a demonstration of solidarity with Ossoli to take his title as well as his name.

Perhaps the real question is, if Ossoli, too, were a republican, why didn't he renounce his title? Why was it so important to secure it for his son? Did the emphasis on the Ossoli title mean that they would have, when times were right, returned to Italy? That is what they both would have wished.

For the moment, with hopes dashed for any livelihood in Italy, Margaret wrote her final dispatch, #37, on January 6, 1850, from Florence, ending it on a note of prophecy that the future would see the final triumph of Italy's freedom and that Mazzini's ideals with time would be accomplished. She and Ossoli had made the hard decision that they would leave Italy for her homeland. Ossoli recalled a prophecy that he should shun the sea for it would be fatal to him. Without an alternative, the couple overcame their misgivings and premonitions, and sent farewell letters to friends in Rome ("I am so sad and teary leaving Italy that I seem paralyzed," Margaret wrote the Storys). Their last night in Florence they visited the Brownings where Margaret said it was a good omen that they were sailing in a ship called the *Elizabeth*. She left for Elizabeth's son a gift Bible from her son prophetically inscribed "In Memory of Angelo Eugene Ossoli." "Such gloom she had in leaving Italy! So full she was of sad presentiment!" Mrs. Browning was to remember.

Margaret's presentiment was accurate: she faced death all the way home. First the captain died of smallpox, then Angelino caught it and struggled once more for his life. The irony of Fuller's much used quote, "Let women be sea captains if they will!" is that on her ill-fated journey home from Italy, after the captain's untimely death en route, it was his widow Mrs. Hasty who instructed the mate on navigating the ship and became a virtual sea-captain. Always in Margaret's mind was the intense inner quandary that the person she had become could never go home again to America.

During the night of July 19, 1850, heartbreakingly close to New York harbor, the ship *Elizabeth* struck a reef off Fire Island. There followed twelve torturous hours for Margaret, Ossoli, and their child, clinging to the wrecked ship before they were swept away, one by one, into the ocean that also claimed her manuscript. Some, including Mrs. Hasty, saved themselves by clinging to planks from the wreckage and letting themselves be washed ashore, though when young Horace Sumner, brother of statesman Charles Sumner, tried it he sank immediately. From Katherine Anthony's psychological biography of Fuller comes the theory that Margaret submitted to being drowned by not trying to save herself, Ossoli, and the child. "Many years before she had written, 'If all the wrecked submitted to be drowned, the world would be a desert.' This is a literal description of how she ultimately met her death. . . . Her death had in it the elements of pagan acquiescence, of consenting to her destiny."[24]

No, I think; she did not go passively, she went willfully, loyal to her commitment never to abandon Ossoli or her child. She had joined Ossoli on the battlements, ready to die with him there; when Angelino was near death she had vowed she would not survive him. At the end they were not separated. Did she know the cruelest of paradoxes, as she waited in the deep to go down—that just because of that anguish and extreme travail her name, and so her work, would surely live forever? That the melodrama of her death would give her eternal life? In her bones she had always known the fact of her early end; it was foreseen in all those dreams, the forebodings about sea and ships . . .

The news of the tragedy reached the Fuller family and friends swiftly. Two days after the event Emerson noted in his journal: "On Friday, July 19th, Margaret dies on rocks of Fire Island Beach within sight of and within sixty rods of shore. To the last her country proves inhospitable to her; brave, eloquent, subtle, accomplished, devoted, constant soul!"[25] With authorization from the

Fuller family, Emerson sent Henry David Thoreau to the scene of the wreck to see what could be recovered. He got to Fire Island five days after the wreck when vandals had already scavenged and there was little to be found. On July 25th, Thoreau wrote Emerson that he was staying only a mile from the wreck and had spoken with the first mate and carpenter from the *Elizabeth*. Someone had found a shift with Margaret's initials on it; Thoreau himself found Ossoli's coat from which he removed a button to take home. Later Margaret's love-letters to Ossoli were found in a little black leather trunk washed up on the beach. The bodies of Margaret and Ossoli were never recovered. The body of Angelino, washed up and buried in a shallow grave on the beach, was taken to Mt. Auburn cemetery in Cambridge for reburial where he lies at the foot of the memorial to his mother, the profile of her daguerreotype likeness carved against a sword and a book within a garland.

From the diary of Emelyn Story, Margaret's friend in Rome, August 6, 1850:

Came home to find letters and the saddest of all news of Margaret and her child and her husband. How deeply I felt it, how sad I was made, I cannot here say; but pale was the sky, dull the face of nature when I thought of the friend I had lost. . . . My mind, last night, was so filled with thoughts and memories of Margaret Ossoli that I found no refreshment even in sleep. The vision of her as I saw her last on the steps of our house, and the memory of those troubled days in Rome, kept coming back to me, and I felt so deep a sorrow that could look neither before nor behind.

Margaret had previous premonitions and dreams of drowning: in September, 1844, at Nantasket Beach, she recorded her dream of falling off the rocks at Nantasket into the ocean. Then she dreamed that her companion, Caroline, was drowning in the ocean and she couldn't save her—"My feet seemed rooted to one spot: and my cloak of red silk kept falling off when I tried to go. At last the waves had washed up her dead body on the hard sand and then drew it back again. It was a terrible dream."[26]

On the way to Italy, she wrote Emerson, "Between Leghorn and Naples, our boat was run into by another, and we only just missed being drowned." In Rome, while young Eddie Spring was in her charge and she became distracted, he came near drowning in a pool in the Pincian Gardens before she got to him. A coach she was to have taken from Rieti to Rome plunged into a swollen river and the occupants barely saved. Her letters are full of Destiny, and laced with images of drowning: "I hope she [Destiny] will not leave me long in the world, for I am tired of keeping myself up in the water without corks, and without strength to swim." Perhaps most prophetic of all was that Margaret, in earlier autobiographical writings, had dubbed herself "Miranda"—the sea-borne child of *The Tempest* who had been set out to sea and suffered shipwreck.

In 1901, a bronze commemorative plaque was dedicated to Margaret Fuller in a gazebo structure on a boardwalk constructed in her memory at Point O'Woods, the site on Fire Island closest to where the *Elizabeth* went down. Julia Ward Howe wrote the epitaph on the plaque and testimonials from leading American women were read at the dedication ceremony. Just twelve years later, the sea that had claimed Margaret Fuller washed away her memorial. It has not been replaced.

Like Corinne, Margaret Fuller paid for her gifts. She fell into something worse than oblivion after her dramatic death by shipwreck at age forty—she became the satirized myth of herself and for over a century was condescended to by biographers, caricatured on the sidelines of literature as an eccentric New England Bluestocking, and left to history more an oddity than a first-rank mind. Fuller's contemporaries probably thought she had reaped what she had sown, though the kinder would have attenuated the harsh judgment by concluding that, horrendous as it was, her death spared her the social censure that might have greeted her return home. After all, she had lingered too long in the land of the lotus-eaters.

Hawthorne's Zenobia, who dies by drowning in *The Blithedale Romance*, the guilty Miriam in *The Marble Faun*, and even the theme of sinful sexuality of *The Scarlet Letter* seem all connected to Margaret Fuller and to Hawthorne's obsessive censure of her. His ferocity seems not only part of a personal pathology in regard to sexuality, but also the standard reaction by some men of letters to feminists. As literary critics Sandra Gilbert and Susan Gubar point out in their *No Man's Land*, such men dealt with feminism by fantasizing about punishing or killing its proponents in order to save the life of male tradition.

Henry James is said in *Portrait of a Lady* to have fashioned Henrietta Stackpole, "a woman journalist studying the position of Italian women," upon Fuller, as well as Olive Chancellor, the feminist figure in *The Bostonians*. It is not hard to imagine the fastidious James being troubled by the turbulence of Margaret's life. He, in Italy after the successful unification of 1870 of which she had been a premature forerunner in the revolution of 1848, mourned the loss of papal pageantry and the passage of the sleepy old town into a modern capital city. He was the aesthete of the past; she had been the champion of progress toward a republic.

I thought of once having been asked, in my research, why I wanted to see Fuller's original holograph journal when it could be more easily read in a printed copy. Not want to see Margaret's own hand? Could the curator not imagine what could be read in that script—nervous, flying, poised, or perfected—as compared to the cold anonymity of print? I thought of Margaret the child, so wanting to please her father and earn his affection when, in a letter to him, she wrote regarding ink blots on the page: "I spoil everything by my impetuosity." That trait of writing in a hurry and throwing herself headlong into her subject, trying to keep up with the pace of her thoughts, is something that remains a mark of her writing style—a style that is frequently overblown, rambling, replete with the allusions of her childhood indoctrination into the virtues of ancient Rome, and unremittingly intense. It is most certainly not the linear, male-privileged standard of unity and coherence and has always been decried by her male biographers and critics as "slipshod," full of digressions, and lacking in surface unity and an overarching theme.

But Margaret wanted, in her words, to communicate "poetic impression"; thus her books have their "wanderings," are multithematic, seemingly fragmented. They are as she is—replete with the vigor of her thoughts and reflections on many things. As she would not be bound by silly conventions in life, so her writing was not bound by linear rules. *Summer on the Lakes, 1843* and *Woman in the Nineteenth Century*, seem idiosyncratic, filled as they are with anecdotes, personal reminiscences and side excursions off the beaten track of her subject. But they are very much of a piece with the woman who had declared that writing was worthless except as the record of a life and that one's book should be an indication of the self.

George Eliot had always intended to write on Margaret Fuller, but aside from two book reviews never did. That she was deeply touched by the American woman is indicated in Eliot's letter to a friend a few years after Fuller's death: "You know how sad one feels when a great procession has swept by one, and the last notes of its music have died away, leaving one alone with the fields and sky. I feel so about life sometimes. It is a help to read such a life as Margaret Fuller's. How inexpressibly touching that passage from her journal—'I shall always reign through the intellect, but the life! the life! O my God! shall that never be sweet?' I am thankful, as if for myself, that it was sweet at last."

Margaret Fuller did know sweetness. It was short-lived, but she knew it would be; Fate showed her its benefices, she said, only to withdraw them. Premonitions about the sea, dreams of drowning: it's as if the very ebb and flow of Margaret Fuller's life with its high waves of elation and then the down-trough of despair had always carried within it the prophetic emblem of her end.

She had always confronted failure and started afresh, but finally there was no more incentive. Did she lose heart with the hugeness of what lay before her even if she were saved—the necessity of earning a living, of making a place for herself and her younger, foreign husband in the censorious milieu of her homeland where he and the child might figure only as curiosities, appendages to her? She was tired, she was drained finally of vital energy and hope; always the decisive one in the relationship, she did not finally attempt the only possible life-saving move—to emulate Mrs. Hasty and try to ride a plank to shore. Ossoli stood by letting her decide, joining in prayer with a servant girl who was the only other Italian aboard. Margaret's last words, heard by a crew member before he jumped overboard were, "I see death all about me." She must have believed that only in death would she find perfect peace and union with her beloved husband and child.

How often I thought of Margaret Fuller when I lived in Rome in a building neighboring hers in Piazza Barberini; how often I had passed the landmarks of her presence in Rome. On the Island in the Tiber, one of the most charming and picturesque places in the city and always revered as a place of healing, is the hospital where she tended the wounded; across the river are the heights of Janiculum Hill where Garibaldi and his heroic followers fought off the French troops who had been called in by the Pope to undo the Rome Republic and restore temporal power to him.

On a return to Rome as a visiting artist at the American Academy in Rome, I was on Janiculum Hill, site of the battles of 1848–49. The area is full of monuments to what Fuller called "these sad but glorious days." From a broad terrace overlooking the city a cannon salute is fired at noon everyday in honor of the gallant fighters for a republic, and there stands the imposing statue of a mounted Garibaldi. Nearby streets are named for all the heroes who participated in those first battles for the unification of Italy. This is where modern Italy had its beginnings.

Across from the American Academy is another of its properties, the historic Villa Aurelia. In Margaret Fuller's time it was a country residence known as Villa Savorelli, the property of a count who furnished candles to the Vatican and was loyal to the Pope. Garibaldi took over the villa and made it his headquarters because of its proximity to Porta San Pancrazio where the French had placed their canon. Badly damaged in the siege, the property was bought some years later by an American woman, Clara Jessup Heyland, who restored it and renamed it Villa Aurelia for its proximity to the old Aurelian wall. In 1909 she gifted the villa to the Academy and it now hosts concerts and conferences in its beautiful rooms. In November 2000, a three-day international conference with thirty speakers was held there to celebrate Margaret Fuller.

And across from the American Academy is another landmark property, the Villa Sciarra, now a public park. There, within the lovely grounds where shaded walkways are named for the prominent, one is called Viale Margaret Ossoli Fuller. There, in the city of her soul, she is remembered as a hero.[27] I often sat there in the park when I was at the American Academy and I liked particularly to think of another New England woman, Emily Dickinson, who though a homebody and not the adventurer that Fuller was, in her own way was still an intrepid traveler through poetry to her predecessor's Italy. Both New England women had, each in her own way, reached Italy.

Emily Dickinson, 1830–1886

2. *The Italian Side of Emily Dickinson*

A few years before my stay at the American Academy in Rome, I had been a fellow resident at Villa Serbelloni, the Rockefeller Foundation's Bellagio Study and Conference Center on Lake Como in northern Italy. Situated above one of earth's beauty spots, the villa is sited on a wooded promontory overlooking the lake with its distant ring of Alps. The beauty of Lake Como was well known in antiquity to the Romans who, by the first century A.D., had established their villas in magnificent locations along the lake. According to scholars, Pliny the Younger's written description of his property indicates that it must have occupied the promontory over the lake at Bellagio where Villa Serbelloni now stands, and where, in fact, fragments of Roman roof tile have been found in abundance in areas around the residence.

If I had known during my stay that Margaret Fuller had visited Bellagio a century and a half earlier, I might have surmised that she was drawn there by Pliny's accounts, so steeped in classical lore was she. Actually, she was there in a moment of difficult personal choice—whether to be practical and continue home to the states with her travel companions or romantically to follow her heart and return to Rome. While in the north of Italy she met Alessandro Manzoni, author of Italy's great novel, *I promessi sposi*, which opens with the sonorous line about its setting on Lake Como, "*Quel ramo del lago di Como che si svolge verso il mezzogiorno . . .*"

Manzoni's beautiful line came back to me each morning when I seemed to be traversing paradise as I left the villa and went through the terraced grounds and gardens to my work room in an ancient chapel down close to the lake. Each morning, from the promontory at the very tip of a headland which juts into the icy blue of Lake Como, I stopped at a view not only stunning but also inducive to contemplation: spread below me and backed by the Alps, the lake branches into two arms: Lake Lecco to the east, and the continuation of Como to the west. It's a compelling image of duality that spoke to me of my own dual heritage from Italy and America. The main body of Lake Como and its continuance was America and the eastern branch was Italy—the two were both joined and separate. And with that view from the past home of an American Principessa, plus the inspiration of a Dickinson poem, came the idea for exploring what Italy had meant in the lives and work of other American women. From the heights over the lake I could see it as diverging into branches, or as one body.

But the view over lake and Alps went further. It gave me the exact visualization of this Dickinson poem:

> Our lives are Swiss—
> So Still—so Cool—
> Till some odd afternoon
> The Alps neglect their Curtains
> and we look farther on!
>
> Italy stands the other side!
> While like a guard between—
> The Solemn Alps—
> The siren Alps
> Forever intervene!

The poem, now numbered 80, was first called "Alpine Glow" as if it were merely some vapid scenic verse when it was published in 1896 under the editorship of Mabel Loomis Todd. Either she titled it or it had been done by Thomas Higginson, who, as co-editor with her of the 1890 and 1891 editions of the poems, had insisted on titles and had "corrected" text and punctuation to make the poems more acceptable. The poem is much more than an Alpine glow.

It was emblematic to me of the pull of Italy and I used it in my introduction to *The Dream Book: An Anthology of Writings by Italian American Women* to illustrate the fascination Italy has always exerted over the Anglo-American imagination:

> It is interesting how many English or American women turned from the Anglo tradition and toward the idea of Italy as a freeing of their human qualities and as an enriching of life. The Brownings went off to live in Florence; Margaret Fuller, in her thirty-seventh year, arrived in Italy as the leading American woman writer and intellectual of her time and found love and motherhood there, writing, 'Italy has been glorious to me.' And Emily Dickinson, from Amherst, thought of Italy as the loosening of trammels, some absolute freeing of the spirit.

Emily Dickinson was a young woman of twenty when Margaret Fuller perished and would certainly have known of her. Although firmly established in our imaginations as the recluse of Amherst, Massachusetts, Dickinson was through her poetry as spirited as Fuller. She is certainly unique, idiosyncratic, and stands quite alone in American literary tradition. In her lifetime she published less than a dozen poems; at her death, more than a thousand others were discovered in her bedroom bureau drawer. She was not reticent in her poetry, but created imagery that was bold and startling with references to an Italy she knew only in her fantasy where it stood for some longed-for, beckoning freedom of spirit.

While I was at Bellagio, Dickinson's poem 80 teased me into considering her proposition that there is another, more vivid side to lives. To every guarded side of a regulated life there is the alternative, that, if set free, would fly to a freedom metaphorically called Italy. One would decamp a "Swiss" life, with its clockwork precision and predictability, for the seductive exuberance of its opposite—"Italy." Emily Dickinson belonged to the same sisterhood of sensibility that had drawn so many nineteenth-century American women of talent to Italy—authors such as Catherine Maria Sedgwick, Julia Ward Howe, and Constance Fenimore Woolson, sculptors Harriet Hosmer and Adelaide Johnson, actress Charlotte Cushman, and painter Edmonia Lewis. It was the combination of my view of Lake Como from Bellagio, the Dickinson poem, and my own personal history that came together in the question of what Italy had meant in the lives of other women who had wanted to "look farther on," beyond the bounds of the ordinary, the securely routine, to "the other side."

Standing guard over Emily Dickinson's curtained and orderly life was the patriarchal Calvinism of her father's New England house (built by his father in 1813) which could effectively bar, like the very Alps, any access (except in fantasy) to the more exotic realm of passionate self-expression in art. I have been to that home in the pleasant town of Amherst. It is where Emily was born in 1830, where she lived (except from age 10 to 25, when her family occupied a house around the corner), and where she died in 1886. It is an elegant Federal-style brick house set back on an elevation above Main Street, adorned with green shutters, and topped in 1855 with an Italianate tower-cupola from which one could see the goings-on next-door in Evergreens, the Tuscan-villa style home of Emily's brother Austin and his family. And Main Street is not at all a commercial strip of shops and businesses but a broad tree-lined residential avenue. Standing as it does on a rise, the Dickinson house, called The Homestead, is commanding and aloof, connoting privilege and sanctuary. The house became Emily's shelter as she withdrew from social activities, from visiting friends and church-going, finally not even venturing to see guests in her own home or making her usual visits next door. I imagined her as a kind of cloistered nun, dressed in white. To the census taker she declared her occupation: "At home." On her gravestone, just three fields away, her epitaph is simply "Called Back."

In willed seclusion Emily built herself; she was her own support, as invincible and strong as a well-built house, an affirmed soul as she declares in poem 1142:

> The Props assist the House
> Until the House is built
> And then the Props withdraw
> And adequate, erect,
> The House support itself
> And cease to recollect
> The Augur and the Carpenter—
> Just such a retrospect
> Hath the perfected Life—
> A past of Plank and Nail
> And slowness—then the
> Scaffolds drop
> Affirming it a Soul.

In 1826, a few years before Emily Dickinson's birth, her father Edward had met Catherine Maria Sedgwick, then the most celebrated female novelist in the United States, whose work he had read and admired for some time. In a letter describing the evening party at which he had been in Miss Sedgwick's company,

Mr. Dickinson remarked on her interesting countenance: "an appearance of much thought, & rather masculine features." He then noted, "I feel happy at seeing a female who had done so much to give our works of taste so pure and delicate a character—and a conscious pride that women of our own country . . . are emulating not only the females but the men of England & France & Germany & Italy in works of literature. . . . Tho' I should be sorry to see another Mme. de Staël—especially if any one wished to make a partner of her for life."[1]

In lawyer Dickinson's careful hedging of a woman's range (an attitude that must have come to bear on his daughter Emily) is his verdict: it was one thing for a woman writer to be a sedate Sedgwick, and quite another to be a rebellious, outspoken Germaine de Staël. A decade after Staël's death, the sway she had held since her extremely popular 1807 novel *Corinne, or Italy* swept Europe and became a transatlantic sensation was still evident in her hold on Edward Dickinson's imagination. The Staëlian legacy had immigrated to stern New England where, though denounced from the pulpit, generations of young women, thrilled by the book's heroine and by the alluring descriptions of Italy, yearned for the glamours of Rome and the brilliance of Corinne. In Emily Dickinson's lifetime the book went through forty editions.

Widely spoken of and known, Germaine de Staël was a figure of great import in the Romantic Movement and influential on several women writers. This formidable personage had swept down upon Italy in 1804–5 in her own emulation of Goethe's earlier journey, and had apotheosized the country in her novel by extolling the genius of its past and elevating its long lethargy of decline into a spiritual value for those of feeling. From all contemporary reports, Germaine de Staël was a daunting presence, discomfiting to many men; Washington Irving, the first American literary personage of standing to travel in Italy, records having dined with her in 1805 in Rome at the home of Baron Humboldt where she astounded Irving with the amazing flow of her conversation and the question upon question with which she plied him.

Mme. de Staël's *Corinne, or Italy* reinforced the romantic spell of an Arcadian Italy, the actual "hero" of this novel-as-travelogue. The book's title could not be more significant—Corinne and Italy are one and the same, while restraint and Northern moodiness is the lot both of English Lord Nelvil, whom Corinne loves, and the dull Englishwoman Lucile, whom he eventually marries.

Corinne was an *improvvisatrice*, something of a rap artist of the day, a sibyl and poetic improviser who could be given a theme and then declaim on it in verse before a public audience—a gift which Staël equates with the Italian genius for spontaneity and emotiveness. Corinne is torn by the conflicted loyalties of a dual heritage but finally chooses the Italy of her Italian mother over the England of her father. The dilemma stands for much more than nationalism or a narrow allegiance to one country over the other. It is art over ordinariness. Under the guise of blatant nationalist rivalries, and the cross-cultural antagonisms between lovers, is the real issue: the difficulty of the superior woman in being creative and being herself independent of a male "protector" or validator. The novel's power is not as a literary text, but in the creation of a myth: Italy (or the Southern temperament) as freedom for the superior woman. The preachiness in *Corinne* is due to Staël's belief that literature should demonstrate a moral or social value.

Mme. de Staël not only raised questions, she also raised hackles. She opened a Pandora's box and aired the essential conflict for those she termed women of genius: that is, how to be true to a creative gift and yet not be driven by emotions nor give in to social convention. For Staël also believed, with a certain contradiction, that it was in Italy (the land of emotion as well as creativity) that the woman of genius could best realize her full potential. As with a later French author, Simone de Beauvoir, Madame asked more of other women than she herself could deliver.

For in her own turbulent life, Mme. de Staël had it both ways. She followed her own bent, but was still "the woman who loved too much" and had a veritable harem of male *cicisbei* following her all over Europe in her pursuit of both love and fame. Caught up as she was in the imperatives of either/or, her life was the perpetual franticness of facing one side against the other. In a sense, she split her own nature into the gifted Corinne and the domestic Lucile and was both. Well aware of her struggle, she still needed constant love and attention from men to sustain her gift. And yet, she was greatly admired and viewed with awe. But not all women can carry it off.

As Lord Byron observed, "Madame de Staël, I grant, is a clever woman; but all the other madams are not Staëls." As late as 1878, reference was still being made to the author of *Corinne* in the passage in Henry James's novel *The Europeans* where, after calling on Eugenia, an American bred in Europe, one impressed New Englander says to another, "Now that's what is called conversation. . . . It must be quite the style that we have heard about, that we have read about—the style of conversation of Madame de Staël."

Many English and American women of talent like Emily Dickinson, George Eliot, Elizabeth Barrett Browning, Margaret Fuller, Harriet Beecher Stowe, and even young Sophia Peabody before she became the self-negating wife of Nathaniel Hawthorne, had been directly influenced by *Corinne*. Elizabeth Barrett Browning's long narrative poem *Aurora Leigh* was her version of *Corinne*, and like Staël's novel featured a heroine with both an English and an Italian side. Constance Woolson's story "At the Chateau of Corinne" was based on her own visits to the site of Mme. de Staël's home on Lake Geneva and bespeaks the French woman's influence even though Woolson's story gives it a bitter twist: the fictional character Katherine Winthrop has to choose between her literary ambitions and marriage to a man who cannot abide Madame de Staël or any other literary woman. He has serious, unspoken objections to de Staël's heroine Corinne as a model of female greatness and offers marriage on condition that Katherine cultivate the "simple and retiring womanly graces" and "write no more" (thus echoing Nathaniel Hawthorne's own warped view of women writers as expressed to his wife Sophia: "My dearest, I cannot enough thank God, that, with a higher and deeper intellect than any other woman, thou has never . . . prostituted thyself to the public. . . . Women are too good for authorship, and that is the reason it spoils them so."[2] Sophia's name as a published author would appear only after Nathaniel's death.) In Woolson's story, Katherine's acquiescence is her downfall and after the marriage her husband "keeps in his study a complete set of Madame de Staël's works as a kind of trophy of what he took from his wife: her independence of mind, her literary aspirations."

In the figure of Corinne, who experienced the flowering of her art and life in Italy and was crowned with laurel on Rome's Capitoline, Germaine de Staël wanted to demonstrate that women could, if they wanted, come into their own in Italy as was impossible elsewhere. That many actual women—poets, sculptors, writers, scholars—did attain personal achievement there is a reality which belies the fictions written by men. If one believed the male account, the gifts of Italy were redeemable only by men and might actually be fatal to women, as they were, for example, to Henry James's *Daisy Miller* and poor Lilia in Forster's *Where Angels Fear to Tread*.

In the Western mode of establishing Either/Or categories, Italy did stand for the Other in human experience: freedom over discipline, innocence over knowledge, and, most romantically, the licentious and sensual South versus a Northern moral temperament. Nothing sums up the tension of contrary positions better than Mme. de Staël's schizoid Corinne with her broad dualisms:

North or South, the hold of reason or the sway of enthusiasm, self-expression in work or self-denial in love. Such bondage to a dualistic notion of experience is the character's undoing. Americans and Europeans alike had yet to absorb the lesson of Eastern wisdom where both parts of one's nature can be accommodated in an ongoing process of alternate rising and falling of differing sides, rather than a final trouncing of one side by the other. All experience is one, not a dichotomy of opposites.

Models of self-realized women following their bent as writers were not lacking to Emily Dickinson; and each reflected in some way the appeal of Italy for women. Catherine Sedgwick, an enthusiastic traveler in Italy between 1839 and 1841, was a reader of Leopardi and sympathetic to the political cause of Italian independence as was Emily Dickinson's chief heroine, Elizabeth Barrett Browning. "My Italy of women" was Elizabeth Barrett Browning's phrase from *Aurora Leigh*, the celebrated and widely read prose-poem which followed the tradition of *Corinne* by having an Anglo-Italian heroine-poet who chose her Italian over her English side and became celebrated for her talent. Emily Dickinson was an avid reader of Mrs. Browning and well acquainted with *Aurora Leigh* which, as a text, was to influence her life. In George Eliot's *The Mill on the Floss*, Emily Dickinson would have come upon references to *Corinne*; Elizabeth Barrett Browning had read it three times over in her twenties. And for Emily Dickinson, who revered Mrs. Browning, it came easily that Italy signified the faraway paradise of gifted women.

Given Mr. Dickinson's association with intellectual circles and his connection with Amherst College, Emily herself would surely have heard discussion of such a well-known personality in American letters as Margaret Fuller. Emily had grown up, in her father's Amherst home, in cultivated and literate surroundings where books and ideas were discussed and reading was part of life. The

Dickinsons were acquainted with the cream of New England literary figures and Emily would have been well aware of Fuller's being called the Yankee Corinne. Given her dominant position in the culture of the times, the name of Margaret Fuller, author, critic, editor of *The Dial*, and closely associated with the Brook Farm utopian experiment and the Transcendental Movement, must have been frequently mentioned in the Dickinson household.

It is known that Emily read the transcendentalists, much admiring Thoreau and Emerson, and Margaret Fuller had once been part of that group. A girlhood friend of Emily's recalled their reading Fuller's translation from the German of *Correspondence of Fräulein Günderode and Bettina von Arnim* soon after its Boston publication in 1842.[3] Fuller's choice of not translating Bettina von Arnim's fictionalized account of her real exchange with Goethe, but, rather, the fervid expression of her friendship with another woman shows Fuller's explicit endorsement of the one freedom women had—letter writing with a same-sex confidante. Nineteenth-century women, confined to domesticity and largely excluded from the male world of ideas and action, exercised their intellectual and imaginative powers in intense, self-revelatory, often extravagantly heated epistles, the correspondents reciprocally inflamed to keep up the pitch of intensity. In letter-writing, the banked fires of their quiet "womanly" lives lit up as if to sear the pages with all that was, otherwise, pent up and unexpressed.

Becoming immersed in adolescence in the impassioned correspondence of those two German women, the author Bettina Brentano von Arnim and Karoline von Günderode, canoness of a religious order, must have had a strong influence on the impressionable mind of Emily Dickinson. There is an interesting linkage between all these women. Fuller herself had intense exchanges with women correspondents, just as Emily Dickinson would. Epistolary friendships among nineteenth-century women thrived.

The friendships, though so intensely expressed, were not sexual affairs, but a valid and potent alternative for women to express themselves in a world where male power was omnipresent in family, society, government, and culture. Margaret Fuller, who longed for a relationship with a man, could still note in her journal when reflecting on a past feeling for a woman friend, "It is so true that a woman may be in love with a woman and a man with a man.... How natural is the love ... of de Staël for De Recamier."

But some present-day academic agendas in the gender wars have meant that friendships between women are being combed over for evidence of lesbian liaisons. Thus, a recent study of the correspondence between Emily and her sister-in-law Susan Dickinson advanced the argument that their friendship was of a committed lesbian nature and that it should be brought to light for the sake of gay students.[4] For, the claim goes, an important way to bolster homosexual self-esteem is to recover gay and lesbian relationships throughout history. Just part of the queer-studies agenda, countered literary scholar Harold Bloom, who finds that Emily's letters were highly inflated and fanciful endeavors, not factual declarations of a lesbian nature, but, in effect, prose poems, carefully staged and programmed.

That Emily and Susan Gilbert loved each other with a typical girlhood crush is certain; the friendship between them became more problematic when Emily successfully promoted the union between her brother Austin and Susan that was to result in a disastrous marriage. But to advance that Emily and Susan conducted their own love affair is unsustainable. Emily's wrought-up communication to Susan was in keeping with the times and the customs, not to mention Emily's own bent for passionate expression of the most ordinary matters as evidenced in all her writing. That some poems were dedicated to Susan and that Susan gave her critical opinion of others, does not make a case. There had been other fervid declarations to other women friends on Emily's part. More astounding is the attempt at proof.

Bell Gale Chevigny's excellent study of Margaret Fuller's life and writings explains female epistolary fervor as part of a broader cultural phenomenon. Chevigny points out the connection of the prevalent nineteenth-century cult of "true womanhood"— whether in Europe or America—and its subversion from the primary goal of making women content to be productive exclusively in the narrow sphere of home life, to the unintended by-product that women (held to be purer, more sensitive, more spiritual than men) would look past the coarseness of the males—father, brother, or husband—with whom they shared their lives to "kindred spirits" beyond the home. Thus was generated the "sisterhood of sensibility" manifested in intense female friendships documented in their letters.[5]

In 1859, approaching her thirtieth year, Emily Dickinson would have read in *The Atlantic Monthly*, which from its first issue in 1857 punctually arrived in the Dickinson home, an article entitled "Ought Women to Learn the Alphabet" by Thomas Wentworth Higginson, the magazine's editor. His piece was an elegant vindication of women's rights filled with mentions of eminent Italian women as well as references to Mary Wollstonecraft, Margaret Fuller, Harriet Hosmer, Florence Nightingale, and Elizabeth Barrett Browning, all of whom, with the exception of Wollstonecraft (who left that experience to her daughter, Mary Shelley), had sojourned in Italy. Higginson wrote of Fuller and Barrett Browning that both were exceptional in that era of undereducated women because they had been educated as were boys.[6]

It was to Elizabeth Barrett Browning, who died in 1861, that Emily's Poem 593 was addressed in 1862: "I think I was enchanted / When first a sombre Girl— / I read that Foreign Lady— / The Dark—felt beautiful—." In addition to Mrs. Browning, who was the inspiration of Emily's poetic vocation, her other main 'heroines' were other titanic literary figures who had triumphed over adversity like the Brontë sisters, George Eliot, and George Sand. Not only her poetry but Elizabeth Barrett Browning's life lit the imagination of Emily Dickinson. It could have been as much Elizabeth's infatuation with *Corinne* and her ideas about Italy as the place for the woman of genius as well as health or finances which determined the choice of Italy as her residence when she and Robert Browning married.

Central to Dickinson's life and work was her reading. She read the Brontës, George Eliot, and Elizabeth Barrett's "Aurora Leigh." Jack L. Capps, in his study *Emily Dickinson's Reading*, would like to think that Robert Browning had more effect on Dickinson than did his wife, Elizabeth Barrett Browning, though Dickinson's very poems and letters show the exact opposite. It was not Mr. but Mrs. Browning in a framed portrait (one of three in Emily's possession) which hung on the wall of her bedroom-sanctuary, and her sister Lavinia described Emily as wearing her hair looped over her ears and knotted in back "because it was the way Elizabeth Barrett Browning did."

Capps claims that Dickinson's interest in the Brontës, like her interest in George Eliot, was in their lives and not in their novels, without divining that it was not the external circumstances of their lives nor the fascination of their relationships with male partners that distinguished them for Emily, but what Barrett Browning referred to as the women's "heroism." "Women, now, queens now!" Emily said of George Sand and Mrs. Browning.[7]

A woman coming into her own, into the realization of her personal voice and the gift of poetic expression, was very likely juxtaposed in Emily Dickinson's mind with her "Blue Peninsula" of delights, the Italy she dreamed of, an image derived from Barrett Browning's Italy in "Aurora Leigh" and signifying a state of delight as hope is fulfilled, a fulfillment so great as to perish from:

It might be easier
to fail—with land in sight—
than gain—My Blue Peninsula—
to perish of Delight—[8]

In *Aurora Leigh*, Aurora, a poet, is caught between her love for her cousin Romney Leigh and her willingness to risk all to realize her gift. It became the classic text of a woman at war with two sides of her nature. That work, beloved of Emily Dickinson, was so influential in her own work that it is said her encounter with it was the Lightening Flash and "waylaying Light" that consecrated her thereafter to a life of poetry much as St. Paul, felled by light, had his conversion on the road to Damascus. Or, the image could be from Canto 33 of the *Paradiso* where Dante, on entering the Empyrean, speaks of being overcome with sudden lightening (*subito lampo*) and dazzling light (*viva luce*). Lines from her poem 1581 make her vocation clear: "And I would not exchange the Flash / For all the rest of Life." Though some critics, unable perhaps to conceive of women following so strong a call to Art, have taken that Flash of "waylaying Light" for religious dedication, the evidence of Dickinson's own words and actions belie it being anything less than intuition into her poetic gift and the courage to follow it when Lightening struck.

In 1862, Emily sent four poems to Thomas Higginson in response to "Letter to a Young Contributor," an article he had written in *The Atlantic Monthly*. She sent him those poems for his advice and encouragement; he responded that he found them "remarkable, though odd," and that since those weren't strong enough to publish, she should send him more. The kindly but baffled editor who became her friend and lifelong correspondent was often discomfited by her unlikely, erratic temperament, finding in what he called her "very wantonness of over-statement" something more probably akin to a suspect Latin strain than New England propriety.

After eight years of correspondence, Higginson finally called on Emily in Amherst in 1870 when she was forty, well into her reclusiveness, and had written him, "I do not cross my father's ground to any house in town." He described the visit in a letter to his wife: "A large country lawyer's house, brown brick, with great trees and a garden—I sent up my card. A parlor dark & cool & stiffish. . . . A step like a pattering child's in entry & in glided a little plain woman with two smooth bands of reddish hair . . . with no good feature—in a very plain & exquisitely clean white pique & a blue networsted shawl. She came to me with two day lilies which she put in a sort of child-like way into my hand & said "These are my introduction" in a soft frightened breathless childlike voice—& added under her breath Forgive me if I am frightened; I never see strangers & hardly know what I say—but she talked soon & thenceforth continually—& deferentially— sometimes stopping to ask me to talk instead of her—but readily recommencing."[9]

Her "nervous force" exhausted him, and in a second letter to his wife he wrote: "I never was with anyone who drained my nerve power so much. Without touching her, she drew from me. I am glad not to live near her." What he felt was the nervous impulse and tension of Emily's imagination that made it unnecessary for her to travel bodily from The Homestead in Amherst; she could imagine what she could not see, as in the case of Italy:

> Volcanoes be in Sicily
> And South America
> I judge from my Geography
> Volcanos nearer here
> A lava step at any time

Am I inclined to climb—
A crater I may contemplate
Vesuvius at Home.[10]

Her poetry is full of volcanoes, and though she never got to see them she had her "Vesuvius at Home." Volcanoes were the vogue. Sir William Hamilton's treatises on Vesuvius gave rise to the popular excursion of travelers from all over Europe to climb the mountain; it coincided, of course, with the excavations of the classical sites of Pompeii and Herculaneum. Goethe came and climbed. Many others did. Mme. de Staël had a dramatic scene between Corinne and Lord Nelvil enacted on the slopes of Vesuvius as they improbably trudged up to the crater. He explains to Corinne why he must return to England; it is to find out the reason his father objected to an earlier secretly arranged match between them. The father's objection, it turns out, was that Corinne, even as a child, was too charming, too talented. As a woman she would, of course, take any husband away from England because "Only Italy would suit her."

Why Italy? Because for Corinne it was synonymous with genius and there one could live more openly, freed for self-expression from convention; there the arts were appreciated, and life, being free from moralizing hypocrisy in a way unknown to more politically and industrially advanced nations, was most suited to women of artistic talent—and, one should add, those to whom, like Corinne, love outside of marriage was no fault. There, as Margaret Fuller was to find, a woman could act out her own nature.

It is compellingly documented in Richard Sewall's biography of Dickinson, and by now well accepted, that she experienced a deep passion for three different men in her life, two of whom were married and completely inaccessible—a condition that protected her solitude. The last, and possibly deepest, attachment occurred when she was approaching fifty, and was for Judge Otis Phillips

Lord, eighteen years her senior and a friend of her late father. The Judge was then widowed and childless and there was no obstacle to marriage should she have wished it. Abstaining from the nineteenth-century woman's mete of marriage and family, Dickinson's abstinence became her treasure. Her great yearning for love went not into married life but into the expression of the other side of herself, the poet's side. The women who had chosen that side, in the literary personifications of Corinne and Aurora Leigh, had already become identified for her with Italy, "My Blue Peninsula."

If one has been indifferently nourished on love as a child, as the case can be made for Dickinson, whose father was "busy with his Briefs" and whose mother was largely missing in any meaningful way, one strives as she did a whole life long to fill the void. Emily sought closeness with many men and women as her correspondence testifies—but at a distance. Wary of personal contact, she emptied her emotions into her poetry and letter writing. If her emotional life were to be solitary, it would not, for that, be impoverished. That was to be her own achievement of heroism.

Adrienne Rich's essay, "Vesuvius at Home," strongly refutes the legend of Emily Dickinson as the fey girl-woman eccentric and the "little home-keeping person," as John Crowe Ransom and other biographers and critics have thought her. An inestimable plus of the women's movement has been the birth of feminist criticism, which has helped us read texts in a new light, shed great insight on what it was to be a woman writer in a patriarchal world that "works from a male/mainstream perspective," and show how much of what women write has to be reinterpreted "to identify images, codes, metaphors, strategies" that are peculiar to women in their use of language.

What emerges of Dickinson from Rich's reading and that of other new critics, is an inwardly conflicted but courageous woman, not so much the mere victim of her deprivations as one who took the pains of her life and worked them to her own uses.

She was conscious of her gift and "husbanded" it, if I can use that weighted term with one who was supposed to be bereft because husbandless in the ordinary sense. Deprived of the nineteenth-century woman's lot of marriage and family, her loss, if that's what it was, became her gift. Her real quest was not for anything as conventional as married life, but for the expression of her other side. Her own life was what she had to transmute into poetry, reaching beyond that life to speak to us all. Given the disappointments Dickinson encountered on a personal level, she guarded her inner self well under the cloak of her reclusiveness and eccentricity. Contrarily, Corinne, Staël's projection of the woman of talent, had been betrayed by lesser spirits and even betrayed herself by loving Oswald and losing her gift and then her life.

Dickinson, who yearned from afar for Italy, did not, as others did, actually get there, except in the imagery of her poetry. Knowing that life was Swiss, and that Italy lay the other side of those barrier Alps, she acted out her own nature by staying where she was, all the while cognizant of those women like Barrett Browning and Fuller who had dared to reach the other side. Her revolution was to literary rules as Margaret Fuller's had been to society's.

Emily Dickinson was not "partially cracked," pathological, or a bereft spinster. She guarded herself and her gift from intrusion and was able to garner from that strength the genius of her poetry, in all some 1775 poems. Born into a world which was constraining to all women, doubly so to women of talent and spirit, she admired strong women who, like George Eliot, Elizabeth Barrett, George Sand, and Florence Nightingale, reinvented their lives on their own terms, who knew and expressed their other side.

As late as 1875, when Emily was forty-five and the great intensity of her richest years of poetry had waned, she cut from *Scribner's Magazine* a reference to the poetry of Vittoria Colonna, the sixteenth-century Italian poet who had maintained a correspondence with Michelangelo. For Dickinson herself had gotten closest to people through correspondence.

If *Aurora Leigh* is the classic case of a woman warring with both sides of her nature, it was, nonetheless, born out of Barrett Browning's own personal triumph. The line of descent goes from Staël, who was a dynamo, through the politically aware Mrs. Browning, to Dickinson, the hero of self-realization, and from her to women of today who are still trying to act out their own natures and take their lives into their own hands. Is it not odd to read in Albert Gelpi's work on Dickinson that in her moments of rebellion, "Emily Dickinson's spirit was, in its feminine way, distinctly and passionately Byronic."[11] Why Byronic, I wonder, why not call it Staëlian? Mme. de Staël was as noted and influential a person, in their day, as Byron, who, predating the hubris of a Norman Mailer, thought to give her the supreme compliment when they met by telling her she thought like a man.

Yet Gelpi does state convincingly that Emily Dickinson went beyond the limits of Amherst and the society of her time to "retranslate her own unorthodox, subversive, sometimes volcanic propensities into a dialect called metaphor."[12] Nowhere is this more evident than in "Our lives are Swiss." Some interpretations seem to miss the import of it. Barton Levi St. Armand, in *Emily Dickinson and Her Culture*, rather tortuously reads that poem in the light of John Ruskin's pious theorizing on the veiling effect in nature (mists, mirage, cloud effects) as meant to be a natural veiling preordained by the deity who has made the world and withheld some of it from man's knowledge.

Ruskin may have been able to read Turner's paintings as a kind of reverent veiling, but it is quite a stretch to apply Turner's misty visions and God's plan for an unsearchable universe to what was in Emily Dickinson's aesthetic consciousness and in her mind when she wrote "Our lives are Swiss." St. Armand would have us believe that Dickinson, swayed by Ruskin, kept to the conservative concept of the necessity of the "veil" in nature, that what she was

after in "Our lives are Swiss" was a rendering of the mysterious-
ness of landscape—no more than that. Dickinson, he says, "was
tantalized by the "unsearchableness" of natural phenomena."
Really?

More convincingly, Dickinson was, according to Adrienne Rich,
"*the* American poet whose work consisted in exploring states of
psychic extremity."[13] That this was obscured by the patriarchal interpretations applied to her life and her work is clear in the kinds
of selections made from her opus either from timidity or from
misreading. She was a unique poet who happened to be a woman
and who had to be made to fit, willy-nilly, the conventions that
society allowed for the type. Thus, squeeze poem 80 into the pi-
geonhole of a Ruskinesque piety and let the Alps stand for "the
type of the world to come, the redeemed and perfected life," even
trying to equate them with a mountain ridge of ancient Palestine!
Many scholars followed Dickinson's earliest editor, Mabel Loomis
Todd, in the attempt to force onto her a religious orthodoxy that
she did not have.

Noted for being, in her own phrase, a phoebe-bird who lifted
material from others to use in her own idiosyncratic way, transforming it completely, Dickinson would almost certainly have
been aware of what was written by another contemporary of hers,
Rose Terry Cooke, who was often featured in *The Atlantic Monthly*.
Perhaps it was Cooke's poem "Beyond" that Dickinson subtly
subverted to her own uses. It is an inspirational poem in which
Italy is made to stand for the soul's reward, joy, surcease—a
promised land over "the steeps God set" attained after a courageous, Christian battle: "For past the Alpine summits of great
pain, / Lieth thine Italy." (Or, did Dickinson slyly recall Hannibal's charge to his weary troops—"Beyond the Alps lies Italy!" In
all cases, a promised land.)

To ignore the exuberance and frolicsomeness Dickinson dis-
plays in her version of getting past the Alps, to read it as a religious message, is to me a distortion. The excitement in "Our lives

are Swiss" of those three exclamation points which splotch the verse, the designation of "Siren Alps" who let down their guard to offer the enticement of Italy farther on, is beguiling not meditative.

And there are truer echoes of sources in Emily Dickinson's own words. In a letter of January 4, 1859, Emily wrote to her cousin Loo, "It's a great thing to be 'great,' Loo, and you and I might tug for a life, and never accomplish it, but no one can stop our looking on." This is recast in poem 80: on some odd afternoon when the mists are gone from the Alps, "we look farther on!" She is thought to have written "Our lives are Swiss" in 1859, as deduced by Thomas Johnson in his edition of Dickinson's *Complete Poems*, and determined from handwriting evidence and references to her reading and correspondence. Rebecca Patterson's 1951 suggestion that Emily Dickinson's great thwarted love was for a woman friend, Kate Scott Anthon, was not well received by Dickenson scholars and critics. But Patterson convincingly linked Kate's significance in Emily's life with "Our lives are Swiss" by quoting a letter of 1860, in which Emily reminded Kate of her past visit to Amherst in February and March of 1859: "It's but a little past, dear, and yet how far from here it seems, fled with the snow! So through the snow go many loving feet parted by 'Alps.' How brief, from vineyards and the sun!"[14] The vineyards and sun, which stand for Italy, also stand for the delight of Kate's visit. Italy was a topic of their conversation, for they took great pleasure in reading together *Aurora Leigh* with its Italian scenes, not to mention the romantic background of the poem's author who herself had fled England for Florence. For Kate the fervent dream of Italy became a reality in her several journeys there; for Emily it was transformed into poetry.

In the effort to trace Dickinson's allusions, everything has been studied—her correspondence, her reading, her schoolgirl studies.[15] In her brief term at Mount Holyoke she studied Samuel

Newman's *Practical System of Rhetoric* and the startling deduction has been made that in the discussion of making proper transitions in composition, she might have gotten her imagery of Italy from reading an excerpt of Oliver Goldsmith's *Traveller*, wherein a comparison of the Swiss and Italians is made. But Emily Dickinson completely reversed the example! Goldsmith described a degraded Italy and then contrasted it to Switzerland, "Where rougher climes a nobler race display." The opposite is true for Dickinson in her poem 80, where dullness is Swiss and all delight lies over the Alps in Italy.

An early biographer, Genevieve Taggard, quoted the whole of poem #80 and attributed it simply to Emily's imaginative following of the Higginsons, who did literally cross the Alps in their journey through Europe. *The Passion of Emily Dickinson*, by Judith Farr, quotes from poem 80, "The solemn Alps— / The siren Alps," to the old effect of their "connoting (like all mountains) a summit of feeling"; for Farr, lofty peaks are again meant to be equated with moral uplift. But Emily Dickinson's range of feelings and how she expressed them went far beyond the commonplaces of her day; she did not treat her mountains like all mountains within the guidelines of expectation, nor anything else in her natural world.

In an early work of the 1960s, David Porter, in his book *The Art of Emily Dickinson's Early Poetry*, had thought of the poem as signifying, perhaps, any longed-for goal, with the Alps standing for the experience of death separating one from the longed-for immortality, represented by Italy; or, the poem as a geographical analogue for life, death (the Alps), and resurrection (Italy). But in the library at Villa Serbelloni an edition of Emily Dickinson's complete poems contained a note from Porter himself dated December 1985, when he was a resident there; he had written, "Emily never visited Italy, and misplaced Mt. Etna in Naples, but she was Italian at heart! See poem 80."[16] And in a more recent book on Dickinson, Porter added more possibilities to his earlier interpretation: "Our lives are Swiss was meant to draw on the whole cultural typology of that single term—to represent it symbolically." Elsewhere he states, "My concern has been to discover and preserve her otherness. Her audacity required an inordinate freedom that needs still to be respected." She may not have gotten to Italy in person, but in spirit and soul she was there.

Supposedly Emily Dickinson was a reclusive New England nun writing of bees, butterflies, death, her soul; actually she shows a defiant, steely willfulness in life as in her poetry and many of her images are daring, sumptuous, baroque. She transcends the supposed image of herself much as Bernini's sculpture of St. Theresa in ecstasy at her mystical union with Christ (and Dickinson, too, saw herself as the Bride of Christ in poem 817) betrays more than the official description would have. I often saw the Bernini sculpture in the church of S. Maria della Vittoria when I lived in Rome. St. Theresa's ecstatic facial expression and lassitude of body more clearly show the mark of physical orgasm than of mystical union. As more than one visitor to Bernini's St. Theresa has thought, if that is divine love, I have known it, too.

And when Emily Dickinson turned that pious commonplace of the Alps upside down, her biographers could not or would not read her clearly—they went back to the sentimental clichés of the Alps as an extension of God and managed to misread Dickinson's casting of them, instead, as a bothersome barrier to the delights beyond. To view Dickinson's poetry merely as sublimation into language or patriarchal theology of a missed heterosexual or lesbian love affair is to misread a strong and original voice by striving to adjust it to understandable norms. Ted Hughes speculated that a woman's only possible substitute for the man lost to her was the Universe in its divine aspect.[17] Thus, he concludes, "the marriage that had been denied in the real world, went forward in the spiritual."

But that won't do any longer; no more squeezing women into the apparatus of patriarchal attitudes in order to explain what is unique and complex about their creative works. Let Emily be seen for herself—a strong, impassioned poet of great intensity who invented a language "dense with implication." Not a perennial child-woman dressed in white, nor the reductive "Belle of Amherst" as played by Julie Harris with her recitation of Emily's famous recipe for black cake (nineteen eggs and two pounds of butter!) in the popular theater version, nor the mythologized Emily Dickinson whose very countenance is changed from the authentic daguerreotype likeness of her plain face with hair severely pulled back to a retouched one where an added frilly ruff around her neck sets off a face made more attractive with wavy, curling hair, fuller lips, and accentuated eyes. Reseen by Adrienne Rich and other feminists, Emily is, instead, "a mind engaged in a lifetime's musings on essential problems of language, identity, separation, relationship, the integrity of the self; a mind capable of describing psychological states more accurately than any poet except Shakespeare."[18]

Like Corinne, the heroine of Staël's novel, two sides of her nature seemed to war in Emily Dickinson: she was in love with the Italy symbolized in Barrett Browning's life and work, and yet she also valued the cool discipline and the austerity associated with the North. In poem 525, "I think the Hemlock likes to stand," Emily makes an unfavorable contrast of "Satin Races" with the northern hemlock that thrives on cold. This echoes the thought of Emerson's "Prudence" and Ruskin in *Stones of Venice*, both of whom believed that a severe climate made better people. Still, Emily Dickinson's poetry is replete with references to the South, to dark people. She herself is characterized as a Brave Black Berry (554) who wears a "thorn in his side," but concealing the pain, offers gifts of herself to passersby. Her friend, then sister-in-law,

Susan Gilbert, was "The love South" or referred to as Egypt, Domingo. Kate Anthon, like Sue Gilbert (and Mrs. Browning, Mme. de Staël, George Eliot!), was dark haired and dark eyed.

For me, it is likely that Dickinson, like Corinne, saw her gift as primary in her life. That she did not marry need not be seen as pathological, nor as a reason to get religion. On the contrary, says Rich "Dickinson . . . was heretical . . . and stayed away from church and dogma."[19] In Emily's letter of 25 April, 1862, to *Atlantic Monthly* editor T. W. Higginson who has asked for details of herself and her family, she describes her mother and father, sister and brother and writes "They are religious—except me—and address an Eclipse, every morning—whom they call their "'Father.'" She often transmuted religious images, texts, or even rhythms to her own secular use as in, for example, the conclusion of poem 18: "In the name of the Bee / And of the Butterfly— / And of the Breeze—Amen!" And her other correspondence and poetry bear out Dickinson's distancing herself from dogma. Her religious explorations were not for ritual or theologized laws, but, in the true sense of the term *religio*, for binding herself to values of an ideal life, and were in service of her inner knowledge of self and its relationship to the cosmos.

When Dickinson writes about her gift she often uses the language of love or religion because those, in her time and in her culture, were the archetypes she had to work with. But it was her particular "slant," her highly original poetic gift and the expressing of it, that was uppermost, and though this was always acceptable in the male artist, it was viewed as perverse in a woman until feminist criticism gave us a new lens for viewing. The problem is not what to make of Dickinson's celibacy, but how to amend those societal attitudes toward unmarried women that constrain critics to look for "normal" explanations for Emily's singleness.

Love, Nature, and Death are said to be Emily Dickinson's great themes—yet ambivalence, the teasing switch of genders in her poetic voice, the split between alternate sides of the same person seem just as cogent; primary, it seems to me, is the search for meaningfulness in life within the self. She was immersed in a search for something Divine which was represented by her art—the nearest she could come to attaining "Divinity."

In choice and perfect words, a baker's dozen, Emily Dickinson rendered the incantation of Italy in the symbol of the rose, the perfect flower, the sublime design of Dante's *Paradiso* as *candida rosa*:

> Partake as doth the Bee,
> Abstemiously.
> The Rose is an Estate—
> In Sicily.[20]

Italy could reside in one's soul—a quality of independent artistic spirit as strong as could be gleaned from any actual trip. The books that stick strictly to the American traveler who actually set foot on Italian soil have missed those who went there on the wings of fantasy as Emily Dickinson did. Imaginatively, without social stigma, a woman of genius could lead an independent life and develop her talent. In every sense Corinne guided her own life. As did Aurora Leigh. And, in the Italy of her imagined other side, so did Emily Dickinson while at home in Amherst, Massachusetts.

Contemporary with Dickinson was another American maiden lady, the author Constance Fenimore Woolson, whose destiny, unlike the homebody poet's, was to be a constant traveler. It is a paradox that Woolson, in contrast to Dickinson in her own lifetime, was a successful and well-known author only to become in our time relatively unknown. For whereas Emily Dickinson was always at home yet fame found her, Constance Woolson was ever in search of both home and fame. She rests now permanently in Rome where I came upon her grave.

Constance Fenimore Woolson, 1840–1894

Miss Constance Woolson?

VENEZIA

3. *Constance Woolson and Death in Venice*

On a sunny February day when I stood in the Protestant Cemetery in Rome at the 150th memorial service for John Keats, who was buried there in 1821, it was just a month since my husband had died suddenly in Rome and I was remembering him, poet, too. After the service for Keats, I wandered a bit in that lovely and haunting spot, once a scorned waste area located at the edges of the city overlooked by the ancient Pyramid of Gaius Cestius and designated for the burial of non-Catholics. By the nineteenth century, it was a walled and flowering oasis, greened with cypress and filled with evocative names, with nostalgia and serenity. Markers now point the way to the gravesites of Goethe's young son and Antonio Gramsci, founder of the Italian Communist Party. Shelley's stone, inscribed *Cor Cordium*, is on the slope near the old Roman wall. And if I had been familiar with her work at that time I would have noted that next to American author Richard Henry Dana lay the ivy- and violet-covered mound of his compatriot and friend, the nineteenth-century novelist Constance Fenimore Woolson, 1840–94.

I was not alone in not knowing of her. In Eleanor Clark's *Rome, and a Villa*, the chapter on the Protestant Cemetery mentions the burial places of artists and clergymen, even noting Edith Wharton's aunt and uncle, before mistakenly writing, "Novelists none. . . ."

Constance Fenimore Woolson, a great-niece of James Fenimore Cooper, grew up in Ohio, then spent much time in the postbellum South becoming a successful writer of regional novels. In her lifetime a uniquely connected and successful author, she chose to live abroad the last fifteen years of her life. It was in Italy that she was befriended by Henry James, who politely praised her fiction but maintained a distance from the closer connection she seemed to invite. She remained single her entire life. Her quest, to reconcile her woman's nature with her art (epitomized in her poignant query, "Why is it that literary ladies break down so?"), came to tragic end when, alone and ill in Venice, she jumped to her death. Henry James called her gravesite "the most beautiful thing in Italy almost. . . . It is tremendously, inexhaustibly touching." His words seem to prenote his story "The Beast in the Jungle," of a life wasted when love went unrecognized. I see Woolson's shadow in his work, and his in hers.

Italy had been a destination in young Connie Woolson's imagination since her school-days at Cleveland Seminary where she was set dreaming by the evocative name of a classmate, Italia Beatrice. "There were romantic horizons to me in the name!" she recalled years later when she had already lived much in Italy and found it as she had imagined. And hadn't James Fenimore Cooper, the illustrious great-uncle on whom she had been raised, found his greatest delight and pleasure there, too? Italy was the country in Europe Woolson most loved; and although her long residence at Villa Brichieri in Florence was a happy period that provided the closest approximation to a fixed home she had had in twenty years, she could not, as Margaret Fuller did, embrace Italy wholeheartedly as destination and destiny. Rather, she came and went moved by uncertainty and some inner longing, but always returning, hoping, perhaps, that it would be for her what it had been for Shelley: the paradise of exiles. Essentially hers was a misconnect with Italy.

Aside from seeming the model of May Bartram in "The Beast in the Jungle," or the spurned spinster niece in *The Aspern Papers*, or the forsaken Milly Thiele of *Wings of the Dove*, who was Constance Woolson in her own right? I wondered. She seems the epitome of the woman writer, the seeker of some resolution between life and art that is the quest of creative women. She was greatly conflicted in her life; always insecure both as writer and person, she felt herself on the margins of both society and literature.

For me, she embodies a mirror image of Italy. The lure of so much promise of beauty, health, love, or whatever fulfillment for so many, Italy has a dark verso to the bright side. Some who journeyed to Italy—Keats, Shelley, Woolson—reaped not the bright promise but, rather, promise denied and then despair, death. "I blame the glamour of Italy . . . she was seduced by a country, not a man," says Lilia's brother-in-law in Forster's *Where Angels Fear to Tread*, indicting the country not the husband for her death. One can easily lose one's way there.

Constance Woolson had begun to use the background and expatriate society she found in Italy as story material, and perhaps she had hoped, in addition, to have there the frequent, if not permanent, company of Henry James, for whose acquaintance she had come to Europe with a letter of introduction, finally meeting up with him in Florence. Miss Woolson was forty, a self-declared spinster three years his senior when she first met Mr. James, the meta-bachelor. It was a meeting of elitist minds, of literary sensibilities, and of reciprocal esteem. The habit of writing and uprootedness was one part of her life, Henry James became another. In their years of friendship they remained, as they addressed each other in letters, Miss Woolson and Mr. James.

Always alert to place and people, Constance Woolson had soon noted the advantages in Italy for women of a certain age as compared to her native land. All older women, whether married or not, had a much better time in Italian society, she wrote her niece in America, "They are not 'shelved' as they are at home, they are important, considered. . . . There is no doubt, Libbie, that one keeps young longer over here." Nevertheless, Italy could also be the wrong place for a woman like Woolson who so prized duty and New England stolidity above all else, and made a hard virtue out of sacrifice. Alone, in her middle years, with an increasingly bad hearing ailment and a history of depression, too difficult must have been the contest between her repressed nature and the surrounding society of hedonists and lovers; and the contrast with her lonely evenings and her own work-bound life must finally have been too hard for her to reconcile. Italy as the golden, unobtainable Other has the drastic effect of putting a bleak life into even bleaker relief. If only she had not fallen ill in Venice, where melancholy can be unbearably compounded by the grey misty winter season, she might have recovered from the low spirits that, as always happened, enveloped her upon the completion of a book like post-partum blues.

As an author, Woolson let her heroines validate repression and sacrifice to an extraordinary extent. One who got off with a close call was Margaret in "A Florentine Experiment," thanks not to her own inclination but to an interfering aunt who performed as deus ex machina to bring Margaret and Morgan together, and helped also by fortunate coincidence. Woolson had to resort to such a solution because, on their own, her heroines were partial to self-sacrifice or too proud to act on their own behalf.

If Constance had ever hoped for a companionable arrangement with Henry James, she lacked the so-called feminine wiles, or the unflinching demonstrativeness needed to overcome his resistance. She was steeped in innuendo, just as is May Bartram in "The Beast in the Jungle" and, like that character, Woolson died waiting, waiting fruitlessly . . . for, as James's biographer Leon Edel noted, James's love, when it wasn't self-love, had for years been expended on ethereal heroines of the mind.

When you have Six / You're in a bad fix . . . goes part of a popular jingle Connie Woolson's mother recorded in her *Recollections*, describing in turn with a couplet the arrival of each of her nine children. Constance, star-crossed from birth, was the sixth Woolson child; she arrived on March 5, 1840, in Claremont, New Hampshire. Two days later an onslaught of scarlet fever struck the household and within two weeks three of the five older children had died—a bereavement that so affected her mother that it led her father to move them off to Cleveland, Ohio, while Constance was still an infant. There, in what was then the "Western Reserve" territory, Connie grew up and was educated, clinging always to a proud sense of herself as New Englander by birth and later, by inclination or affectation.

She became her father's devoted companion on excursions and trips as they explored the environs and summered on Mackinac Island in the still-wild Great Lakes region where she accumulated a store of natural lore. "I have walked to the shores of Lake Erie," she remembered, "driven all through the 'coal country' and the 'corn country' with my father; I know all the hills and dales and rivers; I have sailed up and down the Ohio; I have been to the harvest fields and even helped; have gathered the apples and been to state fairs." She is remembered today on the island where a spot is called "Woolson Rampart."Always, to the last, she kept the memory of her dashing father whom she recalled as having so much romance about him.[1] And all her life she remained active and interested in the world around her; as she had once rowed up Florida bayous and explored the great swamps, so in her last year she visited and described all the islands of the Venetian Lagoon and learned to guide her gondola as expertly as the *gondolieri*.

In Connie's adolescence Woolson child number eight died before reaching her first year. Then came two more grievous losses: her twenty-year old sister Emma died shortly after marriage, having contracted consumption from nursing her young husband before his death; and Georgiana, the eldest sister, so vibrant and beloved, died in childbirth at age twenty-two. Through this sad attrition, Connie became the eldest Woolson child followed by her sister Clara and brother Charley, the ninth and last child and only son, the mother's favorite.

A daguerreotype of the sisters as children shows Connie with the dark hair and piercing look of her great-uncle Fenimore, and Clara more delicate looking and with lighter coloring, softer gaze. In her fifteenth year, Connie was a decidedly pretty girl whose long dark curls framed an oval face of finely molded features. To the last, as photos taken in her fortieth and fiftieth years show, she was an appealing and attractive woman; her countenance had taken on a pleasant fullness, her hair was still luxuriant and dark, she did not show her age. But still she would write home that she was "no handsomer than of old," always convinced that she was neither attractive nor socially adept.[2]

Constance was in Cleveland at the outbreak of the Civil War and she threw herself enthusiastically into the Union cause, participating in various fairs to raise money. Her future publisher, Joseph Harper, in his memoir of the publishing business, recognized her as one of Harper's star authors and provided an astute insight into her character when he noted, "The war for the Union was the great romance of her life."[3]

Her emotions had run high with excitement during the years of conflict from the dedication and the involvement that the war effort demanded. This was the period of the only romance she ever referred to. Briefly she had fancied herself in love with Zeph Spaulding, a friend from childhood who had been co-editor with her of a summer newspaper produced at Mackinac Island, and whom she met again when he was a colonel in the Union army. She quickly talked herself out of love saying it was simply due to "the glamour that the war threw over the young officers" which made her fancy she cared for one.

Did she harbor a morbid, unconscious fear of marriage and motherhood stemming from her family history? Or, did her realization of having inherited her father's hearing impairment along with his disposition to periods of depression dissuade her from any commitment? She had witnessed her mother's hard life of loss, precarious means, and family troubles. Taking everything into account, Constance may have simply dismissed the possibility of marriage for herself. Her public explanation, as found in a letter, is lofty and unconvincing: "My idea of love is, unfortunately, so high . . . that nothing or nobody ever comes up to it."

The unexpected death of her father in 1869 was another blow to her emotionally, but on a practical level the loss provided the impetus necessary for her to become a professional writer. The Cleveland home was broken up. Clara and Charley had each married; Connie was left with her mother. Never again would Constance (not a prophetic name!) know a constant and fixed home setting. Still, those years provided her with the new satisfaction of being successful in her profession. She began writing travel sketches of the northern Lake country she knew best. She was an enthusiast of Bret Harte's "local-color" and influenced by him to try her hand at fiction. Her first stories were collected and published as *Castle Nowhere* in 1875, the title story of which is a kind of gothic fantasy of an escaped criminal who builds a "castle" on a secluded island, living off the wreckage of ships lured by his lights while bringing up an orphan girl in his care.

Her wanderings began as she accompanied her ailing mother south for the winters, first to St. Augustine in Florida, and then to Virginia, Georgia, and the Carolinas. Summers they returned north to New York or to Cooperstown, founded by Mrs. Woolson's grandfather, Judge Cooper. Pomeroy Place, a spacious red brick home given by the Judge to his daughter at her marriage, was Mrs. Woolson's beloved girlhood home in Cooperstown when there were still Cooper relatives to visit, like Aunt Susan, the novelist's daughter, beloved keeper of family tradition and herself the author of the delightful *Rural Hours*, the cycle of a rural year which predated Thoreau's *Walden* and about which Constance wrote an article full of appreciation for its "exquisite truthful descriptions."

Publishers highlighted Woolson's James Fenimore Cooper connection and it served her well. Connections always count. Just as Uncle Fenimore had understood the distinction of his mother's maiden name over his father's surname and had signed himself Fenimore Cooper, so she became Constance Fenimore Woolson. Name recognition brought her immediate results. She was hailed by reviewers as the inheritor of the Fenimore Cooper tradition and was enabled to start a literary career with more momentum and acceptance than might have been the case for her early work. Her success continued unabated to the end. Her first novel, *Anne*, sold 60,000 copies and in England she was amused (and gratified) to see it advertised as "The New American Novel By a Niece of Fenimore Cooper." Woolson became a strong voice in the new "local-color" school, and her sketches and stories appeared in a constant stream for over twenty years in the leading American magazines of her day.

At first I feared the worse from Woolson the writer—a genetic disposition inherited from Uncle Fenimore, whom we all know and are sure we should read but hardly ever do, agreeing with Mark Twain's roasting in his sketch, "Fenimore Cooper's Literary Offenses. . . ." Occasionally Woolson indulges in melodramatic and improbable situations or a peculiarly stilted speech as in a story like "Felipa" where the Minorcan-descended child of the Florida barrens speaks in an incongruously rhetorical way. Like Fenimore Cooper, Woolson too was prolix where she might have been succinct. Yet at her best, she is deft in characterization and the realization of place, and endowed with a flair for subtle wit that she used with too-sparing touches. Her novella, *For the Major*, set in Far Edgerly, a postwar mountain community of North Carolina, is wonderfully redolent of its time and place, and perfect of its kind. Her personal correspondence was humorous and pert, disclosing a freer and more entertaining person than she was in her authorial mode.

In St. Augustine in the early 1870s, Woolson met a vacationing critic from New York, Edmund Clarence Stedman, with whom she began a long friendship and correspondence. In letter writing her range is wide—she writes of books, walks, nature, commentary on local customs, literary appraisals, and life on the move: "I live in trunks and have not even a shelf to call my own." To Stedman she reveals a lot of her apprehension as a writer. Responding to his advice not to be afraid to make her work strong and dramatic, she counters, "But I am afraid. That is the very point of the difficulty. I shall write it—and run!—Probably to Australia," or, flirtatiously, "I think of going to live on a desert island. Will you pay me a visit once a year?"

She has his photo stuck up on her wall—he looks like a brigand with his full beard, she says; and always she sends regards and compliments to Mrs. Stedman. After a visit to the Stedmans in New York in September 1874 where she met the writers Elizabeth Stoddard and Mary Mapes Dodge, Constance wrote a curiously revealing thank you note to him: "I could not help thinking . . . how glad you must be in your inmost soul that your wife was not a writer. . . . How much prettier and lovelier a thousand times over was Mrs. Stedman in every motion, look and tone than the best we other three could do! What is the reason that if we take up a pen we seem to lose so much in other ways?" Woolson was torn by her marked ambivalence about women writers—yes, intellectually she wanted to believe they can soar as men do, be fulfilled in life as other women were, but emotionally she found all evidence against it. Though her adult life revolved about her writing, she was deeply divided about women who wrote. She read and admired Charlotte Brontë, George Eliot, and Elizabeth Barrett Browning and yet felt that a woman must renounce something—either love or ambition: "Why must it inevitably be so?" she had once quizzed Stedman. "But perhaps it is 'compensation'; as we gain money or fame, just so surely must we lose that which in our hearts we prize a great deal more." She seems not to have drawn the lesson from the women she admired who had both.

She hated the word poetess—uses poet for both genders. Is careful misogyny a tactic that she uses to dissemble with men like Stedman and later Henry James?—she obviously wants their help and praise and thus will take care not to alienate them by affronting them with irritant views. Yet elsewhere she takes exception to their restrictive look at women writers, and her future story "Miss Grief" will be precisely about a woman writer outreaching her male mentor.

Years later, in her story "At the Chateau of Corinne," set at the Coppet home of Mme. de Staël, author of *Corinne*, the apotheosis of the woman of creative genius, Woolson reverses the situation and has her protagonist Katherine give up her literary ambition and marry the man, John Ford, who has derided her poetry. There is deep irony, bitterness even, in her ending to the story, which derives from the tension between Woolson's intellectual rejection of such sentiments and her awareness of their continuing force. Even as she assigns the women artists in her fiction either death ("Miss Grief") or diminished lives (Katherine in "Chateau" and Ettie in "Street of Hyacinth"), her authorial voice is assured, ironic, controlled. She is relating the woman writer's constant dilemma—being caught in the *Corinne* conundrum of art or heart.

Letter writing provided the distance that made her boldly confide to Stedman: "About the writing I am much obliged to you for the interest you take in it. . . . I have a tremendous need of encouragement." And finally she confides in him the dilemma that torments her life: "why do literary women break down so, and . . . act so? It almost seems as though only the unhappy women took to writing. The happiest women I have known belonged to two classes: the devoted wives and mothers, and the successful flirts, whether married or single; such women never wrote." She disclosed even her tendency to be "overweighted with a kind of depression that comes unexpectedly and makes everything black." Depression lasted all her life and she recognized it for the deadly enemy it was for "it creeps in, and once in, he is master. . . . I think it is constitutional, and I know it is inherited."

Gallantly, she had devised three strategies to resist the onslaught: the first was to hang on and courageously outlive it; second, was travel; and the third, to pump up one's self-esteem, was a technique she passed on to Southern poet Paul Hamilton Hayne, who, impoverished by the Civil War, despaired of being able to support himself as a writer.

She never reconciled the split in herself; she remained convinced that it was an either/or proposition even as she envied the triumph of George Eliot's life. "How can you say George Eliot was unhappy?" she furiously replied to a friend. "I think that she had one of the easiest, most indulged, and 'petted' lives I have ever known of." It wasn't just that George Eliot craved affection, Woolson observed, it was that she got it "law or no law, custom or no custom." Here was a woman who flaunted convention and still had it all, buffeted and made secure by her devoted companion George Lewes and then, at his death, by a husband twenty years her junior.

Woolson's stories of the South reflect her long sojourns there and her continuing emotional involvement with the War Between the States. Her study of Northerners and Southerners compared two cultures, as Henry James did when he focused on Americans against a European background. Writing to Stedman, Woolson recalled that on a train trip to Florida by way of Tennessee, the station names of towns called out recalled battlefields, and "many of us were with tears in our eyes . . . the war was the heart and spirit of my life, and everything has seemed tame to me since." Identical words would be spoken by one of her characters, the expatriate Mrs. Churchill in a story called "The Pink Villa," set in Italy and written a decade later: "No one can be a warmer American than I am, Philip—no one. During the war I nearly cried my eyes out; have your forgotten that? I scraped lint; I wanted to go to the front as nurse—everything. What days they were! We lived then. I sometimes think we have never lived since."[4] Yet, for all Mrs. Churchill's patriotism, neither she nor the other Americans at her pink villa recognize Whitman's "Pioneers! Oh pioneers" when an English guest quotes him.

Woolson's affinity for the Southern United States was a preparation for her love of Italy; after all, in its slowed rhythms, vividness, preoccupation with beauty, and its sense of tradition and lineage, Italy is itself a Deep South. And again, her angular, strict heritage had the same perplexity about indulging in love for Italy as it had for the American South. Woolson often juxtaposed Puritan with Southern cavalier, or the Anglo-Saxon mentality with the Latin. The more inclined she became to Southern life, the more, it seemed, she insisted on her Northernness. "I am very strongly 'New Hampshire' in all my ways," she wrote Paul Hayne. "I have a row of tall solemn Aunts up there—silent, reserved, solitary, thin, and little grim; I am as much like them as the kind of life I lead will allow."

It is the displacement theme of Woolson's life: she was displaced from her true New England heritage; she was displaced from the joys of womanhood; she was displaced by her gender from full recognition as an author. But then Woolson was rife with ambiguity: she called Nathaniel Hawthorne one of her Gods—he who makes plain in his fiction as well as in the *French and Italian Notebooks* (part of Woolson's library) what he thought (not well) of women writers. She treasured a flower from Hawthorne's coffin and a letter of his written in reply to one from her requesting an autograph to be sold at a fair during the war.

Constance was thirty-nine years old when her mother died. Having performed as a dutiful Victorian daughter and given years to her mother, she then found herself alone and despondent. It was thought a trip abroad with her widowed sister Clara Benedict and niece Clare (who would become the lifelong, devoted memorialist of her aunt), would help Constance get over the major depression that had hit her. She went abroad and took her work with her. She was never to return to the United States.

Constance Woolson landed in England in late 1879 armed with a Cooperstown cousin's letter of introduction to Henry James. She was well acquainted with his work and had written appreciatively of it in critical pieces for *Harper's* and *The Atlantic Monthly*. She missed him in London (he was in Paris blocked by record snow), and went on with the Benedicts to the warmer air of Mentone, a formerly Italian town on the French Riviera near Monte Carlo. It was, in a sense, her first taste of Italy—the olive groves, the scent of lemon, the blue skies, the people in the hills still speaking Italian. She was charmed; she loved the climate, the views to the sea. Mornings she wrote; the afternoons were for excursions. She visited a former castle of the Genovese Doria family that had been made into a convent school by an order called the "Sisters of the Snow." On January 21st she was in the village of Sant'Agnese on the saint's day. Was she mindful of Keats' "The Eve of St Agnes" when one is said to dream of one's future spouse, or did she think of herself as another Sister of the Snow?

By spring she was in Italy. It was while she lived abroad that she produced the major part of her literary work. Though her four remaining novels retained their setting in the American South, Italy became the background of almost every story she wrote from then on. It was the next "region" she drew on her local color canvas. And why Italy?

As a child visiting in Cooperstown, Connie had been regaled with Aunt Susan Cooper's stories of her own youth abroad and how she had been courted in Paris and once danced to the two-piano playing of Chopin and Liszt at a private ball. She told of her father's intense life-long love for Italy and recalled how it was enough to have something Italian in an atmosphere to make him happy. James Fenimore Cooper was the first American writer to be intensely affected by personal contact with Italy. Conversely, for Europeans it was only with him that Americans began to be perceived as having a literature.

Fifty years after Uncle Fenimore's sojourn there, Constance found Italy for herself. She might have recalled that he had doffed his hat in reverence when the coachman called out "Italie!" as the coach left Switzerland and they entered what he called "the glow of Italian warmth." When it came time to leave, he wrote his friend Horatio Greenough, the American sculptor residing in Florence (who there produced on congressional commission a colossus of George Washington seated bare-chested with a toga flowing around his lower parts which prudish officials would not permit to grace the Capitol, warehousing it instead at the Smithsonian): "Italy, Master Horace, haunts my dreams and clings to my ribs like another wife."[5] Back home at The Hall in Cooperstown, he continued to respond to Greenough's letters from Florence: "Italy! The very name excites a glow in me, for it is the only region of the earth that I truly love. I tire of Switzerland, France I never liked, and Germany, though pleasant, excites no emotion, but Italy lives in my dreams." That encapsulation of his experience of Europe exactly anticipated Constance's.

While in Florence, Constance actually came in contact with Horatio Greenough's daughter, the venerable Miss Greenough, who had an apartment in the Villa Castellani and could well have served as a model for some of the elderly expatriate ladies Woolson depicted in her stories, as in this passage from "Dorothy": "For detached American ladies who haven't yet come to call themselves old—for the cultivated superfluous and the intelligent remainders—there is nothing like Europe."

Florence enchanted Constance. It was during its celebrated May season that, in 1880, she finally connected with Henry James, who became her assiduous companion and guide to that city's art treasures. Strangely coincident with their meeting was the appearance of her story "Miss Grief" in the May 1880 issue of *Lippincott's Magazine*. What is particularly uncanny in the story, written well before she met James, is that the male narrator, an established writer, is approached for counsel by an aspiring writer, Miss Grief—quite suggestive of the real-life successful Henry James with Miss Woolson in the role of neophyte seeking a master. After they met in Florence, Henry James and his work became a dominant influence and presence in Constance Woolson's life. Her regional stories changed in tone to studies of manners or of Americans abroad after she began her expatriate life. The words of a future character, Ettie Macks, to her sought-after mentor, Raymond Noel, seem to echo Woolson's own life: "Why, Mr. Noel, I came to Europe to see you!" she says to the astonished critic.[6] It might just as well have been, Why, Mr. James. . . .

Slyly, Connie affected a certain nonchalance, as she put Mr. James at the end of her list of enthusiasms when she wrote to family: "Florence is all that I have dreamed and more . . . here I have attained that old-world feeling I used to dream about, a sort of enthusiasm made up of history, mythology, old churches, pictures, statues, vineyards, the Italian sky, dark-eyed peasants, opera-music, Raphael and old Michael, 'Childe Harold,' the 'Marble Faun,' 'Romola,' and ever so many more ingredients—the whole having, I think, taken me pretty well off my feet! Perhaps I ought to add Henry James. He has been perfectly charming to me for the last three weeks."[7]

What Henry wrote home to his Aunt Kate had more of a bite: "This morning I took an American authoress on a drive— Constance Fenimore Woolson whose productions you may know, though I don't. . . . Constance is old-maidish, deaf and 'intense';

but a good little woman and a perfect lady."[8] Actually, when James first met Woolson he found that she was hard of hearing only in one ear, so that it was merely a matter of speaking to her good side to insure that nothing said was lost on her. But he always magnified the disability and, in describing her in his correspondence, never left it out, repeatedly calling her "impracticably deaf" and old-maidish. Here was the onset of the condescending, affably derogatory tone in James that his biographer Leon Edel would take up in regard to Constance Woolson.

At their first meeting, Henry James was favorably impressed by Miss Woolson's devotion to his work and by her family connections. It was natural for one as concerned with status and family line as he was to refer to her as "our dear friend Fenimore," "the excellent Fenimore," etc. But his emphasizing of her great-uncle's identity over her own can also be seen as his unconscious assertion of male authority over women writers.

It wasn't only James's courtly charm that swept Woolson off her feet, but foremost his magisterial gifts as a writer that made her seek him out in the first place. When they strolled and conversed in the Cascine Gardens and she told him of her problems with rewriting, she was amazed to hear him reply, "Oh, I never copy"—his original draft of a work was his only one. Was it permanently unknown to Woolson that James did, in fact, rewrite? Edel gives quite a different picture of him at that very moment in Florence in 1880 when he was hard at work on *The Portrait of a Lady* and telling Woolson he never recopied. In fact, he worked over each chapter of that novel, "every part being written twice," as he himself related.

A dozen years later, still under the impression that he got perfect copy at first try, she wrote him of her own despair in revising and mentioned that "added to your other perfections was the gift of writing as you do, at the first draft." She at that time was working on the serialization of *For the Major* for *Harper's* and described to him the great fatigue of the work: six consecutive weeks at ten hours a day, then two more weeks working thirteen hours per day. She had to take two weeks just to recopy, working from early morning to evening while enduring hand cramps. "You, master of all the situations in which you find yourself, would never have been caught in any such position."

Henry James's mastery, his absolute confidence, his sublime gift made her despair of her own slow plodding way. It took her years to complete a novel, working steadily but slowly, and when she was focused on a long work, she infrequently wrote short fiction or travel pieces. Only thirteen short stories of hers appeared in the magazines that were serializing her novels while she was abroad. The disparity between James's rapidity and ease of production and her own labor kept her psychologically abject for their entire friendship, as she reiterated that the utmost best of what she wrote could not touch the hem of his poorest.

It seems unsporting that he did not communicate his own difficulties to Woolson, but he basked in her awe; he accepted an adoration which could not have been other than undermining to her, confirming what she had always been told and had such ambivalence about but now had to acknowledge—the natural superiority of the male artist over the female. "A woman, after all, can never be a complete artist," she wrote him.[9] Was it irony, or inner defeat? Both, perhaps, as Woolson veered both ways in her own mind.

Woolson, too, was busy writing during the period of that first encounter with James. Her story, "A Florentine Experiment," appeared in the October 1880 issue of *Atlantic Monthly* and contains descriptions of landmarks and Florentine art works based on her excursions in Florence with him. The story is quite a projection: Margaret, a maiden lady abroad with her aunt, meets Trafford Morgan, the mysterious suitor of Beatrice, her widowed close friend who is at that time away from Florence. Morgan's interest moves from the absent Beatrice to the present Margaret. In his self-absorption and conceit, he becomes convinced she's smitten with him.

In a nice parallel with the Florentine days of Miss Woolson and Mr. James, Morgan refers to the times when he and Margaret roamed the galleries as the attraction between them developed. Scenes take place in the cloisters of San Marco, in the Medici Chapel, in the Duomo, in the Boboli Gardens; Woolson's characters converse on art in remarks that repeat the didactic conversation of Henry James as he charmingly instructed Miss Woolson on the masterpieces around them and as had already appeared verbatim in Woolson's letters home.

Margaret senses the conceit behind Morgan's charm, and at his proposal retorts, "You do not love me; I am not beautiful; I have no fortune. What, then, do you gain?" He blandly answers that he gains a wife who adores him. Perhaps Woolson, too, from her feeling of unworthiness had felt both gratitude and resentment at the egotistical condescension that lay beneath James's fine, courtly manners. In "The Florentine Experiment," Margaret is outraged by Morgan's presumption and, in a scene that must have given much pleasure to its author, upbraided his huge conceit before rejecting him flatly.

The story, however, has a happy ending. After an absence from Florence, Morgan comes to realize that he did, in fact, really love Margaret, not just her devotion to him. He has profited from the author-directed insights into his character. Returning to Florence to make amends, Morgan pleads with Margaret, "Is it too late?" Of course it isn't, and Woolson fulfilled for her fictional double a fantasy she'd never realize for herself. James's friendship with her would remain, in his description, a "virtuous attachment" at discrete intervals.

"A Florentine Experiment" is interesting for reintroducing that polished, rather cold and arrogant, but charming, grey-eyed male character who was to appear in other of Woolson's stories and was redolent of The Master himself. He is the duplicitous narrator of "Miss Grief," the celebrated critic of "The Street of the Hyacinth," and the cold-blooded John Ford of "At the Chateau of Corinne."

Was Woolson so enchanted by Henry James that her secret, unexpressed (except in fiction) wish was to give in to him, let him indeed be the Master as she lets Katherine from "Chateau" give up literary ambition in order to marry John Ford? In "Chateau," Katherine's losing her wealth and thus being amenable to John Ford's proposal on condition that she give up her "literariness," would be the equivalent of Woolson's forsaking her writing. Writing is equivalent to wealth since the income she derives from it has supported her, made her comfortable and independent. Perhaps subliminally, Constance (in the guise of Katherine) would give up her literary ambition for the sake of marriage with the grey-eyed, expressionless Henry James (in the guise of John Ford).

For the purposes of the story, marriage was the proper, conventional ending for her readers; but Woolson's covert irony regarding Katherine's sacrifice of her creative bent for the sake of marriage and security gives it a bitter edge and tension. Woolson is totally ironic as she provides John one last cynical gesture that is a gratuitous, hurtful revelation to Katherine that he might have foregone. We are left to wonder what bliss will come of this match when John Ford, having derided Mme. de Staël, keeps her volumes in his study, on the shelf, a reminder that Woolson herself used the term "shelved" for women who were not allowed to circulate freely. Certainly, in light of Woolson's life and death, the story reveals a remarkable tangle of motives and a deeply rent nature.

Convincing and keen in her stories of the American South, Woolson is less so in her Italian stories and even those much praised in her day seem strained today. "The Front Yard," the title story to a posthumous collection of her short fiction, especially strikes me as a curious perversity. Woolson presents Prudence Wilkins as a forty-five year old Yankee spinster in Italy who belies her given name and heritage and is guileless enough to be taken in by a handsome Italian waiter eighteen years her junior who, after they're married, reveals he has children and dependent in-laws from a previous marriage. This charmer spends Prudence's savings, and when he dies after a year of marriage misguided duty to his extended family keeps Prudence from returning home; the rest of her life is spent in a rude dwelling outside Assisi pining for a proper "front yard" such as she remembers in her New Hampshire town. Just as Constance was inconstant in her homes, so Prudence was imprudent in love. Where, in the figure Woolson depicts, is New England character and horse-sense? Why does Prudence become a slave to a family of "singing, indolent Umbrians" who exploit, cheat, and rob her?

The most striking thing about Woolson's Italian stories is how little she uses them to write about Italians in a non-clichéd way. Italy is simply a background for expatriate Americans who very much like the ease and culture of their lives abroad, but still view America as their homeland. Woolson places her Americans in places she knows—Sorrento, Paestum, Rome, Assisi, Venice, Pisa, and Florence—without ever penetrating the particular character of those places, much less the lives of the people who actually live there. Italians are simply marginal accessories to American characters—servants, gondoliers, peasants, and the like. No one evinces interest in contemporary Italian matters— indeed, the only reference to the recently unified Italian nation is in "A Pink Villa" when mention is made of the unifying monarchy in the New Italy not as a political achievement but as a social grace—"it's a pretty little court they have now at Rome, I assure you, with that lovely Queen Margherita at the head."[10] Woolson's expatriate stories became, like the novels of Henry James, mainly a study of manners of a certain strata of American life—those with sufficient income and leisure to live abroad.

The two expatriate authors, Woolson and James, lived out their own story of circumspect manners with each other. Admiring him, she admonished him, too, about his ignorance of how women love. She maintained a strong bond with him, mostly through correspondence since they were not often together in the same place at the same time. His writings, she told him, had become her true country, her real home. She clearly valued her friendship with him, the exalted author, while he liked highlighting her connection with an illustrious American literary heritage and a family of landed gentry. He spoke or wrote of her familiarly as Fenimore, la Costanza, or mockingly as the *littératrice*, or contritely as the best and tenderest of women. Always, he kept the upper hand.

Gradually Constance became more incisive in her correspondence with Henry, sarcastic, even, and aggressive, daring him to portray love in his work by allowing his characters that emotion. She wrote long, long letters; he answered in brief notes, filling the page with over-large writing and a huge signature which took up half a page. Or, he would send frequent, sprightly telegrams which could almost stand in for witty conversation and distract from the insufficiently answered letters.

An illuminating insight of James's ability to deflect what he didn't want to address was recorded by Thomas Hardy in his diary when he noted that James had a ponderously warm manner of saying nothing in infinite sentences. So, too, in his dealings with Woolson: he created a semblance of warm friendship that was more politesse or a game of male gallantry and social charm on his part, misinterpreted on hers. The tie that bound them was her idolization and his total acceptance of that devotion, which he described as *sans bornes*.

Why, she asked rhetorically, should he answer her long letters, "I am not important, you know, and my letter is naturally like its writer."[11] Her work could never be compared to his, nor her life compared to his brilliant social one, so full of notable people. As she repeats her criticism of the cold lack of love displayed by his fictional characters, one catches only too well her complaint of his lack of emotional involvement with her.

Indeed, the expression of love in art was the most interesting duel between them: he complained that Woolson's novels were almost exclusively based on "the complications of love . . . the question of engagement and marriage," a love interest that was preeminently the domain of women writers, so that there was no "tangle and overgrowth" of other worldly or social issues at stake. For her part, she takes him to task in regard to *Daisy Miller* and *Portrait of a Lady*: "why not give us a woman for whom we can feel a real Love? . . . perhaps let some one love her very much; but, at any rate, let her love, and let us see that she does; do not leave it merely implied . . . take the one further step, and use your perfect art in delineating a real love as it really is."

If Woolson criticized James in her letters, she immediately tempered that criticism in the very next line: "Forgive me—if you dislike what I have said . . . if your judgment pushes away all these suggestions of mine, I yield. You know best." Yet that isn't quite what she thought, for she was tangled in her own ambivalence. She was both suppliant and defiant toward James; though she revered him, she also competed with him. They were "Harry" and "Connie" on an existentialist see-saw, eternally oscillating between the highs of attachment on the one side, and freedom on the other. How to choose?—there is a perennial thirst for the security and warmth and glow and delight of love as a high; then on the descent, the low of extreme discomfort at the restraints it enforces on one's sense of self. Or, there is the exhilaration, the sense of achievement and independence while riding high on freedom until it, too, sinks to the low of loneliness, isolation, disconnection. The tension between the desire to do what we want versus the need to be cared for by others is the human condition. "Harry" was better equipped to survive—he was favored, after all, in being male, a social lion, wealthy, and firmly planted at home in Lamb House at Rye or in his London digs, the centers to which he unerringly returned after travels. "Connie," a woman alone, was plagued by her history of depression, the social discomfort that increased with her deafness, and by being completely untethered to a home-base.

Her first years abroad Woolson spent mainly in Italy—Florence, Venice, and Rome—leaving for Switzerland, as was the custom, during the hot months. After not seeing Henry James since their meeting in Florence three years earlier, in 1883 she established herself in England where he lived and once again had his occasional company in person and not just by letter. At this time she became acquainted with his ailing sister Alice and became one of Alice's preferred friends. Constance recognized the tragically unexpressed gifts of her new friend; she interested herself in Alice's condition and recommended that her American doctor in Florence, Dr. William Baldwin, visit Alice when he was in London. Constance wrote Dr. Baldwin about her, "If she had any health, what a brilliant woman she would have been."[12]

And to Alice she stated what she did not to her male friends, that she favored medical education for women and that they receive it in the same classes with men. "It is the only way, in my opinion, to widen the feminine mind. . . . Do not suppose from that that I think the feminine mind inferior to the masculine. For I do not. But it has been kept back, & enfeebled, & limited, by ages of ignorance, & almost servitude."

Did the two women discuss suicide? It was a favorite philosophical topic with Alice, who, at age thirty had made her desire to commit suicide known to her father, who, after a solemn lecture, granted his permission. Woolson's rapport with Alice James was that of two gifted women who understood themselves to be restricted by their times from fully realizing themselves but who nonetheless determined to remain in charge of their own fate. In Woolson's novel *Jupiter Lights*, the despondent heroine, Eve Bruce, asks, "Is it wrong to try to die?" Constance's brother had taken his life when only in his thirties. And she herself had often told her friends not to mourn her at her death for the end would come as blessed relief.

Constance was religious; she believed in an afterlife and expressed wonder that anyone could doubt immortality since it was clear to her that "a future existence seems the only solution to the riddle of the present one with its bitter disappointments, its heavy cares, its apparent injustice to so many." When her brother-in-law Samuel Livingston Mather died regretting never having seen her again because she was "wedded to Europe," she felt guilt-stricken until reconciled to seeing him in the afterlife. "God be thanked," she wrote his son, "for our firm and beautiful belief in immortality."

In 1885, after receiving Christmas week tidings from Henry James about the suicide of Henry Adams's wife Clover, Constance wrote John Hay that she planned to leave England for Italy. She had spent a relatively secluded period in England working steadily on her novel *East Angels* with the pictures of a smiling Howells, the poetic Hay, and a cynical Henry James above her work-desk, and only occasionally having the company of the last-named at the theater or, once, on a trip to Stonehenge. By 1886 Constance acknowledged her craving to return to the sun and warmth of Italy.

She got first to Venice, and, as her gondola shot out into the moonlit Grand Canal, experienced a throb of joy which she described in a letter: "I think I felt compensated for all my years of toil, just in that half hour." She made her way to Florence where

Henry James' letter to his friends, the Bootts, had prepared the way for her, since, as he wrote, she "appears to know few people there" and acquaintance with the Bootts, father and daughter, would give her joy. "She is," he wrote Francis Boott in a curious mix of endorsement cum warning, "a deaf and méticuleuse old maid—but she is also an excellent and sympathetic being."

The Bootts welcomed Miss Woolson and eventually she rented rooms in a wing of their Villa Castellani, located on the Bellosguardo height outside the city, known for the magnificent views and celebrated in the opening of Elizabeth Barrett Browning's long narrative poem, "Aurora Leigh": "I found a house at Florence on the hill of Bellosguardo. . . . What evocations of great creative spirits the place was endowed with!" Nearby the James Fenimore Coopers had also lived in a villa outside the city walls some fifty years earlier, and Galileo, too had lived at Bellosguardo for a number of years. Woolson's windows framed a view of the tower where her idol Nathaniel Hawthorne had composed *The Marble Faun*.

Constance developed a close friendship with the Bootts, liking the sentimental songs which the father composed and eventually creating a demand for one of them when she cited it in her story, "Dorothy." Boott in turn gave Constance mementoes of Elizabeth Barrett Browning. Other reminders of creative, fruitful lives were everywhere in Florence. It must have seemed to Constance Woolson that her best work was forthcoming, that life could be sweet in such surroundings.

Before leaving to spend the hot summer months in Switzerland, as was her custom, Constance took a lease on Villa Brichieri adjoining the Bootts at Bellosguardo. The Brichieri villa, too, had been distinguished by a host of creative residents: its rooms had rung with the conversations of the Trollopes, Walter Savage Landor, Bulwer-Lytton, and Robert Browning. Once, the frail Elizabeth Barrett Browning had come, too, and sat for three hours looking out at the view that would inspire the locale of *Aurora*

Leigh, and distinguishing the sofa upon which she reclined so that it was ever after known by her name. Ruskin's discovery, Francesca Alexander, the poet and artist of *Roadside Songs of Tuscany*, had lived there, followed by the English writer Isabella Blagden. A guest of Blagden's for long periods in the 1850s was the American sculptor Harriet Hosmer, chief of those American women artists in Rome whom Henry James had dubbed "the white marmorean flock." Hosmer, a vigorous and independent-minded New England woman, used to descend the tortuously winding path past farmyards of chickens and goats, walking to town daily to breakfast with her great friends the Brownings at Casa Guidi.

In the period from Constance Woolson's reentry in Italy in 1886 when she lived in a veritable Italian paradise at Bellosguardo until her leave-taking in 1889, she became deeply attached to that beautiful spot. It was to be a happy period of her life abroad, both her life and her work were going well and Henry James, too, came to Villa Brichieri to add to its renown, staying a few months on two separate occasions.

The first time he arrived was in December 1886 when he accepted her suggestion of subletting quarters on the lower floor of the villa while she occupied her own apartment on the upper floor. She was still at Villa Castellani and would not go to her new lease of Villa Brichieri until the first of the new year. Some books James gave her—his *Bostonians*, an edition of Shelley, George Eliot's *Romola*—are dated from this period. He inscribed *The Bostonions*, "To his padrona Constance Fenimore Woolson, her faithful tenant and friend, Henry James, Bellosguardo, December 1886." On Christmas eve he wrote a letter from Villa Brichieri to John Hay regarding Constance, his temporary landlady: "I see her every day or two—indeed often dine with her. She has done a brave thing in settling herself here for 2 or 3 years in a somewhat mouldy Tuscan mansion."

The place was anything but mouldy. Enclosed within high tawny walls, it is still palatial with a grand terrace overlooking great distances, a continuing delight to Constance. "I have been house-keeping here since January 1st," Constance wrote a friend in the states, "and it is an immense success in every way. . . . The situation is unrivalled, for owing to its position it commands not only the 'sweet Val d'Arno,' as Ruskin calls it, but all Florence with its domes and towers. . . . Not far off is the villa where my uncle Fenimore spent two summers, sixty years ago. My cousins write that they were the happiest summers of his whole life." She was further delighted to discover Uncle Fenimore's *Excursions in Italy* in a Florentine library.

Her apartment in the villa had nine rooms plus a kitchen and servants' quarters. Her Angelo was an excellent chef and handyman for whose services she paid $10.00 a month. And then she had Assunta and another maid. "All goes like clock-work, and I have no care at all. . . . Once a week I am 'at home'—as everyone is at Bellosguardo on that day. When it is pleasant, all of us here are overwhelmed with callers. . . . The other days I have to myself, and spend the mornings in my little writing-room—which overhangs the Val d'Arno—and my afternoons rambling these enchanting hills. You will see from all this that I am very happy here. I am indeed . . . happier than I have been for years—with this enchanting landscaping and a home of my own."

From Florence Constance wrote to Alice James's companion Katherine Loring in London: "I am grieved to hear that Miss James has been suffering. Tell her that an exclamation burst from me irresistibly, night before last—namely—I wish she were here this minute! . . . The broad doors stood wide open; the moonlight outside lighted up my old garden, and the dark, rugged outline of Hawthorne's tower; perfume from a thousand flowers filled the room; and I was so happy to be here that it was almost wickedness!"[13]

If Henry James appreciated her devotion to his work, he must also have thought her repaid handsomely by his attention to hers. With a superb "bread and butter note" Henry James repaid her Bellosguardo hospitality with no less than a critical review dedicated to her in *Harper's Weekly*. He must have already been working on it at Villa Brichieri during his first December stay, since it appeared in the issue of February 12, 1887, only weeks after he departed Florence for Venice. When he returned in March, his excellent Fenimore would have still been exhilarated by the piece devoted to her. Excluding only a page of biographical notice in which he gave her background and, of course, her relationship to James Fenimore Cooper, and retitling the essay "Miss Woolson," it was included the following year in his book *Partial Portraits*, boosting her reputation even further since the volume contained only nine contemporary writers. She was in the company of George Eliot, Turgenev, De Maupassant, and others of that rank. Henry James, Edel explained, was "not without a Napoleonic propensity to remember those who were loyal and those to whom he was devoted."[14] She became identified by literary historians as the first writer adequately to interpret the postwar South and to record it with evenness, not allowing her Union sympathies to blind her to reality.

In targeting her conservatism, James had, above all, quite overlooked the striking example of Woolson's own life, which is stunningly the contrary of conservative: with total independence she supported herself and realized herself as a writer. Woolson, a well-paid professional woman, went about on her own setting up residences where she would, traveling as she wished, maintaining a rigorous work schedule, attaining success, beholden to no one.

When, in the spring of 1887, Henry James returned ill from Venice, Constance offered him his former quarters at Villa Brichieri. The site and the climate worked its magic, as he wrote to a friend in London, partially paraphrasing a Dantean description: "I am completely restored and have taken, till the first of June, part of a delightful villa on this enchanting hilltop just out of the gates of Florence, where the most beautiful view in the world—as beautiful, and somehow as personal—as a lovely woman—hangs before me as often as I lift my head. As soon as I can stop making love to it I shall go back to England—somewhat ruefully, for I feel myself again somewhat tainted with the taste for living abroad."

Italy, he found, was perfectly irresistible and he entered one of the most productive periods of his career, producing some of his most celebrated tales and the brilliant short novel, *The Aspern Papers*. The mode of life, living under Fenimore's roof, and having her excellent Angelo prepare his meals, suited him but he made no reference to their shared living in his letters, implying only to a caller whom he entertained one evening along with Constance that she was an old and valued friend who happened to be at Bellosguardo. He seems to have taken Woolson's kindnesses for granted and if he suspected any fantasy on her part for a closer attachment, it was transferred to the fictitious Tita, the spinster in *The Aspern Papers*.

The tale derived from a story he had heard in Florence concerning Claire Clairmont, the aged former mistress of Lord Byron who had in her possession some of Byron's and Shelley's papers which an American collector desperately coveted. At Claire Clairmont's death, when a middle-aged relative inherited the papers and exacted marriage as their price, the would-be buyer fled in horror.

In *The Aspern Papers*, James transfers the story to Venice where the aged Juliana, once mistress of American poet Jeffrey Aspern, lives on cared for by her middle-aged relative Tita. Again there is an avid collector to whom Juliana denies all access to the papers. When, at night, he is discovered rummaging through her desk, she cries out famously, "Ah, you publishing scoundral!" (Perhaps Henry James was unaware that the cry echoes one from Woolson's much earlier story, "Miss Grief," where the aunt accosts a critic as the cause of Miss Grief's death with the accusing cry, "You, you—YOU literary men!") At old Juliana's death, the price for the papers is again marriage with the great-niece and again the horrified collector flees.

Henry departed Bellosguardo. Clara Benedict was her sister's next visitor at Villa Brichieri and she extolled it in rapturous letters home: "It is all so beyond what I had expected, so much more beautiful . . . we are living like queens, and we shall be thoroughly spoiled . . . and the rent of this whole delightful, furnished villa, commanding one of the most beautiful views in the world, is less than half what I pay for two inferior rooms in New York!" Certainly one of the great advantages for the expatriates was how well and how cheaply they could live abroad. It was not a minor consideration.

Mrs. Benedict also made great mention of the constant talk that went on between them: "we wander about these beautiful hills and talk, we go out on the balcony, have a cup of delicious tea, and talk . . . and we sit in Connie's pretty parlour, before an open wood fire in the evening, and talk. And we go to bed talking; and we wake up and talk!" It's hard to imagine, with all that talking, that Woolson's deafness was the insurmountable impediment that Henry James made out. It's as if he made it seem so to himself in order to vacate himself from the possibility of any kind of closeness with her. Yet the "virtuous attachment" and discrete occasional visits continued. Constance had grown used to Henry's company. In the fall of 1888 a rendezvous was arranged in Geneva where they stayed in separate hotels a mile apart, worked at their work, and met in the evening to dine together. It was perhaps to such virginal tryst that Alice James referred when she wrote home to brother William, "Henry is somewhere on the continent flirting with Constance."

As Constance's lease came to an end, rather than renewing she began to speak of leaving and Henry James reported to Francis

Boott, "Fenimore's mind and talk are full of her last year or two at Bellosguardo . . . she constantly speaks of giving up her villa. I can't imagine why unless to mortify the spirit." Yes, the theme of renunciation that is so much a part of her fiction may play a part here, but James is disingenuous if he refused to see another motive, especially as her next move was to England where he resided. If she had been reading Dante in Florence as all cultivated visitors did, she would have been moved by the line in the fifth canto of the *Inferno* which depicts the great love between Francesca da Rimini and Paolo: *Amor, ch'a nullo amato amar perdona.* . . . The line declared that no one loved can be absolved from returning love and was beloved by all sentimental Victorians.

The fact is that the "so deeply-rooted Fenimore," as Henry thought of her in her Florentine home, is ready to give it all up—give up a place she loved to attempt once more the English climate she abhorred. Had she overstressed the inconveniences and negatives of her beloved Villa Brichieri so as not to arouse his suspicion? James, seemingly none the wiser, reported that she "left Florence with a kind of loathing . . . for the crowds, the interruptions and invasions, the final rapacity and trickery of the unmasked Brichieris, and the conditions consequent upon her extravagant propensities for "packing—the most unenvious virtue that ever a woman was cursed with, and the blight of her whole existence." He was right about that—the blight of her existence was the packing and repacking of her trunks as she looked for home.

Travel, as she had long ago counseled Paul Hamilton Hayne, was one way to combat depression. So, before resettling she traveled to Greece and Egypt with the Benedicts. The rest was will power and work. She wrote more travel pieces, kept up her correspondence, kept on the move, worked hard, and was repaid with steady publication and having to turn down offers of more.

By the spring of 1890 Constance Woolson was back in England braving a climate she disliked, living first in Cheltenham, then Oxford, for the pleasure of occasional visits with the Master. During this period she was writing what was to be her last novel, *Horace Chase*, again laid in the American South. It was an exception to the previous ones in which women had been central characters, for the self-made man for whom the book is titled is the focus of Woolson's attention. Was she giving up her self-sacrificing, renunciatory female characters at last? Was she ready to examine other complications of life? After three years of hard work on it, and the decision to return to the Italy that she loved best of all, did it mean that she, too, was finished with sacrificing her likes and preferences for what turned out to be, after all, a *fata morgana*, an illusion?

Woolson's time in England had not been pleasant. "Our poor Fenimore, at Oxford, which she likes," Henry James wrote to Boott in Florence, "has had a very painful illness—an affection of the head, brought on by trying false drums (a new invention) in her ears. But she is better, though her hearing isn't. I go to see her next week."

Before Alice James's death in 1892, she sent a last message to Constance that remains a mystery but seems to have alluded to some pledge on Henry's part, a pledge that Constance confided to her nephew.[16] Then, repenting, she wrote him that what she had done was "simply the relief of having family to talk to . . . whether it was safe or not, wise or not, prudent or not" to have done what she did, she could not tell. She has decided again to return to Italy even though her leaving England means "giving up being near my kind friend Mr. James." But, she adds, he will be coming to Italy every year. Was that his pledge to the dying Alice who passed it on to Constance?—that he would continue looking in on their Fenimore in his own deliberate way?

Alice's message remains a cryptogram in the Woolson–James relationship, never to be decoded just as they intended that their correspondence to each other would never be read by others. But the weighted language, the hint that something might not be "safe or wise or prudent," certainly gives it a ring that can't be disregarded. By mutual agreement, Constance and Henry destroyed each other's letters as soon as read and replied to; that four letters of hers—totaling almost forty revealing pages!— survived was probably due to their having been mailed to Henry James in America while he was on a home visit. Somehow the letters were left behind, became mingled with brother William's papers, and were only discovered when all parties were long gone.

Alice was fond of Constance; they had a bond in their separate afflictions and in their intellectual compatibility. Even so, strange it is to think of Alice on her death bed asking to have read to her Woolson's story "Dorothy" about a young American in Italy wasting slowly away because she simply does not want to live. That so-called Bellosguardo story evoked a setting and people very dear to Woolson. In it she named her friends Francis Boott and John Hay as composers of a song particularly dear to Dorothy. Through depicting Dorothy's attachment to her Bellosguardo villa and her sickness at leaving it, Constance reflected her own difficulty in uprooting herself from Villa Brichieri.

In the spring of 1893, a year after Alice James died, Constance Woolson packed her trunks once more to leave England for Italy. Her completed novel *Horace Chase* was being serialized in *Harper's Magazine* and she was preparing the book version. She had a bout of influenza in London which laid her very low, making her naturally depressed spirits even more so.

Fourteen years abroad had passed. Woolson, deciding this time to locate in Venice, had indicated to Henry that she would spend the rest of her life in Italy, but he had skeptically written to Boott, *chi lo sa?* He knew her past restlessness and how she alluded every so often to settling in a cottage in Florida with her books, a dog, and possible summer sojourns in Cooperstown (so picturesquely nestled into the south tip of Otsego Lake and the site of so much tradition where she told him to come visit to enjoy rowing on the lake, the gorgeousness of the Northern fall, the pears, and Uncle Fenimore's gentleman-of-leisure library). This time Italy did turn out to be for the rest of her life.

Again, Henry James, in his multitudinous correspondence, mentioned to a mutual friend, "you will have heard of our excellent friend CFW, of her at last actual domestication (for which a permanent flat is indeed still needed) at Venice. She is looking at palaces. I hope to see her there in autumn." Elsewhere, Henry James the writer had given a morbid estimate of those attracted to the watery city: "The deposed, the defeated, the disenchanted, the wounded, or even only the bored," he wrote "have always found in Venice a sort of repository of consolations."[16]

But Woolson found ample consolation there including, once again, agreeable echoes of Uncle Fenimore who had been inspired by the history of the Serene Republic to write *The Bravo*, his first novel with a European setting. And the English general from whom Constance leased Palazzo Semitecolo on the Grand Canal, was a James Fenimore Cooper enthusiast. Forty years earlier, the General told Constance while entertaining her grandly at tea, he had been in the United States and had made it a point to go to Cooperstown for several days because of his great admiration for Fenimore Cooper's novels which, he added, he knew by heart.

Constance Woolson's final notes from Venice give a picture of her life there: she rose at 4:30 A.M. to work in the cool of early morning, took breakfast, worked again, and then toward afternoon went out to the Lido to bathe. "These baths are, to me, quite perfect; the best I have ever had . . . the water is soft, and the little waves lift one up so lightly that I almost swim. I go out as far as I can and just float and float." Then home to dinner and all evening out in her gondola enjoying the gliding rhythm over the waters and feeling that nothing in the world can be more beautiful than the lagoons by starlight. She was content with her life in Venice— even the fact that "society" was so laid back and easy to take or not, as one wished. She loved her expeditions in the lagoons, discovering and cataloging the islands, her walks on the Lido with her little dog Otello, *detto* Tello whom she paraphrased in playful dog-language letters to her niece Clare Benedict. She seemed to be planning a future in Venice, engaging in house-hunting and writing the Benedicts to join her in the spring when her friend Henry James would also arrive.

She must have recalled the exuberant, euphoric days of her first stay in Venice a decade earlier in the spring of 1883; she must have hoped to recapture them. Two 1883 letters of hers sent to Henry James in America have survived to describe her being happily ensconced in a third floor suite above "no less a personage than Symonds, the English writer on Italian arts" who occupied the second story. He appears in her story "The Front Yard" where an American tourist, arrived in Assisi, "read Symonds and wondered about exploring the ancient town."

She described her lodging with its two small balconies on the Grand Canal, balconies so small that she treated them as fresh-air sofas and demanded cushions for them from the *padrona*—red cushions, no other color would do. And there she would sit with her views of the Canal; or, from a side-window "the harbor, the Riva with its masts, the fresh green of the Public Gardens . . . San Giorgio Maggiore with its angel-topped pink tower. . . . Behold me then, established. I am here at last. Here at the perfect season of the year—and I have no plan for departing."

She pictured for him her days—getting up very early and looking out the arched windows, seeing to the pots and pots of flowers, more looking from the window, writing until four in the afternoon.

> Then I put on my straw hat, go down my lighthouse stairs and either take a gondola and float luxuriously through all the color until six; or else I go, on foot, to all sorts of enchanting places—Santa Maria dell'Orto—over myriad bridges, losing my way all the time and enjoying it, and wondering only now and then how I shall ever be able to get away from Venice; whether the end of the riddle of my existence may not be, after all, to live here, and die here. . . . I come home—having dined on color—to my tangible dinner—first, of course, stopping in at St. Mark's for a few minutes, as a fit close for the beautiful day. Then, immediately after dinner, out I go again in another gondola. And when respectability requires that I should come within at last, I come. And then I sit in my red-cushioned balcony, and watch the lights on the gliding gondolas, and the colored lanterns of the music-barges . . . and make out Schubert's "Serenade." Isn't this being as happy as Fate allows us—no, I mean allows *me*—to be?

She offered him a gift: "I have something for you . . . two Greek coins set by Accorisi of Florence as scarf-pins."[18] Of the three coins she had purchased at Paestum, she had kept for herself the one depicting an owl (her emblem, the "solitary old bird?"), and offered him the ones of Bacchus and a Boeotian shield. Perhaps in an allusion to the provenance of the family fortune from the New World Syracuse, she says she had hoped to find him an ancient "Syracusan coin." Then she assures him of her discretion: "Nobody knows of my coins—the ones destined for you." Leon Edel commented in a footnote that later photos of Henry James show him wearing a tie-pin that fits Woolson's description of one of the coins.

Her happiness, her past joy, culminated in a kind of threnody of bliss as she recalled to James that he knows the very scenes that she was presently enjoying, and that his writings captured them so perfectly that "they voice for me—as nothing else ever has—my own feelings; those that are so deep—so a part of me." Her letter included a graphically provocative lure: "I am so shamefully well . . . the back view of me as I depart from you, is like that of a Veronese woman!" Meaning, of course, ample, fleshy, rotund, beckoning. An intriguing word-picture from spinster to bachelor. She ended her last 1883 letter with very poignant, quite transparent words: "The lagoons, the Piazzetta, and the little still canals all send their love to you. They wish you were here. And so do I."[18]

Ten years after that letter, Constance Woolson was in a different state of mind; in December 1893 she made a new will. On Christmas Eve she was at the Lido recording in her notebook the sad words seen on a tombstone of one who had died at age forty-five, "worn out by misfortunes and a too sensitive disposition." She would soon be the reverse age: fifty-four. And she followed her notes with this reflection:

Upon seeing the sharp peaks of the Dolomites and the great snow masses of the Alps from the point of the Lido on Christmas Eve, 1893, the thought came to me that they are riding along through immeasurable space, they are the outer edge of our star, they cut the air as they fly. They are the rim of the world, I should like to turn into a peak when I die; to be a beautiful purple mountain, which would please the tired, sad eyes of thousands of human beings for ages. For "I will lift up mine eyes unto the hills, from when cometh my help," is an almost universal aspiration. George Eliot wrote: "O may I join the Choir Invisible," etc., but I should rather join the mountains, and be an object of beauty and have nothing to do with the eternal sorrow and despair of poor human beings.[20]

Constance spent a solitary Christmas declining all invitations. A few days earlier she had written her nephew Samuel Mather a nostalgic and moving letter recalling her long-ago feelings for the Civil War sweetheart of her youth. "I should like to see him again . . . if I could get him alone, I dare say we should have a very friendly and funny talk. But, meanwhile, we should both be inwardly thinking . . . what an escape I had. It was only the glamour of the war that brought us together. Every girl wanted to have a soldier-lover in those intense years." Even toward the ebb of her life, she kept her cool irony (the habitual cover-up under which she hid her feelings) and continued to pretend to be that "solitary old bird" who put all the best of herself into her work.

In thinking of Constance Woolson, I am reminded of Dorothy Wordsworth whose tense and responsive mind was, later in her life, to snap under the strain of repressed emotion. She was a talented woman who lived in the shadow of her brother William and was unrequited in her affection for Samuel Taylor Coleridge. He made a disastrous marriage, she became mad. That sad personal history in the annals of English literature is matched by the "virtuous attachment" between Henry James and Constance Woolson.

On New Year's Day, feeling the strain of illness and fatigue, Constance wrote to a *Harper* editor that she was "profoundly discouraged," feeling that she had little or no more literary work to do. By mid-January she had a recurrence of influenza and was attended at home by a nurse. In the very late hours of January 24th, Constance sent the nurse out of the room on some pretext and then fell or jumped from the second-story window of the back bedroom in Palazzo Semitocolo to the pavement below. Was it a deliberate leap to death, or accidental loss of balance due to delirium? She was philosophically certain of another, better life ("Yes, we shall live again—and go on living, and then, if we have been faithful here, we shall be happier . . ."), but she had also been a hardy hanger-on who knew how to weather her low points.

The next day, January 25, the *New York Times* ran the notice of the death of "the authoress who wrote stories, sketches and poems in charming profusion." Two days later the paper ran a piece calling the death a suicide according to information received from a European correspondent, and ended the brief notice by reporting that "Miss Woolson suffered from influenza for four days, but she had been eccentric for a longer period." Eccentric, yes, not in the delightful, daffy way of English characters, but in the precise meaning of off-center: indeed, of no center.

Having first heard of Constance Woolson's death from her sister, and only subsequently of its violent form, Henry James was so greatly shocked and horrified, he was unable to attend the burial in Rome. Years earlier when he had received the news of Clover Adams's suicide he had been able to weigh it philosophically: she had "succumbed to hereditary melancholia," and the act provided a "solution of the knottiness of existence." With Fenimore's death there were too many intense personal reverberations for him to be detached: "I have a dismal, dreadful image of her being alone and unfriended at the last. But what sudden disaster overtook her—pneumonia supervening on influenza? That her funeral is to be in Rome—where she would have wished—is in some degree a comfort. But poor isolated and fundamentally tragic being! She was intrinsically one of the saddest and least happy natures I have ever met; and when I ask myself what I feel about her death the only answer that comes to me is from what I felt about the melancholy, the limitations and the touching loneliness of her life."[20]

The equanimity he counseled in letters to Constance's distraught sister and niece could not, apparently, be summoned to ease his own anguish; he wrote compulsively, reciting the details and explanations and his reaction over and over again to many of their mutual friends including Mrs. Bronson in Venice: "But it is all too pitiful and miserable to dwell on—too tragic and obscure . . . this publicity of misery, this outward horror and *chiasso* round her death was the thing most alien to her . . . and therefore, to my mind, most conclusive as to her having undergone some violent cerebral derangement. Nothing could be more incongruous with the general patience, reserve and dainty dignity, as it were, of her life."

He proved an excellent friend and support to the Benedicts, meeting them in Genoa in spring and staying with them throughout the six weeks of packing up Woolson's effects and settling her affairs in Venice. He destroyed the remainder of his correspondence to her, was given his choice of some of her books, and received on loan from Mrs. Benedict, at his request, a small Italian painting that had been Connie's favorite and was to hang in his parlor at Lamb House for many years. He did his last bit for his "excellent Fenimore" and, as he wrote to his brother William, was sadly confirmed by the evidence of her lapse from sanity: "The sight of the scene of her horrible act is sufficient to establish her utter madness. . . . A place more mad for her couldn't be imagined."

The Benedicts departed and he, worn out and wearied from the ordeal, left for Ravenna from where he wrote William about "the great hole bored in my time and my nerves by the copious aid" required by the poor clinging, helpless Benedicts. But, he ended with a flourish, let's not talk of them, actually writing *"non ragionam di lor!"* the famous passage from Dante's *Inferno* about not wasting thought on the miserable souls who lived without blame and without praise and so deserved neither heaven nor hell but are left forever in an antechamber nowhere.

That fall of 1894, on a visit to Oxford, Henry James actually sought out the same lodgings Woolson had occupied during her last residence in England and stayed there himself. At that time he noted in his journal the beginnings of a story, "The Altar of the Dead," in which a man establishes "an altar in his mind, in his soul" which is then realized in a chapel where he goes to remember the dead. It is his touching pledge to the memory of Fenimore. It would take Henry James almost ten years before he would settle in his own mind her sad end and he did so through the fictional character of John Marcher in "The Beast in the Jungle." Marcher had flung himself upon the grave of May Bartram who had waited so patiently and fruitlessly for him, and through Marcher, James expiated his own grief and guilt.

Given a nature already prone to depression and the inroads that influenza could make into that already vulnerable state of mind, nothing is less surprising than that Constance Woolson's remedies for fending off depression could not, at last, save her. She was in the wiped-out psychic state which she said always came over her at the completion of a book, and perhaps, most embittering of all, she may have recognized her delusion in thinking that James, too, would make his home in Venice. His oblique reference in a letter to friends implies this: "I expressed myself clumsily to Miss Woolson," he wrote the Curtises, "in appearing to intimate that I was coming there [to Venice] to "'live.' I can only, for all sorts of practical reasons, live in London."[21]

It is not difficult to find Palazzo Semitecolo in Venice. At the *traghetto* stop near the Gritti Hotel I got in a gondola-ferry that goes from that side of the Grand Canal to the other side where, between Peggy Guggenheim's Palazzo Venier and the monumental Church of the Salute at the Canal's majestic opening, I found Constance Woolson's last residence, a pretty *palazzetto* that is now marked D. A. Salviati and Co., a venerable mosaic company that would have been familiar to her one hundred years ago. The rear of the *palazzetto* is on the narrow Calle del Bastion and this is where, having leapt from her bedroom window, she lay crumpled on the pavement, an indistinguishable heap of white that two passing Venetians came upon just after midnight. One tapped the curious mound with his walking stick; a low moan was heard. They called for help, Woolson's servants rushed out and carried her into the *palazzetto*; she never regained consciousness.

There is a terrible severity, almost denigration, in how Constance Woolson's friends responded to her death: John Hay who arranged her burial in Rome wrote to Henry Adams, "We buried poor C. W. last Wednesday . . . laying her down in her first and last resting place—a thoroughly good, and most unhappy woman, with a great talent, bedeviled by disordered nerves. She did much good, and no harm in her life, and had not as much happiness as a convict."[22] Like James's fictional Daisy Miller with whom she also identified (perhaps because Winterbourne was obtuse to her love), she found home at last in Rome's beautiful Protestant Cemetery.

Her friends' comments annul the courage, the striving and dedication of the woman and distort her life into a woe begotten affair. She made great efforts to live, to connect with life, to depict it, as she saw it, in her writing; her deafness made her more comfortable alone, reading, writing, and walking with her dog. But she did not, after all, invalidate herself as Alice James did, and make a career out of receiving sickroom calls. She achieved much despite many obstacles—not only of the times and society she was born into, but also those of her physical disability and her own convoluted nature. That she did as much, and as well, as she did was her real monument.

It should be noted that the anxiety Henry James manifested in his words about "poor Fenimore" could have actually been a transference of his own fear of isolation and solitude. He was to some extent reading his own anxiety and fear of loneliness into Woolson's state. When he was seventy he said about the quiet of his home in Rye, "I can no longer stand the solitude and confinement, the immobilisation, of that contracted corner." He fled to the crowds, the taxis, the light, the noise, the movement of London. He saw in Woolson's isolation something he could not have borne.

Homeless for half of her life, Constance Woolson had once written Henry from Leipzig, "I suppose there never was a woman so ill fitted to do without a home as I am." She compared herself to a beaver she had seen at the Zoo there—an American, as she!—who had constructed a pathetic dam out of a few boughs just as she did with her things in hotel and pension rooms.

Constance Fenimore Woolson was of those nineteenth-century American women writers who achieved prominence in their lifetime only to be posthumously eclipsed by male contemporaries whose names entered the texts of American literature even as the women were forgotten. For a short time after her death in Venice, Constance Woolson was still read thanks to the publication of two posthumous collections of her Italian stories, a travel book, and reissues of some earlier work in the late 1890s. Then her name and her works receded from memory until she was revived in Leon Edel's life of Henry James. There she is treated as the "regional Authoress" of tales for popular American magazines, and a devoted fan of Henry James who attempted in the fourteen years of their friendship to extract more attention from him than he was willing to give.

The focus on regionalism and novels of manner that had been Woolson's strength was played out, and whatever progressive notion her work might have embodied about woman's state was too buried under irony, too indistinct to make an impression. Constance Woolson transposed woman's struggle between her creative bent and the socialized imperative of her destiny into fiction with an embittered ironic cast because there was no answer. Her signals, to herself and to others, are crossed.

In 1938 Clare Benedict dedicated a Constance Fenimore Woolson House on the campus of Rollins College in Winter Park, Florida. The house, appropriately of Mediterranean style, is for the use of English department faculty and students and contains a museum room where Woolson's papers, Italian furnishings, and memorabilia, including the framed "Reflection" written in Venice on her last Christmas Eve, are gathered. Listed in the catalogue of Woolson's personal library are several books which had belonged to her Uncle Fenimore, and those given her by Henry James. Included in her collection, perhaps to compensate for her having once negatively reviewed it when it first appeared, is a later edition of Henry's *Roderick Hudson* in which is inserted his photo and autograph. There are volumes in French and Italian, including those of an Italian novelist contemporary with Woolson, Matilde Serao.

A dedicatory plaque names Constance Woolson rather astonishingly, "Laureate of Florida both in Verse and Prose." Surely, with her sense of wit and irony, she would have been amused, perhaps even pleased. The plaque is on the little house in the South where she had once thought to make her home until the fatal charm of Italy beckoned and kept her. Woolson's happiest years had been at Villa Brichieri, outside Florence, and if she had remained there she would have had as neighbor in nearby Villa Curonia a radically different compatriot and a certain subject for her stories. In the environs of Woolson's quiet, writerly life, the heiress Mabel Dodge, a completely different type of American woman searching for her self, was to set up residence and begin her Italian life in a radically different style.

Mabel Dodge Luhan, 1870–1962

4. *Mabel Dodge Luhan: In Search of a Personal South*

Mabel Dodge, acquiring the attire and attitude of a Renaissance personage, was the willful mistress of Villa Curonia in Arcetri outside Florence from 1905 to 1912. Among her string of names—she was born Ganson, then acquired Evans, Dodge, Sterne, and Luhan through marriages—Reticence was not one. One biographer entitled her work simply *Mabel*, putting her in the category of those greats known by first names only—Michelangelo, Raphael, Leonardo, kings, queens, and saints.

Born in Buffalo, New York, in 1879, Mabel was a preeminent American exemplar of the genus Mistress of the Grand Salon and Patroness of All. With the publication of her four-volume autobiography in the 1930s, when such frank accounts from women were not usual, she became a memoirist for her era as well as the symbol of the sexually emancipated, self-aware New Woman in control of her own destiny. She created a sensation, which was what she always intended. After reigning in her Tuscan villa as another "Lorenzo the Magnificent," she returned to the United States, finally settling in Taos, New Mexico.

After her several marriages and moves and "cosmic" transformations of the self, Mabel emerged as the first of a new breed of celebrity—she was famous for being famous. She entertained notable people, and her grand achievement was to get D. H. Lawrence and his wife Frieda to move to her place in Taos, New Mexico. It was there that she made her last stand with her fourth and final husband, the Pueblo Indian Antonio Lujan, a man of few words, indeed almost inarticulate. But then for words Mabel had always sent out for company. Ironically, by providing not only Lawrence but other eminent writers and artists (Willa Cather, Georgia O'Keeffe, Thornton Wilder, Robinson Jeffers, Andrew Dasberg, Aldous Huxley, et al.) with material by her very presence and surroundings, she unwittingly obscured her own work.

Commentators on the life of the flamboyant Mabel have tended to see her residence in Italy as simply one of several phases in her pattern of taking up and dropping enthusiasms and locations as she did partners. From hometown Buffalo to the villa in Tuscany, then to Greenwich Village followed by the Croton countryside until she finally created an adobe compound in New Mexico, Mabel repeated her formula of making a setting, animating it with a collection of creative guests, and installing a man at its center.[1]

Mabel's lasting identification is with Taos and, after my own journey there, I came to see its affinity with Italy and how Mabel's experience of Italy had prepared her for that final stage of her life. Her sensory awareness of and pleasure in color, form, and appearance, and her appetites and sympathies were all distinctly more of a meridional than nordic bent. Thus, in the personal search that landed her in the Southwest she could identify with its Italianate qualities, for it was the part of her homeland most influenced by Latin rather than Anglo values.

Mabel had observed about D. H. Lawrence's wife that "Frieda had a German mind, indelicate and robust, not like the Latin mind that he himself so admired," intimating that the Latin sensibility resided, instead, in her.[2] Lawrence and Mabel, therefore, were the proper soul-mates. She knew it to be true because she and Lawrence were the same kind of people, in tune with the instinctive South rather than the rule-obsessed North.

But to start at the beginning: Mabel was nothing if not voluminous and melodramatic. She had none of the ladylike self-effacement of Constance Fenimore Woolson, nor the patrician aloofness of Marguerite Caetani. The woman was, in our terms, a spiller. Her life story is told in volumes of striking exhibitionism and vivid detail organized around the theme of her search for her true identity and the place in the world where she could realize her transcendent being; everything that happened along the way was simply her preparation to lead the white world to recognize and adapt the spiritual gifts of the American Indian way of life. Mabel's symbolic self, she felt, embodied no less than the decline, fall, and potential rebirth of Western Civilization. Mabel was also nothing if not grandiose.

The only child of a wealthy Buffalo family, Mabel Ganson was born in 1879 and, according to *Background*, the first volume of her *Intimate Memories*, grew up in an unloving and repressed household. She wrote in her original foreword, "Here I begin, as they say, to give myself away. But this is what anyone must do who writes a true history of himself—and I feel a gladness rising in me at the thought of it." The claim is grandiloquent; the telling is often partial or selectively slanted in her favor, especially when she's discussing ex-husbands or lovers. Her upbringing on Delaware Avenue in Buffalo's "gilded quarter" left her lonely and frightened, a neglected child in a household so alienating and peculiar that her father lowered to half-mast the flag which always flew in front of their residence when her mother, a cold and contemptuous woman according to Mabel, returned from trips to New York.

Mabel's claim that she was forever damaged by the materialism of the society into which she was born was firmly grounded. And yet she lived and thrived on that materialism, dependent her whole life on an annual allowance of some $14,000, handsome in those days, and usually doubled by additional hand-outs from her mother. When presented with a doctor's bill for $10,000, unaware that it was for Mabel's psychoanalysis, the mother commented, "So much!—well, I can't see that you've lost any weight."³ Mabel's never-ending flow of money permitted her to do what she wanted.

And what Mabel wanted was to wield power over people. She exerted her fascination over Karl Evans simply because his engagement to someone else made him irresistible to her. They had a hasty secret marriage that her shocked family rectified two months later with a full-blown society marriage. Then came the birth of Mabel's only child, about whom she had rhapsodized in the abstract during pregnancy only to lose interest once he was born.

But then she paid little attention to anything that was not herself and her emotions. When President McKinley was assassinated attending the Pan-American Exposition in Buffalo in 1901, the whole city reeled; only Mabel seems not to have noticed. As she was to claim years later when she objected to her lover John Reed always perusing the morning papers in front of her, "I have never read the news in all my life except when it was about myself or some friend or enemy of mine."⁴ The year after the McKinley assassination, Mabel's young husband was accidentally shot and killed on a hunting trip and she was a widow at twenty-three with a small child.

She was not inconsolable. Omitted in her memoirs, but revealed by biographers, was the affair begun early in her marriage with Dr. John Parmenter, who attended Mabel in her pregnancy and may have fathered the baby he delivered, who was also named John. Willful and reckless Mabel had been in love and that, to her mind, was reason enough for the affair. Buffalo society and Mrs. Parmenter thought otherwise; divorce would have ruined the doctor. Mabel's mother packed Mabel off with her little son and two nurses, one for each of them, and sent them to Europe, ostensibly for Mabel to recover from a nervous breakdown brought on by widowhood.

On board ship in July 1904, Mabel met a young architect from Boston, Edwin Dodge, who had studied at the École des Beaux-Arts and was also on his way to Paris. By chance, they were staying at the same hotel; he pressed his suit, she rather calculatingly accepted—he was, after all, very good with young John; she needed a protector and remarriage was a way to build a new life. She did not love him, but they shared an interest in structure and design and he won her with the promise of their working together to make something new and beautiful that would use his architectural skills and her decorating talent: a Renaissance villa. As she very openly says in her memoirs, "Houses have always been my antidote for love!"

She and Dodge were married in October 1904, but depression overcame her as they wintered on the Riviera. In early 1905, her spirits revived when they carried out the plan they had formed: to go to Florence and recreate the Renaissance. Mabel taught her young son to quote Hannibal's charge to his troops, "Beyond the Alps lies Italy!" while pointing dramatically in the proper direction. For Mabel, Italy represented the Life she longed for, with the Alps just the newest barrier, after those of Buffalo, to realizing that life.

The basis for Mabel's skills in attracting people, and her celebrity status, was laid in the Italian phase of her long, dramatic life. Italy represented for her the possibility of transformation: there she could make herself over into the woman she felt herself to be, the new Twentieth-Century woman; or, better, a Universal Woman as reflected in these lines from a poem of hers published in 1914:

> I am the mirror wherein man sees man,
> Whenever he looks deep into my eyes
> And looks for me alone, he there descries
> the human plan.[5]

When, in the fall of 1905, Mabel Dodge flung open her hotel window in Florence and inhaled the night air's centuries-old aroma, she found a challenge: "Its unfamiliarity made a kind of arrogant anger rise in my heart, and I found myself saying to the indifferent old city, lying there . . . 'I will make you mine.'" In her early fascination with Florence, fully recounted in *European Experiences*, volume two of her *Intimate Memoirs*, she felt the essence of place first. Exploring the hilly roadways above Florence, winding past walled villas, she echoed Henry James who had thirty years earlier strolled the same route: "In the uninvaded privacy of those silent walls, behind the trees, if one could by some miracle penetrate those mysterious enclosures, surely one would come face to face with some exquisite and intense life such as one had never known."

Edwin and Mabel Dodge set out to find a south-facing villa for, contrary to the Tuscan custom of facing homes north and east in order to insure coolness for the summer, she wanted a place full of sun. Additionally, she wanted space and plenty of land to reign over. Leaving Florence by Porta Romana and heading southward on the Viale della Poggia Imperiale, the Dodges came to the locale called Arcetri on the western fringe of hills where Galileo had spent his last years in home exile. His place, known as "The Jewel," was within sight of the Dodge's Villa Curonia which was said to have been the country house of a physician to the Medici. Reaching their villa on a steep road with sharp turns was a challenge for their turn-of-the-century Renault. Looking down toward Florence, as Mabel described the scene, they could see the church of San Miniato in the foreground and beyond that the round dome of the Duomo with Giotto's tower outlined against it; Florence itself "lay far below in a huddle of pale opal colors" backed by that "tumbled heap of solid shapes," the Appenine Mountains.

By agreement, Edwin purchased the Villa and Mabel's share of expenses went for renovation and furnishings—a total of some forty to fifty thousand dollars, an enormous sum in those days, contributed by her mother. Mabel played her part to the hilt, searching out antiquities, lovely fabrics, and all kinds of special effects—what she called "the million billion organized glints and sparkles." Outside, white peacocks ornamented the lawn and the characteristic terracotta planters of Tuscany held oleanders and jasmine on terraces. It was understood that they would live there forever.

Villa Curonia, so-named by previous Russian owners for Kurland in their homeland, became a showplace on which Mabel expended her decorating energies creating inside and outdoor settings for receiving guests. She robed herself in gowns of old damask or velvet that hung, Renaissance-style, in heavy folds from the shoulders with great full sleeves slashed open from shoulder to wrist and bound with bands of old gold braid, and wound around her head scarves of silk, turban fashion, innovating a fashion that, she said, was then taken up by the Russian Ballet. Thus costumed, Mabel was painted and photographed by the several artists she summoned.

To enhance the villa's pedigree, the Dodges claimed that some of the facade could be attributed to Raphael, and Brunelleschi was said to have designed the cortile that Edwin successfully excavated from its encrustation of ugly brick and plaster. He also added a loggia and the ninety-foot great room where, Mabel reported, Bernard Berenson stood on the steps leading into it and exclaimed, "Ah! No one can build rooms like this any more." Muriel Draper, however, described it as a less than perfectly proportioned room approached by an inadequate flight of stairs and whose walls were covered in "rich man's red brocade."[6] In that *gran salone* Mabel had gathered old paintings, tapestries, statuettes, gilded boxes, china dogs, Venetian glass candelabra, figurines, and bric-a-brac on a number of Renaissance refectory tables. The villa, a friend noted, was the perfect reflection of her personality.

Edwin had redesigned the main entrance to lead into a court-yard hung with long Sienese banners. Mabel, arriving by car, would rush to the entrance to get there ahead of the servants for she loved to push open the huge heavy doors with her own weight before they could be opened for her. She felt grand as she made her entrance, "trailing long silks and chiffon veils."

She loved the long house running east and west the width of two large rooms, and situated on a height from which silvery olive groves sloped down and roses climbed the outside walls, one of which was a twenty-foot stone embankment that supported the grand terrace. The Italianate garden was bordered by flame-like cypresses and filled with gardenias, daphne hedge, and statuary. For Mabel it was perfect.

But another, more acrid appraisal, recorded by Logan Pearsall Smith, was given by Janet Ross, an eccentric Englishwoman who had lived in Florence so long that the Dodges seemed mere parvenus to her. Mrs. Ross was the author of two very well regarded volumes, *Florentine Palaces* covering city residences and *Florentine Villas* the surrounding area, the latter book dedicated to her kinswoman The Countess of Crawford, owner of Villa Palmieri. Mrs. Ross's books, based on the exemplary eighteenth-century work of Giuseppe Zocchi, provide background, stories, and engravings for the most important villas and palaces together with maps which locate them within the city or in close proximity. Villa Curonia is not among the prominent villas mentioned, although the road to reach it passes by two that are: Villa Poggio Imperiale and Villa Capponi. After a visit to the Dodges at Villa Curonia, Mrs. Ross, in high dudgeon, pronounced it "absolutely hopeless and uninhabitable . . . all their improvements terrible and they themselves the commonest people she had ever known."[7] Adds Logan Pearsall Smith, "As we drove away she almost popped out of the carriage in her anxiety to point out walls that were sure to fall down and she counted at least sixty trees that were certain to die. If any of them survive the effect of her evil eye it will be a wonder."

Villa Curonia had not the severe lines of the traditional Tuscan villas and Edwin Dodge made not wholly congruent additions to the old edifice. Still, it was sufficiently grand and the Dodges survived the snubs of the aristocratic Florentine families and the established Anglo-American gentry by importing their own company. At times, Mabel was like either the most foolish or the brashest of some of Henry James's fictional American characters abroad: foolish because, on her first arrival in Florence she let herself be talked into renting a provisional residence at a considerable price with the proviso that the owners could stay on in their own quarters; brash, at the Actons' villa, when she assumed she could buy any of their furnishings she desired. Another time Mabel turned up, uninvited, at Contessa Serristori's ball when she decided that if a guest of hers was invited, then she was, too.

Mabel was described by her portraitist, Jacques-Émile Blanche, as the domineering, strong-willed, clever American woman who with New World money tries to acquire the Old.[8] Mabel, in her memoirs, had a different twist: her need for love unsatisfied, she began to buy things, create interiors, ambiance: "I had turned to beauty . . . for my sustenance, and my thoughts were of a life made up of beautiful things, of art, of color, of noble forms." She also began to collect the locals; one was sculptor Pen Browning, son of Robert and Elizabeth Barrett Browning, and another was Bindo Peruzzi di Medici, the last of the Medici family and a grandson of an earlier American expatriate in Italy, William Wetmore Story.

Mabel's writing is at its best when descriptive of Florence and its environs, detailing the people she so keenly observed. She is gifted at word portraits, warts and all, and at recreating conversations. When she does err it is usually due to her impatience at verifying facts. Despite her years in Italy, Mabel's rendering of

Italian is idiosyncratic, as in *fourbo* or *avocate* or *babo* or the Frenchified *désinvoltura*. She mentions "shading cypress trees" even though a compact, spear-like cypress does anything but give shade.

She felt she had at last found a society that could accommodate her spirit . . . she dreamed of the beautiful people who had inhabited the Renaissance villas, and she approached the Renaissance from a purely aesthetic perspective. It was a total involvement with antique objects of which she wrote: "There is so much thought and feeling given to them. To their discovery, their attainment, their disposition, in one's house. It's almost like a love affair."

Anglo-American society in Florence was at its peak when the Dodges resided at Villa Curonia. Bernard Berenson was at I Tatti; Lord Acton's son Arthur, at Villa La Pietra, was a distinguished antiquarian known as the rags-and-bone man; Leo Stein walked over from his place in Settignano to get the view from Mabel's terrace; everyone came calling, everyone knew each other; everyone was moneyed and precious and interesting. Life consisted of visits, or motoring around to make rare finds in some out-of-the-way spot before someone else did; or travels, including occasional trips home to the United States so that one could return to Italy relieved not to have to live in that unrefined land where the money came from. In Italy the food was good, climate fine, one's allowance always arrived and it went a long way in the Tuscan hills where help cost practically nothing and was always so cheerful.

Pledged to boring fidelity with Edwin, Mabel engaged in teasing flirtations as an exercise of her power over others, for power, she declared, was her most profound enjoyment. She was not past making overtures to her chauffeur or her son's tutor and relished being serenaded by a young Franciscan friar from the monastery nearby. Edwin, either dull or exceedingly indifferent, "seemed to ignore the principal motives of what, to me, engineered the existences of us all," i.e., exercising her magnetism to "draw men here and there like flies to honey." She gloried in herself as a predatory woman whose success lay in her instinctive knowledge of other people's weak spots. Comparing herself to the hapless Edwin, her vanity was forthright: "I so deep, so fatal, and so glamorous—and he so ordinary and matter of fact."

During those Florentine years Mabel's Renaissance persona was captured in several portraits. Jacques-Émile Blanche, summoned from Paris to paint her, found a difficult subject—an enigma in search of enigmas. He saw an impassive countenance hiding her thoughts: "No smile flitted across her lips; she had the slow movements of a fleshy odalisque, worn out by the heavy perfumes of the harem." She posed for him as a regal presence seated in a throne-like chair and garbed in Renaissance robes and turban, her small son kneeling at her feet and gazing up at her.

Jo Davidson, a renowned sculptor of the era who had done portrait busts of all the world's eminent, was also invited to Villa Curonia. In his memoir, *Between Sittings*, he mentions her enigmatic smile that made him wonder, "What is she plotting now?"[9] To some she was a mute Buddha figure who sat remotely silent in shimmering satin, absorbing the ideas and opinions bandied about by others. When compared to his vivid representations of other personalities, Davidson's bust of Mabel is uncommonly bland. Full-faced with bangs and large knobs of hair over her ears, Mabel had composed her features in an inscrutable gaze, a not-quite smile on her lips.

Artist Blanche, however, had a chance glimpse of an unaware Mabel that told him that the woman who posed in the rich velvet robes was a cover-up for another self. Unobserved, he had seen Mabel coming from a farmplace dressed in a plain cotton skirt, holding a blue parasol and a basket of eggs in her other hand. That simpler, countrified persona was also Mabel.

But mostly she reveled in her showy accomplishment. "Making a Home," a chapter in *European Experiences*, details, room by room, every furnishing and object placed in them. She had wanted space and grandeur but her residence must also "have the poetic and tender charms of unexpected corners and adaptations to small, shy moods, twilight moods." It would allow one to be both majestic and careless, spontaneous and picturesque; always framed and supported by a beautiful authenticity of background.

If a certain ambiguity exists in "small, shy moods" cheek by jowl with exhibitionism, Mabel's motto took care of that: emblazoned on thick, white writing paper her violet monogram was positioned inside a silver circle around which Walt Whitman's words pursued each other: "Do I contradict myself? Very well, then, I contradict myself." But only she was allowed to contradict—later on she would accuse D. H. Lawrence of being a deplorable fellow because she thought him a veritable mass of contradictions.[10]

As a newcomer to Florence, Mabel was taken in hand by an aging Lady Paget, then at Villa Bellosguardo, who, says Mabel discerningly, was kind but always retained in her manner an awareness of Mabel's "American outlandishness." Lady Paget instructed the Dodges, once Villa Curonia was renovated, to invite *tout* Florence—they would come. The Dodges held a 5–7 P.M. At Home. Mabel described the setting: "almost Renaissance, the wide doors open, the dining room table laden with fruit and flowers and luxurious things to eat—a Medicean feast; and the guests strolling in a poetic twilight against the garlanded background of a spacious fete; music and soft light and roses in the midst of the damask and velvet hangings. Tintorretish." As dusk fell, a soloist burst into "Oh, Evening Star" from Tannhäuser.

Villa Curonia gave Mabel the art of hostessing. She also absorbed an Italian tolerance for non-conformity and irregular relationships. Yet despite her bounty and elaborate settings, Mabel's entourage was considered a step lower than "the best" society.

Mary Berenson, in her personal copy of Mabel's *European Experiences*, made the notation: "Mabel Dodge made friends with all the people in Florence whom we consider particularly undesirable."[11] Arthur Acton's son Harold, using Shelley's phrase, recalled Villa Curonia as "a paradise of exiles" and "a sunny place for shady people." He also found some of her memoirs of special "period" interest, for exposing the behavior of Anglo-American dilettanti in the carefree time before World War I.

It was a perfumed existence, the sweet scents of jasmine and gardenia always in the air, a life of exquisite effects. Mabel paid attention to detail: she had old bricks smashed into gravel so that the resulting orange-pink path richly contrasted with the solid dark-green of the bordering boxwood. From the pathway one entered a hall to the pleasant awareness of the outdoor colors repeated in the orangey-pink velvet Spanish altar cloth spread over a Bolognese credenza that reposed on dark green carpeting.

When perfection had been reached at Villa Curonia, Mabel and her friend Muriel Draper tried to buy an old feudal estate that had been expanded over the centuries in every architectural style from thirteenth to late eighteenth century. Some twenty kilometers from Florence, just beyond the village of Montagnana, loomed the enormous Castello di Montegufoni, a kind of Tibetan lamasery set on a hill. It was a huge, stark pile; seven original buildings had all been fused into one great complex containing over a hundred rooms and encircling five separate courtyards. Large enough to house about three hundred men, women, and children, it had become a virtual village occupied by peasant-squatters after the owners had given up living there.

The castle, when Mabel and Muriel saw it, had its own post office, a chapel, some shops in the arcades which closed an open side of one courtyard, a *limonaia* housing over two hundred lemon trees, a central bell-tower replicating the one at Florence's Palazzo Vecchio, secret passages, and possibly a prison in its subterranean depths. The squatters were about to be turned out; the place was to be sold. The two American women started figuring whether they could extract enough from their respective incomes for the purchase and the extensive restoration that would be called for. Despite the cattle in the great hall and goats in the *salone*, "We wanted it, we wanted it terribly," Muriel wrote in her memoir, *Music at Midnight*. "My computations took a very short while; Mabel's much longer, but even she decided in the end that it was beyond our reach." The Tuscan Castello di Montegufoni was bought, instead, by Sir George Sitwell, father of the noted English family of writers and eccentrics.

The most significant of Mabel's visitors at Villa Curonia, for the influence it would have on her life, was Gertrude Stein. A mutual friend had first taken Mabel to one of Leo and Gertrude Stein's evenings at 27 Rue de Fleurus in Paris. As recounted by Alice B. Toklas, "Everybody brought somebody . . . to the house Saturday evening. One evening a number of people came in . . . and among them was Mabel Dodge. . . . She was a stoutish woman with a very sturdy fringe of heavy hair over her forehead, heavy long lashes and very pretty eyes and a very old fashioned coquetry. She had a lovely voice. . . . She asked us to come to Florence to stay with her."[12]

Always ready for new experiences, Mabel had been excited by her exposure in Paris to the new thinking in art and literature. She did not invite Gertrude and Alice idly; she bombarded the two with letters and telegrams until they finally arrived at Villa Curonia in July 1911. Mabel's keen eye and descriptive talent was trained on her guests: "Gertrude Stein was prodigious. Pounds and pounds and pounds piled up on her skeleton—not the billowing kind, but massive, heavy fat. She wore some covering of corduroy or velvet and her crinkly hair was brushed back and twisted up high behind her jolly, intelligent face. She intellectualized her fat, and her body seemed to be the large machine that her large nature required to carry it. Gertrude was hearty. She used to roar with laughter, out loud. She had a laugh like a beefsteak. . . . Yet with all this she was not at all repulsive. On the contrary, she was positively, richly attractive in her grand ampleur."

And here is Mabel on Alice Toklas: "She was slight and dark, with beautiful gray eyes hung with black lashes—and she had a drooping, Jewish nose, and her eyelids drooped, and the corners of her mouth and the lobes of her ears drooped under the black, folded Hebraic hair, weighted down, as they were with long, heavy Oriental earrings. . . . She looked like Leah, out of the Old Testament, in her half-Oriental get-up—her black hair—her barbaric chains and jewels—and her melancholy nose. Artistic."

Mabel, as described in turn by Alice, "reigned in white, usually in a long silk dress and a white turban. Her room was white— whitewashed walls, white curtains—but the room she gave to Gertrude was hung with gold and crimson silk. . . . Besides her numerous guests, her husband Edwin, and her young son, she had a dog, Climax, and a monkey, Emma Bovary."[13] Alice was there when Mabel cooed to her young son as he stood on the edge of a balustrade threatening to fly off, "Fly my dear, fly if you want to." Edwin Dodge, Alice noted, merely said, "There is nothing like a Spartan mother."

One evening Alice made conversation with dinner guest André Gide until Mabel made a late appearance. After dinner, stretched out on one of the long sofas as was her habit, Mabel conversed in a low voice exclusively to Gide who sat opposite, leaning over her. Another guest, finding Mabel's action inhospitable and highly ridiculous, danced about the sofa with an imaginary partner. But, noted Alice, this did not disturb Mabel who always did as she pleased.[14]

Mabel disliked Alice making herself indispensable to Gertrude and usurping Leo Stein's position with his sister. The initial visit was long enough to establish ill-feeling between Mabel and Alice, but not long enough for a clash. That came when Gertrude and Alice stopped again at Villa Curonia after a trip to Spain.

Gertrude was put in Edwin's room, for he was away on a business trip to New York. After everyone was asleep she would sit at Edwin's table in the room next to Mabel's and write. It was at this time that she composed *Portrait of Mabel Dodge at Villa Curonia*, alternately titled "Mabel little Mabel with her face against the pane . . ." It began with its most quoted and intelligible line: "The days are wonderful and the nights are wonderful and the life is pleasant." Gertrude wrote automatically, letting thoughts ooze up from deep inside her and scrawling lines onto paper which she tossed to the floor. In the morning Alice would collect the pages in no particular order and type them, as delighted as Gertrude at what the unconscious had transmitted.

Mabel was at the time pursuing an ardent interest in her son's twenty-two year old tutor who she said was in love with her just as a matter of course. One night, as Gertrude worked, the young man crept down the corridor to Mabel's room. There they clung together on her bed in the moonlight, chastely locked in each other's arms, according to Mabel, "while Gertrude wrote on the other side of the wall, sitting in candle-light like a great Sibyl dim against the red and gold damask that hung loosely on the walls." Perhaps that was the night that Gertrude penned the lines: "There has not been that kind abandonment. Nobody is alone." As she lay clutching the tutor, Mabel wondered if Gertrude could hear their heavy breathing through the walls. In fact, Gertrude begins three consecutive lines with the words, "So much breathing. . . ." Perhaps because nothing more came of the young tutor's visit the sketch ends, "There is not all of any visit."

Mabel was thrilled with the cryptic *Portrait* from the great Stein. Intent, perhaps, on minimizing allusions that were all too recognizable, she interpreted the symbolism as so obscure that only by feeling it could anyone get the key to what Gertrude was saying.

Gertrude's earlier portraits (of Picasso and Matisse, for instance) were quite accessible, but as Jo Davidson said of Mabel's portrait, "if it were not described as a portrait on the cover, who would suspect what it was all about."[15] Leo Stein raged against the work. Bernard Berenson had always thought Gertrude Stein's writing "meaningless Incantations"; nevertheless, Mabel risked sending him a copy of the work. The important thing for Mabel was her name in the title of a work by Gertrude Stein.

Portrait of Mabel was the ultimate thank-you note from a guest, and Alice Toklas recorded how it came to be printed. Houseguest Constance Fletcher, who resided in Venice (and years before had relayed the news of Constance Woolson's suicide there to Henry James), told Mabel, "We must have this printed at once, I will do the correction of proof, it will not take any time to have it printed."[16] Mabel then proposed to bind the little booklets in modern prints from old Florentine woodcuts. It was Mabel's initial error in referring to the characteristic decorative paper known as *carta fiorentina* (produced by the renowned old firm of Giannini that still operates in Florence opposite the Pitti Palace), as "wall paper," an error that has been repeated ever since to describe how Gertrude Stein's work was bound.

It was during the second Stein visit that Mabel flaunted her flirtatiousness when she sensed that Gertrude was attracted to her. The formidable Stein threw Mabel a look across the lunch table one day so electrifying that Alice left the room in tears. It was Alice's jealousy that, *poco-poco* as Mabel put it, severed the friendship between Mabel and Gertrude.

Critic and author Carl Van Vechten had also been Mabel's guest at Villa Curonia, thus it duly appeared as Villa Allegra in his novel, *Peter Whiffle*, with Mabel Dodge cast as "Edith Dale," "a new kind of woman, or else the oldest kind." Van Vechten casts himself as the narrator. Concerning the villa he explains that "Edith" had occupied herself in transforming it into a perfect environment for the amusing people with whom she surrounded herself. . . . Then, with her superlatively excellent taste she rushed about Italy in her motor, ravishing . . . divers bibelots until the villa became a perfect expression of her mood. When every possible accent had been added, she entertained in the evening. Eleanora Duse, a mournful figure in black velvet, stood on the loggia and gazed out over the hills towards Certosa; Gordon Craig postured in the salone; and Gertrude Stein commemorated the occasion in a pamphlet, printed and bound in a Florentine floral wall-paper, which today fetches a good sum in old bookshops, when it can be found at all. To those present at this festa, it seemed, doubtless, like the inauguration of the reign of another Lorenzo the Magnificent.

"Edith Dale," as was her custom, left her guests a good deal to themselves during the day when she breakfasted alone on her balcony, read for an hour or two, then sometimes disappeared, even for several days, on visits. "We usually met her at dinner when she came out to the garden-table, floating in white crepe de chine, with a turban of turquoise blue or some vivid brilliant green."

But the ultimate parody of Mabel at Villa Curonia came from Cornelia Otis Skinner, a humorist of past years, in her "Brief Digest of the Intimate Memoirs of Mabel Fudge Hulan":

That summer I moved to Florence. Everyone of importance followed me there. They all lived in the villa. Some had to sleep on the stairs or in *cinquecento* chests. . . . The place was vibrant with the iridescent quality of my aura. In some curious way I became the reincarnation of Lucrezia Borgia . . . so much so that when I spoke to Berenson about it he lost his appetite. I was majestic and picturesque . . . glamorous in asphodels and conch shells and an exquisite Etruscan toga my spaniel had dug up near the Farnese cesspool.

I would wander about the *boiseries* of my *pied-à-terre, ad libidum*, suffering from a combination of *Weltschmerz* and *dolce far niente*. D'Annunzio drove up in a Bugatti *couleur de rose*. He had mistaken my driveway for the one next door. He said, "Please forgive me, Madam." [Actually his words were "*Scusi, signora*."] His lips were rich and red . . . as if he'd been eating pomegranates . . . or raspberry gelati. The wind howled sexually.

Gertrude Stein and Alice Toklas spent the summer with me. Also a little man from Mallorca whose name I have forgotten. He collected cactuses. My husband was along too. I have also forgotten his name. I did not love him. I never love my husbands . . . that is why I never remember their names. X was there . . . caught in the golden net of his love for me . . . his response to my magnetic intellect. I played with him as a cat with catnip. His wife resented me. She came from Maine and was incapable of the finer emotions.[17]

Such were the evenings at the Villa where Mabel the Magnificent reigned. The food and wine superb, the surroundings incomparable with the faint perfume of the lemon trees and gardenias wafted in through full-length open windows, the after-dinner coffee served on a terrace overlooking the valley of the Arno and the surrounding hills.

Before Betty Boop, Mabel Dodge was the "It" girl: her expressed creed at that time was "Let IT happen . . . let IT decide. . . . Have faith in life and do not hamper IT or try to shape IT."[18] This reliance on intuition, passivity, and hunches was, of course, completely contrary to Mabel's lifelong need to control people and events. She may have said, let things happen, but what she did was manipulate, shaping things her way.

The day came when Mabel had "done" Ponte Vecchio, done Florence, done Italy. The day came when even her Florentine collection of people and friends became like the collection of paintings at Ponte Vecchio: "I have seen them . . . they began to bore me." Once the villa was furnished and decorated and she had provided the perfect backdrop, what was she to do with herself? What it had taken the Florentines a century to accomplish for the glorious period known as the *cinquecento*, Mabel did in the biblical seven fat years of her own personal renaissance. And then she moved on.

Mabel's return to the states in the fall of 1912, ostensibly for her son's schooling but actually to get rid of Edwin, signaled her sea-change from lady of the villa to avant-garde arts patron and social activist. In New York, she leased an upper floor in the substantial corner residence at 23 Fifth Avenue of General Sickles, a Civil War veteran. A break-through to a contiguous Ninth Street apartment gave her additional quarters for servants and guests. She decorated the large main rooms in dazzling all-white, having her caretaker at Villa Curonia send her the polar bear rug from the *gran salone*. She set about meeting people, retained Domenico, her indispensable servant from Florence, but dispensed with husband Edwin on the welcome recommendation of her analyst. Edwin obligingly departed and Mabel began a career as hostess and lover to some of the personalities whom she entertained in what was to become America's most celebrated salon.

In February 1913, Mabel was approached to be a contributor to the famous Modern Art Show at the Sixty-ninth Street Regiment Armory. She, in turn, made that show her personal launching pad by connecting the cubist art being displayed for the first time in America with the writing of Gertrude Stein. Mabel had promised to publicize Gertrude in America by taking bound copies of *Portrait of Mabel Dodge at the Villa Curonia* with her to New York. When coupled with the name of Gertrude Stein, Mabel's name spread. Then Mabel's piece, "Speculations, or Post-Impressions in Prose," appeared in *Arts and Decoration* magazine in March 1913, prefaced by the editorial note: "This article is about the only woman in the world who has put the spirit of post-impressionism into prose, and written by the only woman in America who fully understands it."

That piece, Mabel claimed, was the first thing ever published in America about Gertrude Stein's writing. It was certainly the most publicized and Mabel was astute enough to accompany her article with Stein's *Portrait of Mabel Dodge* so that her name became as prominent as Gertrude's. As she discovered in those heady New York days, "if Gertrude Stein was born at the Armory show, so was 'Mabel Dodge.'"

The publicity in America was gratifying to Gertrude Stein until she began to begrudge Mabel's ride to fame on her coattails. It caused the rift between them which Leo Stein explained to Mabel: his sister's reaction was that there was some doubt as to which was the more important, the bear or the one leading the bear. Though Gertrude Stein cooled toward Mabel, she continued to be interested in gossip about her. She asked Carl Van Vechten for news of Mabel's becoming an Indian. In a 1924 prose piece, Stein, referring to her relationship with Mabel, called it "a history of having a great many times not continued to be friends."

They were never to meet again. Decades later, when Mabel was living a year in California and Gertrude Stein was visiting the site of her childhood home in Oakland (where she made the trenchant remark, "there is no there there"), Mabel tried to call her old friend, but Alice said she could not be disturbed. "It was evident," wrote Mabel in her memoirs, "that Alice's painful memory of her humiliation at the Villa Curonia, years before, when Gertrude had cast such a meaningful glance across the luncheon table . . . had remained with her."

Without the intellectual mastery and commitment to social causes of a Margaret Fuller, nor the creative imagination of an Edith Wharton reflecting her times in writing, Mabel used her acquaintance with notable people in every field to create her own fame. At 23 Fifth Avenue, she surrounded herself with creative, interesting personalities and became a salon hostess who offered stimulating company along with lavish buffet suppers at her Wednesday evenings. The salon had been the idea of Lincoln Steffens, the popular muckracker-journalist. "Have Evenings!" he instructed her. And so she did. "I wanted to know everybody," she wrote in *Movers and Shakers*, the third volume of her *Intimate Memoirs*, "in particular . . . the Heads of Things. Heads of Movements. Heads of Newspapers. Head of all kinds of groups of people. I became a species of Head Hunter."

Mabel's salon attracted an eclectic mix of social reformers, socialites, anarchists, publishers and editors, and Greenwich Village writers and artists of the pre–World War I era. Chroniclers of the period provide lists of impressive names—everybody who was anybody was there. The evenings became so popular that they were organized by theme: Margaret Sanger spoke on her Birth Control Movement as well as on Sexual Freedom, or Free Love as it was called then; John Reed and Walter Lippmann were featured on Socialism night; Big Bill Haywood, whose presence in Mabel's salon was a real coup for her, was the star attraction of Trade Union night; Gordon Craig, father of Isadora Duncan's children, conducted a drama evening; Poetry night was led by Edgar Lee Masters who had just published *Spoon River Anthology*, but the occasion was something of a bust since Amy Lowell walked out and Edwin Arlington Robinson sat mute, refusing to participate.

Margaret Sanger left a telling description of her hostess: "brown bangs, outlining a white face, simply gowned in velvet, beautifully arched foot, beating the air."[19] For two hours Sanger watched that "silken ankle in its violent agitation," finding it expressive of a rudderless dilettantism. Mabel, for her part, was an immediate enthusiast to Sanger's doctrine of pleasures of the flesh as a means to growth of the soul.

When New York newspapers withheld coverage of the Paterson silk workers strike, Mabel made a remarkable suggestion to Union boss Bill Haywood: "Why don't you bring the strike to New York and show it to the workers?" Inspired, she explained, by the idea of her never realized plan with Gordon Craig to put on a cinquecento pageant in Florence, she went on to suggest the hiring of Madison Square Garden to reenact the strike's closed mills, the police turned into gunmen, the murder of a striker, the funeral with the mill hands following the coffin and women dropping red geraniums cut from their window pots onto it. Not only was Bill Haywood enthused, but a young man at the meeting sprang up and cried, "I'll do it!" and proposed to Mabel that they work together. Thus did John Reed come into her life. Mabel began her very public affair with Reed as well as her all too transitory interest in social issues.

Reed, a brilliant young journalist a decade younger than Mabel, was invited to accompany her to Italy to stay at Villa Curonia immediately after the strike reenactment. He said he drew inspiration from her; she realized in him a passion that had been missing from marriage. But Reed always had other things on his mind besides Mabel. Already in Venice she was annoyed by a lover who went around exclaiming, "The things men have done!" His admiration for the city seemed to detract from her. There was one last summer at Villa Curonia before World War I broke out.

Van Vechten, in his recollection "July–August 1914," describes being at Villa Curonia when the war started and everyone (except Mabel, who was expecting the arrival of John Reed) was anxious to leave Europe on the first ship back to the states. At first that summer, Mabel had seemed ready to give up New York and go back to living at Villa Curonia where she had returned each summer since leaving Italy. But with the war she realized she couldn't keep people coming to her and she gave up the place altogether.

Van Vechten describes Mabel's mood as that of Madame Ranevsky in "The Cherry Orchard": facing the sad inevitability of losing her beloved home. She had very practically made arrangements for the rental of Villa Curonia to an American woman who would be arriving in October with six girl students. Of course, they never did arrive: the war did. Mabel, still dressed in white, on leaving Villa Curonia forever, told Van Vechten, "I've made a perfect place of this and now I'm ready for whatever will come after the war. I am through with all property, as every one else will have to be." Perhaps she thought so. While living a regal life at Villa Curonia, she had written to H. G. Wells that she was sympathetic to socialism and wanted a school extolling that ideal for her son—did Wells have any suggestions? Wells may have been abashed, but Mabel never was.

Mabel followed Reed to Paris where he was covering the war for his paper. She herself wrote "The Secrets of War" for *The Masses*. But "work" had never appealed to her and she lacked the discipline for a journalistic career. As Reed's ardor waned, so, too, did her interest in the political activism she had supported in her salon. Her enthusiasms often peaked and then, as she put it, "I just switched on one viewpoint and switched off another."

Her attention then turned to Nature and Beauty, both embodied in Isadora Duncan's expressive new form of naturalness in dance. Mabel had long admired Isadora Duncan and had known her and Gordon Craig in Florence. After seeing Isadora dance in New York and finding her "the most truly living being I had ever seen," Mabel was easily persuaded to buy a studio building and house in the countryside outside New York for Isadora's sister Elizabeth to found a school where young children could be trained in the new dance forms. Writing of her switch from social causes to Aesthetics, Mabel quite glibly commented on how she had gone from siding with the Paterson silk-mill workers to working with the very management they had struck against because the mill owners were disposed to contribute to her Duncan School of Dance in Croton-on-Hudson, New York.

It was in Croton, a river town some thirty miles north of New York, that I first heard of Mabel Dodge. Arriving from Europe with my Italian husband, correspondent for an Italian paper, we settled in Croton to be near but not in the city. A new friend, the artist and writer George Biddle who lived on Mt. Airy Road, had stories and lively history about former residents. Gloria Swanson once owned the Longue Vue estate off Mt. Airy; atop a hill was the large brown residence that had been the Duncan dance school; just across the road was Sharkey Cottage, the old four-room house with a tiny attic and a guest shack that Mabel Dodge had leased in 1915. A few years after Mabel, the cottage became famous as the place where John Reed settled in with his bride, Louise Bryant, and wrote his famous *Ten Days that Shook the World* on the Communist revolution in Russia. Reed died in Russia at age thirty-three, a Hero of the Revolution, and was interred in the Kremlin wall. In 1969, the fiftieth anniversary of Reed's death, the then owners of the cottage were surprised by a party of some forty people, delegates to the United Nations, who assembled in front of the house on Mt. Airy Road (derogatively called "Red Hill" by the villagers) to honor their hero.

John Reed's final exit from Mabel's orbit was described by another Croton resident, Max Eastman, publisher of *The Masses*: "I remember his stamping out of her bedroom in the small hours of the night, slamming the door and plunging away in a heavy rainstorm, none of us knew where. I felt that Mabel was on the hunt again, and that I was in a dangerously convenient position. She seemed to be sending out waves of more than the usual potency in my direction. . . . All she ever said was: Max, why don't you arrange your life?"[20]

Max Eastman ran his free-spirited journal of the American left from 1911 to 1917, and had Mabel guest-edit an issue after her notoriety with the Armory Art Show made her a public figure; she also contributed opinion pieces from time to time. Eastman is among the many who, in their reminiscences, mention Mabel; he understood her paradoxical nature which hovered between passiveness and magnetism when he wrote,

> She seems never to have learned the art of social intercourse—a rather dumb and stumpy little girl, you would say, and move on to someone who at least knew how to make conversation. You would move just to escape embarrassment, but before long you would be around there trying to talk to this little girl again. For there is something going on, or going round, in Mabel's head or bosom, something that creates a magnetic field in which people become polarized and pulled in and made to behave very queerly. Their passions become exacerbated; they grow argumentative; they have quarrels, difficulties, entanglements, abrupt and violent detachments. And they like it—they come back for more. Many famous salons have been established by women of wit or beauty; Mabel's was the only one ever established by pure will power.[21]

Max Eastman bought a house just down the road from Sharkey Cottage and the drift of artists, writers, editors, and intellectuals from Greenwich Village to Croton began in earnest. "Suddenly that summer," as our friend, designer Don Wallance, used to say, "they all went up to Croton." Croton became a staging area for many twentieth-century American idealistic, artistic, and social-reform movements, giving the village an unusual density of bright and accomplished men and women quite out of proportion to its size, and making it the Village North.

With Reed gone, Mabel moved on to artist Maurice Sterne, whom she had noticed at a Duncan dance recital in New York when he cast at her what she described as a dark brown look. Maurice Sterne's artist's eye saw her as an exotic fortuneteller, saying that she looked and dressed like one and stirred up an appropriately feverish and expectant atmosphere.

With Maurice she moved to Finney Farm in another part of Croton and installed him in a studio in an outlying house, attempting to change him from painter to sculptor. Finally, she relates, she had to marry him to carry through her plan. It was on a boring August day of 1917 that Mabel decided she and Maurice Sterne should go up to Peekskill and be married. Afterwards she described lying in the hammock on the wide porch of the farmhouse feeling "terribly alone" as she faced Maurice in the big rocking chair opposite her. Next day, the *New Herald* carried the news: Mrs. Mabel Dodge secretly married to Russian artist . . . 'No romance,' says Maurice Sterne, 'we just decided to wed.'"

When my husband and I lived in Croton-on-Hudson, we had friends at Finney Farm. The old farmland had been divided and modern homes occupied sites, including the Breuer-designed home of designer Vera Neumann with its huge Alexander Calder mobile overlooking grand views to the river. All these decades later, and despite new building in the vicinity, the large old white farmhouse with the turquoise-colored shutters and the wraparound porch described by Mabel is still as she knew it. Even today the red outlying buildings below the farmhouse remain, as does the romantic shell of the roofless cement barn where Elizabeth Duncan and her pupils long ago gave dance performances in Grecian garb, and theatre was staged.

The connection with Croton and Maurice Sterne marked a new, but tormented, phase in Mabel's life. Leo Stein, unlike his sister Gertrude, remained Mabel's life-long friend and stayed with Mabel at Finney Farm when he was in the states during World

War I. Much later, recalling that period, he wrote her, "In the first place, way back when I saw you in Provincetown and you were at your first hesitation about Maurice you said you wanted to get settled. You tried it at Finney Farm, and of course it was a failure, partly because of Maurice, partly because as 'Chatelaine of Finney Farm' you had no sufficient outlet."[22]

True, Maurice was a mistake, but he turned out to be a fortunate one. Immediately after their impulsive marriage, Mabel sent him west to paint, refusing to accompany him on what she called his "lonely honeymoon." He wrote her on November 28, 1917, from Santa Fe the prophetic letter that not only called her to the Southwest but gave her a mission. "Dearest Girl, Do you want an object in life? Save the Indians, their art—culture—reveal it to the world!" A month later, Mabel joined Maurice in New Mexico. She stayed the rest of her life, certain that she had at last found the place, after Italy, where she could realize herself.

In December 1917, Mabel joined Maurice in Santa Fe, the city with a Latin name and a Latin look to its plazas, courtyards, graceful arches. Bells pealed, there were smells of cooking over wood fire, vendors with donkeys ambled along the streets and called out their wares; colorfully blanketed Indians and Mexicans stationed themselves in the arcades where they passed the time of day and sold their pottery or weavings. It must have recalled to Mabel scenes of cloaked peasants at market in small Italian towns. What she responded to in the still natural surroundings and in the people connected her to the past experience of the Mediterranean world: there were the markets with the colorful arrays of foods fresh from the fields, the craftspeople with their hand-made wares, the solemn traditional ways of life and the ritual celebrations in a rhythm altogether different from that found in frenetic New York.

Within a week of her arriving in Santa Fe, Mabel and Maurice drove off to Taos. "Here," she declared, "I belong, and here I want to stay." Following her pattern, Mabel separated from Maurice as she became interested in the Pueblo Indian Antonio Lujan (whose name, when she married him, she spelled Luhan in accord with its Spanish pronunciation). To marry him she had to pension off his wife, an Indian woman named Candelaria, just as she did Maurice.

Maurice Sterne's marriage to Mabel and her arrival to join him in New Mexico, followed so soon by her infatuation for Tony Luhan, is characterized in George Biddle's foreword to Sterne's book of recollections, *Shadow and Light*, as "a long ring-fight . . . pure burlesque . . . Italian comic opera." Once Maurice recovered, he started painting successfully again and his career flourished with a one-man show at the Museum of Modern Art in New York and honors from the Uffizi gallery in Florence. His reputation shone brighter than ever. He happily remarried and returned to Italy to paint in Anticoli where his name and fame live on in the street of that Italian hill-town dedicated to his memory.

Mabel had felt a mystic pull to Tony Luhan from the first time she set eyes on him because, she relates in her last volume of memoirs, *Edge of Taos Desert*, his visage had already appeared to her in a vision; he, too, she goes on, had a premonition of a white woman's coming to him who would look like Mabel. One can almost sense her restless mind weaving and fashioning the myth of Tony and Taos into her life, embroidering it in fanciful designs and brilliant colors just as she did the needlework she enjoyed. Since Tony is mostly silent, or barely intelligible, one gets the impression of Mabel creating for him much of his significant cosmic talk; creating, in fact, his character to meet her needs.

As Mabel entered her newest "cosmos," as she called her transitions, she had what she called her conversion to the Indian way of life and tried to change in appearance to appear more Indian. A photo of Mabel in those years shows her wrapped in a blanket, her hair bobbed and straight; another photo is of the strikingly handsome and solemn Tony Luhan with long plaits of hair over his blanket. Mabel looks forthrightly at the camera, a dog at her feet. She seems at peace. To arrive there she had undergone years of other experiences.

During the New York and Croton interludes when Mabel merely leased residences, perhaps she thought she would never again be a property owner. But it was another question when she got to New Mexico. There she bought property galore and regained the enthusiasm for building and decorating that she had in Italy. Despite the great contrast of the American Southwest with the green hills of Tuscany, Taos and the surrounding country does have an uncanny affinity with the south of Italy, the stark and ancient territory that had been the Magna Graecia of the ancient world. Both shared the same sense of ease and harmony so often found in backwater cultures in contrast with the hurried, frenetic, complex culture of the industrialized world. Mabel had, in her words, Italianized herself, and would transplant the vital root of that experience to New Mexico, her ultimate destination. She showed it in her need for harmony with her surroundings, her bond with nature and with the simple broad base of daily life in which every phase is honored as ritual handed down from and connected to eons past. The rural life of Tuscany combined with the artistic achievement of Villa Curonia had been the perfect harmony.

Even the way Mabel relished her food in Italy signified her sense of harmony with her surroundings. Describing motor trips in the Tuscan countryside she wrote, "At lunch I used to eat with great intensity the nutty, coarse bread, rubbing it in salt as one does radishes, and I consumed great dishes of pasta, washing it down with goblets of the good wine, and the food had its own special imaginative quality that it derived, for me, from the simple modes that had produced it: the women, baking, were richly happy, and lively with true life; the men, pressing the grapes, were quickened with the sap. I felt the warm stream, magnetic and alluring, that flowed from the Italian peasants. . . . When I ate, I gathered their life into myself . . . I felt I was one with them. . . . I took the Holy Communion of Italy and Italianized myself."

After Croton-on-Hudson, it was in New Mexico that I refound Mabel. While visiting Santa Fe, Antonio and I planned to drive to the ranch Mabel had given D. H. Lawrence some miles outside Taos. We had heard of it from our artist friend George Biddle who had been there and painted a compelling portrait of Frieda Lawrence that we had seen in his Croton home on Mt. Airy road. We never did reach the Lawrences' Kiowa Ranch, what with tire blow-outs and other mishaps. It was as if Mabel, who all her life believed in her psychic power over others, was still possessive of Lorenzo and forbade our arrival at his shrine. That frustrated visit I described in a piece called "The Spinsters of Taos" where I also related the affinity, for me, of New Mexico to Italy: "It was clear that we were no longer in the standard USA with its iron obtuseness and businesslike bent; it was more like the Mediterranean world where the warm dramatic color of Catholicism is peopled by devils and miracles and is rich with superstitions and lore. What was the sanctuary of Chimayo, where we stopped on the way to Taos, but the Old World with its suffering saints and amiable sorcerers and, marvelous to say, even a pit of miraculous mud in a dirt-floored chapel off the main altar? We could have been in Sicily."

And so, I imagined, it might have seemed to Mabel in her search, like Lawrence's, for a personal South. Lawrence had found that in Italy he could "live in a certain silent contact with the peasants who work the land. . . . It is they, really, who form my *ambiente*, and it is from them that the human flow comes to me." That was precisely Mabel's feeling, half a world away, with the Pueblo Indians of Taos. Their civilization, like that of the Mediterranean world, endured like a barrier against the overwhelming technology of the modern era. It was to such an unbroken, spiritual connection to the land that Mabel sought closeness.

Just as years earlier Mabel had exulted in going "beyond the Alps," so she refound that euphoria at the edge of the Taos desert. If she had experienced in Italy a simpler country life combined with real work, rather than the artifice of high life in the Villa, she might have achieved satisfaction years earlier. It was, after all, a farming community that Mabel ended up with in Taos. Jacques-Émile Blanche's intuition of the essential Mabel, the simply dressed woman he had glimpsed carrying a basket of eggs, seems to confirm a buried part of her. It recalls her love of nature, dogs and horses, and hunting trips to the Adirondacks. All that had got overlaid by the overdressed, exhibitionist character she became in an overdecorated environment. Italy was displaced but seemed never to have receded from her memory; her exposure to the basic verities of life in the Old World prepared her for those of the American Southwest.

When Mabel left Italy in 1912, she was thirty-three years old—Dante's symbolic age of renewal on the road of life, a coincidence that couldn't have escaped her, imbued as she was with feelings for symbols and disposed to find meaning in such synchronization.

Maurice Sterne's artistic sensitivity had discerned in Mabel an attachment to what he called the exotic, and he felt that much of Mabel's interest in him was his connection to the Mediterranean through his Jewishness. Despite his birth in Latvia and a background of German culture and language, he had always maintained that his heritage, his looks, and certainly his temperament, were Mediterranean. Maurice had been to Bali to paint and had already experienced the Otherness of that culture—a matter of great import to Mabel. Knowing his belief in the connectedness between all so-called exotic peoples and the complementary civilization of the Mediterranean, Mabel wanted him to portray her "like those archaic heads of the early Greek things."[23]

Just before arriving in the Southwest, Mabel had been writing a syndicated column for the Hearst papers that, without mentioning Freud by name, circulated his ideas to a mass audience. One of her first columns was "Growth of Love," in which she outlined the progression from self-love to love of objects, then to sexual passion, and finally to the mature growth as Love of Humanity. In her life she was striving to replace self-feeling with fellow feeling, and her strong, immediate attraction to Taos had been her appreciation of the communal strength of the Pueblo Indians there who, she felt, had much to teach the white man.

By fall 1924, seven years after her arrival in Taos and the year after her marriage to Tony, she had reached another crisis of boredom, frustration, and melancholy. For a while, she considered moving east, even leasing Finney Farm in Croton-on-Hudson again and returning to Dr. Brill for analysis; she considered divorcing Tony. He simply rebuffed her with silence. Mabel found he was the one man she could not send out of her life. And he quite tellingly identified her lack of inner stability by describing her as always "goin' by, goin' by, just like water." As much as Mabel longed to dispense with the modern world and her old anxieties, she could not. In her promised land, she still had fears, bouts of depression, nightmares, and a continuing need for psychoanalysis. Uncertain of her future, on a trip back to New York she visited an occultist who gave Mabel the motive and embellishing myth for her to return to Taos: she was told that she had been singled out to be the bridge between Indian and white people, and Taos was to be "the beating heart of the world." Such cosmic significance was what Mabel had always wanted of her life. She fell back on what had always sustained her—creating and decorating a home—but more than a home, a hacienda complex. That turned out to be the Los Gallos compound of several houses and farm buildings that Mabel created in Taos. Despite intervals of restlessness, including a year of moving Tony and her new household of Indian servants to Carmel in California to be near the poet Robinson Jeffers, she would remain in Taos the forty-five years that were the remainder of her life.

Mabel suffered neurasthenia: often an affliction of the bored and helpless. Among the parade of saviors whom she consulted, her analyst Dr. Brill told her work would save her and suggested writing in some disciplined, planned way. She had, in fact, a talent for the opinion pieces which she had done irregularly for periodicals. What she didn't have was staying power. Her last Hearst column was dated February 8, 1918, and was titled "Mythic Utopia of Taos" as if her life had concluded on that happy note.

In New Mexico, the stark landscape, the huddled adobe dwellings analogous to the stone houses of Italian hill-towns, and the dried-up river beds seem to evoke parts of Italy—the Abruzzi, say, or the islands of Sicily and Sardinia. There is something similar in the natural surroundings and how the native people relate to it; there is the same hybrid Catholicism with its mix of pagan rites.

Years ago, in Sicily, I witnessed a Good Friday parade of the crucified body of Christ in Taormina, where D. H. Lawrence once lived. "It is the mystery that does it," he said of the Good Friday procession and the fearful impression it had made on him by revealing the pagan elements still pervasive in Italy. That was akin to the spiritual sensations Mabel felt on first arriving in Taos and hearing the Indian drums, seeing the dances and rituals. In Sicily, at Easter the resurrection of the green of spring is celebrated in honor of the grain goddess, Demeter, with symbolic grains of wheat baked in the ricotta pies and boxes of sprouted wheat placed at the foot of the Virgin in all the churches. In New Mexico, as a spring rite, Indians dance the corn dance. As for the people, there is much of the same stoic solemnity in the Sicilian as in the Pueblo Indian.

The parallel between the Mediterranean world and the American Southwest surely illuminated Mabel as she read passages from Lawrence's *Sea and Sardinia* and connected his search for values in the Sardinian world to hers in Taos. "I knew when I read him," she explained in her book *Lorenzo in Taos* (using the Italian form of his name), "here is the only one who can really see this Taos country."[24] What she described for him was a place "where the plainest tasks took on a beauty and significance they had not in other places." Just as in Italy. And he, responding, told her he liked the name Taos because it was like Taormina.

"Italy has given me back I know not what of myself," Lawrence had once said, "but a very, very great deal. She has found for me so much that was lost."[25] That "recovery of the lost" theme was very dear to Mabel's heart. It defined her ongoing search. She felt, as she reviewed her life in her memoirs, "I lost a part of the spirit of the place for every human contact I made. . . . People have nothing to do with the *genius loci* . . . in the same way that I lost Florence, I have lost this whole, round earth. . . . I built myself a world to replace the lovely world of nature that I lost and sacrificed for [people]."

Such feelings induced Mabel to think that Lawrence, a true lover of the instinctive, non-machine-made world, would respond in the same way to New Mexico as he had to Italy. Both of them, she felt, had sought that spontaneity of being and naturalness that had taken them, at separate times, to Italy in a quest for a personal South that was the antidote to their upbringings in materialistic cultures. So she wrote Lawrence to invite him and Frieda to come to her new world; his own personal search had taken him to many other southern places, now he should see New Mexico. But mostly she called D. H. Lawrence to her to have him write the narrative of her conversion story—how she found inner peace in Taos through her final alliance with a Pueblo Indian.

For both Lawrence and Mabel, their exposure among the Indians of the Southwest to ceremonies that had pagan resonances added to their critique of Christian doctrine with its denial of the senses. They both felt confirmed that the element of primitivism in traditions, whether in Italy or New Mexico, was superior to modern age austerity of the senses and put one in touch with a physicality that had been lost in contemporary society. The Italian peasants for Lawrence and the Pueblo Indians for Mabel provided links to mediate between mechanized humans and the natural world. Those closest to nature expressed, as devitalized city people could not, the regenerative power of nature and the possibility of rebirth into a new state of being. Mabel had expressed that vividly in her love for the peasant bread and wine of Italy that had been communion for her; and Lorenzo expressed it in his own simplified way of living—he baked his own bread, he and Frieda cut each other's hair, did all the washing, cooking, cleaning, and other chores.

D. H. Lawrence was only the first in a series of notables whom Mabel enticed to the Southwest, ostensibly in her efforts to promote the whole region as having unique artistic as well as spiritual attributes. Despite her lament of having lost the spirit of places to human contacts, she continued to need interesting people around her. With Lawrence she played on his antipathy to what white Western civilization had become—a morass of materialism and technological trappings. The Southwest, she told him, was different; there, say the Indians, is the heart of the world. "*Their* world, maybe" was his response after he came and found himself not only attracted but also repelled by Indian primitivism, and quite antagonistic to Mabel personally.[26]

He grew fractious toward his hostess and scrapped the novel based on her after the first chapter. Aspects of Mabel appeared in his Mexican novel *The Plumed Serpent* and in several stories, the most powerful being "The Woman who Rode Away," which tells of a white woman who suddenly finds her life empty and, turning her back on home and family, rides off in Mexico to Indian country where she passively accepts her role as the sacrifice which will induce the Gods to bring back the old ways.

Unfortunately, Mabel also stood for America for Lawrence: "America lives by a sort of egoistic will, shove and be shoved. . . . I will not shove, and I will not be shoved. *Sono io!*"[27]

Scathingly referring to her cluster of adobe homes as Mabeltown, Lawrence personified in her all of his diatribe against American women in general which, for him, was at the root of America's malaise. Sarcastically, he reported, "Having loudly renounced the sick old world of art and artists, she still filled her life, with suppers and motor drives and people dropping in. She loved to play the patroness, and her relation to the Indians was that of the great lady to her wards." His conclusion?—"she hates the white world and loves the Indian out of hate."

He became infuriated with the belief that Mabel had taken up the Indian not to reintegrate her white consciousness with the aboriginal world, but in order to emasculate the white man intellectually and sexually. "White Americans," he wrote, "do try hard to intellectualize themselves. Especially white women Americans. And the latest stunt is this 'savage' stunt again. White savages, with motor-cars, telephones, incomes and ideals! . . . ye gods!"[28] He referred to Mabel's quarrels with Frieda, Dorothy Brett, and himself as "the vileness of 1923" and cynically summarized Mabel's marital career by saying, "She married two white men, a Jew, and an Indian."

In several fiercely mocking stories, Lawrence introduced a character very much like Mabel to satirize the American lust for accumulating possessions and culture abroad. His 1928 story, "Things," about American collectors in Florence, characterizes the idealists' need to cling to something for support (just as Mabel had always to cling to a man). And a passage from the story "None of That" graphically renders Lawrence's portrait of Mabel in his character Ethel Cane:

> She was extraordinary . . . one of those American women, born rich, but what we should call provincial. . . . She was too much of a personality to be a lady, and she had all that terrible American energy! . . . She was a dynamo. In Paris she was married to a dapper little pink-faced American who got yellow at the gills, bilious, running after her when she would not have him. . . . She knew all the people, and had all sorts come to her, as if she kept a human menagerie. And she bought old furniture and brocades; she would go mad if she saw someone get a piece of velvet brocade with the misty bloom of years on it, that she coveted. She coveted such things with lust, and would go into a strange sensual trance, looking at some old worm-eaten chair. And she would go mad if someone else got it, and not she: that nasty old wormy chair of the quattrocento! Things! She was mad about 'things'. But it was only for a time. She always got tired, especially of her own enthusiasms. . . . If she ever heard of a man who seemed to have a dramatic sort of power in him, she must know that man. It was like her lust for brocade and old chairs and a perfect aesthetic setting.

In reverse, Mabel extolled the Indian for supposedly not wanting "a dismal accretion of cars, stoves, sinks, et al. . . . the blood of their fore-runners is still stronger in them than new needs for THINGS." She was wrong. The younger ones wanted what she had in her own great house, and she had unwittingly disclosed her inner conflict by possessing the very things that she professed to despise.

D. H. Lawrence, feeling a sense of obligation for Mabel's gift to him of Kiowa Ranch, was able to reconcile with her from a distance. Following the experiment of living in Taos in three different periods between 1922 and 1925, Lawrence and Frieda resettled in Tuscany not far from Villa Curonia, which had remained in Edwin Dodge's ownership. Once safely back in Italy, the Lawrences resumed with Mabel what appears a cordial correspondence and even obligingly went to Villa Curonia to pack up and send Mabel some two hundred volumes that they decided were the best of the books she had left behind and then wanted.

It was at Villa Mirenda in Scandicci that Lawrence wrote not the Mabel novel but his explosive *Lady Chatterley's Lover*, first published in Florence in 1928, having first dedicated his 1927 *Mornings in Mexico* "To Mabel Luhan, who called me to Taos." Away from Mabel, Lawrence continued to do things for her and became a generous mentor by mail. She asked his advice and sought encouragement as she embarked on writing as antidote to the depression which again afflicted her. When she asked his opinion about her joining the Gurdjieff community in France, Lawrence responded in a fury, inveighing against all cultists and analysts and their zeal for "adjusting" people. Lawrence, to whom mind control was anathema, reminded her of her once-held faith in intuition and impulse. Prolonged analysis, he felt, had deprived her of her intuitive "IT." But it also gave her material for a book manuscript called *Psychoanalysis for Beginners* that she sent to Bennett Cerf at Random House in 1938, to which he replied: "All of us have given very serious thought to your little book on psychoanalysis, but it is the unanimous feeling that this would be a very bad choice as to your first volume under a new imprint."[29]

As she composed her memoirs over the years, she'd send Lawrence batches for his comment as she did also with Willa Cather and other writers. Lawrence told her they were "hemlock in a cup," and so horribly near the truth it made him sick in his solar plexus. Although he found the pages she sent him "frightfully depressing" for their "long, long indictment of our civilisation," he also told her that her work was the most serious "confession that ever came out of America." The themes of sexual rivalry, sordid little power struggles, and hostility were the real subjects of her work, just as they were his own favorite subjects. But, since she named actual people, Lawrence told her she shouldn't think of publishing yet. She was advised to labor and wait, to let her writings lie still in a safe. She did. Lawrence, mentioning Mabel's memoirs to his friend Catherine Carswell said of them, "I don't care, so long as she dies before she gets to Frieda and me!"[30]

It was he who died first, aged forty-five, in 1930. And Mabel rushed to publish by 1932 a self-aggrandizing account of her genius in getting him to Taos, and his lack of appreciation. She lamented what she had gone through in their friendship ("if that's what it was") without mentioning the great distress she caused him by giving away the precious manuscript of *Sons and Lovers* with which he had repaid her for Kiowa Ranch. *Lorenzo in Taos* was Mabel's first published book and gives the impression that it was written swiftly so that she could establish her primacy over the Lawrence legend and make sure the world connected her name to his, as she had previously managed with Gertrude Stein.

Mabel treated Lawrence much as she did those husbands and lovers who had disappointed her—vindictively. But as her close friend Hutchins Hapgood wrote Maurice Sterne, "Lawrence was always right and she always wrong."[31] Mabel, presuming to be Lawrence's only "understanding" soul mate, had worked every device, emotional and material, to separate Frieda from him.[32] Her possessiveness of Lawrence did not end with her attempts to entice him back to Taos, nor even with *Lorenzo in Taos*. Not able to relinquish the genius whom she felt belonged to her even in death, Mabel made an attempt to steal Lawrence's ashes when Frieda returned from France to inter them at Kiowa Ranch. Historian Paul Horgan, who compared Mabel to the scheming sorceress of Arthurian legend, records that she wanted to filch the ashes and scatter them to the desert winds, thereby returning Lawrence to the great free forces he so loved. Thus would Mabel, who always maintained she knew Lawrence better than Frieda did, upstage her rival. Someone in Mabel's employ warned Frieda of Mabel's plot and Lawrence's ashes were quickly set into a cement block and locked in the chapel at Kiowa built by Frieda's new Italian husband, Angelo Ravigli.

Poor Mabel. Her flamboyant over-sized life was the very stuff of parody. Malcolm Cowley, reviewing her four-volume memoirs, wrote, "When she describes herself, it is almost always in electrical or chemical or mechanical terms—she calls herself a live wire, a dynamo, an engine, a vibration, a blue flame, a clockwork in a cage, a magnet, a chemical compound, but never a human being."[33]

She was constantly written of in stories, plays, and novels and even the "Talk of the Town" pieces which appeared in the *New Yorker* in 1940 and 1945 partake of caricature. By 1947, after the publication of her last book, *Taos and its Artists*, when she was in her late sixties, *Time* magazine identified Mabel as a "Grandmother with graying bangs" and satirically quoted her on modern times: "If more machinery would break down, we'd be better off."

Mabel collected the adverse criticism, quite convinced that it would in time be reversed as was the case with Proust and Lawrence, with whom she compared herself. When all is said and done, here is a woman, both pathetic and disagreeable in herself, with a narrative gift that might have been expanded into higher flights of imagination, but was left to revolve solely around her persona as she sought her true self. Seeking linear progress in time and space, she seemed, instead, to be always spiraling around herself, still prey to the old fears and doubts even as she announced them won and trounced.

But what simpler life had she, in fact, achieved?[34] Los Gallos was a seventeen-room adobe palazzo with 8,400 square feet of living space filled with Italian antiques; it overlooked a compound of five guesthouses, corrals, stables, a barn, and a large gatehouse for servants. Mabel continued to build homes, selling off her Medici chairs and other precious things to Millicent Rogers in order to be able to build yet another house in Embudo, New Mexico.

Even *Winter in Taos*, a lyrical recounting of a day in Mabel's Taos life when Tony is absent and she muses on his tasks and hers, the book which is judged her most successful effort, is a version, with different setting and different husband, of a piece she did years before for Max Eastman's *The Masses* based on a day in her life at Finney Farm when Maurice Sterne is off somewhere and she reflects on their life together. The reality of life with Tony was other: his alcoholism, syphilis, jealousy, her need for intellectual stimulation from others, her interest in other men, his mistresses, his taste for expensive suits and Cadillacs—making their idyll seem more like sparring episodes from *Who's Afraid of Virginia Woolf?*

In her Taos restatement of bliss, she loves the country, the seasonal rituals, riding horseback over the plains, her house pets and farm animals, good food and good company. But when friends leave and with them the talk that Tony compares to the buzzing of flies, the time of winter solitude approaches and her heart tightens up. She feels sorry for herself when Tony is away until she remembers she chose to be there and had built a life and it was best there: "Yes, this was my bed I had made and I would lie on it, and for the most part it was better than others'." And then Tony returns.

Mabel frankly explained her swing between highs and lows in her life as based on her dependency upon a boost from someone else. Maurice Sterne put it in more biting terms: she was a parasitic orchid needing a tree to attach to, a dead battery needing to be recharged with the juice of some man.

In 1940, at the suggestion of her novelist son, John Evans, Mabel tried to reestablish her salon in New York. After a first meeting at which a young Thornton Wilder explicated *Finnegans Wake*, she gave up the attempt. She found herself irrelevant to a younger generation. A few years later she came east again and fared no better with a novel manuscript called "Let's Get Away Together." Having happily described it in a *New Yorker* interview as the story of discharged World War II soldiers who establish a cooperative community near Taos, she said that the idea had been suggested by her analyst, Dr. Brill, and the book had practically written itself. It remains unpublished.

With the invention of the atom bomb, developed and tested at Los Alamos, only seventy miles west of Taos pueblo, Mabel began to speak of leaving New Mexico altogether. It is almost like retribution for her blithe motto of contradictoriness that the "contraption," as Mabel referred to the bomb, should have been born in her paradise. In *The Masked Gods*, author Frank Waters noted the dramatic duality: "Perhaps in no other comparable area on earth are condensed so many contradictions, or manifested so clearly the opposite polarities of all life. The oldest forms of life discovered in this hemisphere, the newest agent of mass death. The oldest cities in America and the newest. The Sun Temple of Mesa Verde and the nuclear fission laboratories of the Pajarito Plateau. The Indian drum and the atom smasher."[35]

In her final years, Mabel appeared in photos as a decorously groomed and permanent-haired elderly woman, as traditional looking as any senior citizen of Buffalo, New York, except for the incongruous figure of the portly Indian male seated next to her. As she grew older and less steady of mind, she would often seem bewildered at Tony's presence—"Who is that Indian?" she would say. "Get him out of here."

Los Gallos, Mabel's great house, renamed Las Palomas, became a bed and breakfast conference center and is on the National Historic Landmark register. Guests can choose, at the top of the line, to stay in Mabel's bedroom suite complete with her hand-carved double bed that was built into the room; or, there is Tony's room, seven steps up from hers; or the first floor rooms named for Willa Cather, Georgia O'Keeffe, and Spud Johnson. A promotional brochure describes the place as "the former home of Mabel Dodge Luhan, well-known hostess and meddler in social and literary affairs."

Mabel, like D. H. Lawrence, found her final resting place in the Southwest. Perhaps as a lasting reminder to the contradictoriness she raised to a philosophy, at her death in 1962 she was buried in the Kit Carson Cemetery in Taos, named for a man she hated since he had spent part of his life as a killer of Indians. Mabel ends as she began in paradox: "Life is not concerned with results," she wrote in her preface to *Lorenzo in Taos*, "but only with Being and Becoming." And yet she had compelled Life, all her life, to produce results for her. The written volumes of her life stand testimony as to whether she achieved her quest for a personal South.

Social Historian Christopher Lasch, author of *The New Radicalism in America, 1889–1963*, which includes a chapter on Mabel Dodge Luhan entitled "Sex as Politics," saw her as emblematic of the social vacuum of modern life and the breakdown of family moral authority. She tended to see all human relations as a form of politics: "Love, friendship, and sex all continued in her imagination to constitute a struggle for mastery; life itself was a struggle for mastery." Actually, she so insists on her significance that the reader comes to share her doubt of it. As feminist scholar Patricia Spacks puts Mabel's life, "Repetitive, undisciplined, self-indulgent, it conveys the essential confusion of the woman whose sense of reality was always vicarious . . . unable fully to exist as a separate self."

She was not, after all, the New Woman who asserted the right to a career, to a public voice, to visible power, and to a presence in colleges, in the professions, or in the workplace. Closer to that ideal was Gertrude Vanderbilt Whitney who, also born to wealth and privilege, went on to have her own avant-garde gatherings in her Village studio, founded a great art museum, and was an artist in her own right.

At times I like to speculate that if, while she was living in Italy, Mabel had met Maurice Sterne when he, too, was residing and painting in Anticoli, the hill-town outside Rome known to artists for its beautiful models, she might have found her right destiny with him in Italy. Sterne felt that though Mabel was drawn to Mediterranean culture, she had never fully plumbed the depths of it and thus never understood all of what Italy offered.

Mabel is known now for her own life as cast in her memoirs; she was an unreliable reporter of others' lives for she often wrote hearsay without fact checking. She could be misleading and inaccurate in her facts, wrong in her conjectures. She seems, at times, like the unreliable narrator of a novel whom we become leery of, her word against our better judgment. Again, as chronicle of American cultural history, Mabel's memoirs reveal her indifference to the great issues of the day except as they impinged on her personal relationships and so are considered by Lasch as "relics of a period which the Depression had made ancient history." But she was too flamboyant a personality, too colorful, to be left out of personal accounts of many prominent people as well as numerous social histories of the first half of the twentieth century.

The bulk of Mabel's writing, weighing in at over half a ton of paper, was sent by her in various shipments to Yale's Beinecke Libary where her erstwhile friend, Gertrude Stein, is also archived.[37] Mabel's papers, including a great deal of correspondence, two novels, poetry, essays, and volumes of her memoirs, including material omitted from her published works to avoid lawsuits with the living, reposed in the library until the collection was unsealed in the year 2000—reposed but perhaps not completely undisturbed, for in the volumes I consulted several sections had been cut out. Nonetheless, like the Phoenix, in a postmortem peremptory strike for her continuing glory, Mabel's ghost may arise with the anticipated new publications and impose itself on the twenty-first century as she did on the twentieth.

In contrast to Mabel was Princess Marguerite Caetani, who showed a complete indifference to posthumous fame and left a dearth of writings about herself in diaries and memoirs. Their life spans of eighty-three years were the same; they were exact contemporaries. Yet, despite similarities in background and having lived through the same times, they were as unlike as two American women could be. Both came from privileged backgrounds, but where Mabel was bold, Marguerite was guarded and reticent. And for me personally, though I found Mabel's extravagant life a good read, it was Marguerite Caetani who, through her founding of the literary publication *Botteghe Oscure*, shone as a beckoning star in my college years and helped me to Italy as destination.

Marguerite Caetani, 1880–1963

5. *Yankee Principessa: Marguerite Caetani*

I was a young, aspiring writer when the excitement of an international literary review from Rome called *Botteghe Oscure* arrived in upstate New York and flung open the doors to the wider world of writing and pointed my way to Italy where it was happening. It was just after World War II ended: the era of Dior's new look, of the debate on Ezra Pound the poet versus Pound the traitor, and of the end of American isolationism. At my university the English department was agog over the new review. Bland-beige of cover and fat in format, *Botteghe Oscure* was named for Via delle Botteghe Oscure, the Street of Dark Shops in Rome, site of Palazzo Caetani from where it was edited and issued twice a year from 1948 to 1960. Welcoming to its unadorned pages the young and obscure as well as the famed, it emphasized the creative writer in his or her original language, not essays on academic topics or critical writing about writing. The multi-lingual review mirrored a new international spirit and opened a larger literary world to a generation of writers who would find each other through its pages.

Botteghe Oscure was the creation of Principessa Caetani—"the legendary aristocrat," Cynthia Ozick, a contributor, rather extravagantly termed her—and everyone wanted to be published in it. The princess was born Marguerite Chapin in 1880 near New London, Connecticut, to a notable family whose origins in America dated back to a truly legendary ancestor, Samuel Chapin, who left

England for the New World in 1635. As a young woman, Marguerite went to Europe aspiring to be a singer. In Paris she met the man she would marry, Prince Roffredo Caetani, the second son of a distinguished Roman family dating back to antiquity. Prince Roffredo eventually succeeded his elder brother as Duke of Sermoneta and family head. With that, Marguerite acquired the additional title of Duchess of Sermoneta and became the last in a succession begun with Lucrezia Borgia. But of Marguerite Caetani's titles the one she must have loved best was Lady Bountiful to not a few of this century's eminent writers. Her wealth and influence in the arts was integral in founding the influential international literary review that was *Botteghe Oscure*.

I was interested in who Marguerite was aside from her titles upon first acquaintance with *Botteghe Oscure*. But as with the name of the review, so Marguerite, too, remains in many ways as shadowy as the original medieval street of the dark shops before it was widened and opened to the light in Mussolini's urban renewal sweep of the 1930s. There is copious correspondence related to the management of *Botteghe Oscure*, but little of personal nature. At Marguerite's death in 1963, her daughter Lelia observed that the *New York Times* obituary functioned "very well as a notice" but was too spare considering who Marguerite Caetani and her work had been.[1] Yet, Marguerite herself had chosen to keep out of view, not even having her name appear in the review until some years after its launching.

Marguerite Chapin Caetani fascinates by her contrasts. On the one hand, she became a public figure, having stepped to the forefront of literary publishing by her financial patronage and editorial involvement with two internationally influential journals (her French language *Commerce* published in Paris in the 1920s preceded *Botteghe Oscure*); on the other hand, she stayed illusive and private despite her celebrated hospitality to friends and artists. Marguerite was not a Mabel Dodge sort of patroness, one who cajoled writers into putting her into their fictions and left volumes of memoirs recording her every thought, word, and deed.

The late writer from Alabama, Eugene Walter, who popped up in Europe on his GI bill just after the start of *Botteghe Oscure* and became Marguerite's right-hand man, explained her reticence as due to her New England ancestry: he recalled to me her saying that real ladies just did not appear in print telling all. That, of course, explains nothing—and quite belies Margaret Fuller who was New England to the core and full of passionate telling; nor does it explain real ladies like Marguerite's friend Iris Origo, nor Vittoria Colonna, her sister-in-law and predecessor as Duchess of Sermoneta, both of whom wrote books of memoirs. History and literature are replete with the words of well-born ladies who do tell all.

The difference is in the rigorous reticence Marguerite maintained over the deep losses of her life: she was five when her mother died, fourteen when she saw the fiery end of her childhood home, and at sixteen she was orphaned by her father's death. And then there is the central tragedy of Marguerite's life, the death of her twenty-five year old son Camillo in a war he and she both detested. The *New York Times* reported his death as the greatest loss the Italian nobility had suffered in World War II, for with him the family line was extinguished.

Marguerite took on the ways of her father who loved to laugh, to be amused: come back to Rome she implores J. P. Marquand, you are much needed since we haven't laughed so well since last you were here; of contributors whose cause she took up at editorial meetings, she would often cast the winning vote because "he made us all laugh so much when he was here last Sunday"; to Eugene Walter she reports how they all screamed with delight at his letters, and what a riot Niccolò Tucci was at Viareggio impersonating a Russian Grand Duke. She loved the beauty of her garden at Ninfa, the power of poetry, and the company of creative souls. What was hurtful was buried deep. What Marguerite left instead of a personal record are the publications she financed and believed in along with the letters attendant to them, the rushed business correspondence she carried on herself with her editors, distributors, and contributors.

There were so many silences in her story and turns to her life that kept suggesting more questions that I set out to find her, if I could, at her beginnings when she was Marguerite Chapin in Waterford, site of her girlhood home on the Connecticut shore, and in the contiguous urban center of New London. A veil of oblivion seems to have descended over her long-ago New England haunts: the old Waterford home combusted and gone from the earth and vital records nonexistent; the familiar New London sidewalks from her youth had become fronted by an empty, darkened hotel, a silent theater, rows of abandoned stores. In her lifetime the city declined into a shadow of its prosperous self, reviving only at the beginning of the new century with the opening of the Pfizer research center.

In Waterford and New London they did not know her name when I asked town clerks and curators and librarians about Princess Caetani, born Marguerite Chapin. She rings no bells in local memory even though her father, Lindley H. Chapin, had built around 1870 a notable estate at Goshen Point occupying one of the finest sites on the eastern coast. The family spent a good part of every year in Waterford and I felt it had to be there that Marguerite was born June 24, 1880, not New London as is often reported. Well-to-do families like the Chapins did not have their children born in a hospital, which, moreover, did not exist in New London at that time, but at home. I searched for, but did not find, her birth certificate in Waterford's town hall, although those of her half sisters Katherine and Cornelia are recorded there.

"They weren't locals," a historical society curator dressed as a dairy maid at a Revolutionary War dwelling told me when I asked her about the Goshen Point residence and the Chapins. "They were summer people. We wouldn't have anything on them." The Chapins dismissed as not local? As summer people?

The Chapin home burned to the ground in mid-November 1894 when the family was still at Goshen Point, and so clearly they were not just fair-weather vacationers. Lindley Chapin died in 1896 before it could be rebuilt and within a few years his widow had sold the property. In 1907 it belonged to wealthy philanthropist Edward S. Harkness, the son of John D. Rockefeller Sr.'s partner and financial backer. Eventually given to the state, the property, still a glorious site, is now open to the public for strolling and summer concerts as Harkness Memorial State Park. How, I wondered, could such an important property built by a descendant of the earliest settlers of New England not be in the local records?

The Chapin clan descends from Deacon Samuel Chapin, who sailed from England to Massachusetts in 1635 with wife and children and in 1642 pushed on from Roxbury to be one of the founders of Springfield. It was this redoubtable Deacon who not only gave his new country a wealth of descendants, but also his physiognomy to the statue by Augustus Saint-Gaudens widely known as "The Puritan." The statue stands in Springfield: a serious-miened, stocky man advancing apace under flowing cloak while clutching a huge tome against his side—for all the world, a man of the book who went by the book. This was Marguerite's forebear, the no-nonsense progenitor who gave America an indelible image of puritan rectitude, and to her a notable hard edge. Generations of other prominent Chapins lived in the Connecticut River valley until the mid-nineteenth century when some moved further south toward Long Island Sound and some into New York City.

The descendants of the old puritan deacon included T. S. Eliot on the side of his mother Charlotte Stearns, and also Noah Webster, Presidents Grover Cleveland and William Howard Taft, Harriet Beecher Stowe, the abolitionist John Brown, J. P. Morgan, and a good many scientists and railroad magnates as well as divines. On the artistic side there were Marguerite's half sisters, poet Katherine Garrison Chapin and sculptor Cornelia Chapin, novelist Isabel Bolton, watercolor artist Lelia Caetani, and impresario and author Schuyler Garrison Chapin. In New World terms, the Chapins are as endowed with notables as the Old World Caetanis whose stem, two golden wavy bars on a blue ground, illustrates their origin from Gaeta on the sea: the Gaetani from Gaeta became Caetani.

Marguerite's father was a gentleman of leisure with a predilection for farming and things French. Her French-descended mother was Lelia Gibert of New York City. At the Goshen Point estate, Mr. Chapin, who had converted to his wife's Catholic faith, had built a chapel for Lelia that included among its adornments nothing less than a Cellini chalice. It would have been in that chapel that Marguerite was baptized and, since the Catholic parish of New London included Waterford at that time, her baptismal record would have read as issued from New London, thus adding to the confusion about her birthplace. Or perhaps she herself simply gave New London as her birthplace because it was better known—a prosperous nineteenth-century city with a thriving port, handsome buildings, and gracious residences including that of her close contemporary, Eugene O'Neill.

Once, New London's daily newspaper, *The Day*, was well aware of the Chapins. The conflagration at Goshen Point made two columns on the front page of November 12, 1894. A reporter almost rapturously recounted the brilliance of the fire and the picturesque scene as hosts, guests, children, and servants fled the mansion with only the clothes on their backs. Only the chapel was spared. Mr. Chapin had managed to save most of his wife's jewels, but her new $1,000 fur coat, a $1,500 piano, dozens of tablecloths at $150 each (newsworthy prices a century ago), and china worth its weight in gold, not to mention generations of family portraits and all the other furnishings of forty rooms (twenty-one of which were family bedrooms) had all burnt to ash or become molten lumps.

In her youth, Marguerite Chapin moved between the Connecticut estate and the family townhouse at 5 37th Street just off Fifth Avenue in New York City, a few blocks from the old Metropolitan Opera House. It was a time and place of privilege for America's moneyed gentry. Though lost to her at such a young age, her mother remained a powerful presence in Marguerite's life, both inspirationally in the French influence and in the naming of her own daughter, and also materially through the Gibert inheritance that came to her.

Both Marguerite Chapin and Virginia Woolf, born within a year of each other, were motherless daughters—we know what effect it had on Woolf, but Marguerite never alluded to her childhood. The single glimpse is indirect, refracted from a memoir by a Springfield cousin, Mary Britton Miller, who became a writer with the pen-name Isabel Bolton and was to appear in the pages of *Botteghe Oscure*. Through the blended voices of young Mary and her twin sister comes the picture of summers spent at an uncle's country place at Goshen Point, just across the way from the Chapin estate where Marguerite lived with her father, his second wife, and the children of the new family, Paul, Katherine, and Cornelia, in the halcyon last decades of the nineteenth century.

Waterford had always been a farming community and Goshen Point on its shoreline is traversed by lush tree-lined roads affording views of seaside meadows, fine for dairy cows which the area specialized in, and spectacular settings for the great houses which once rivaled those of Newport in the Gilded Age. The air there is fresh and briny with the sea, the trees are huge centenarians, corn is high, the waysides filled with Queen Anne's lace and blue chicory, the whole a seascape as beautiful and breezy when I saw it as when little Mary Miller was there. The Chapin property was a large holding of lawns, gardens, and meadow acreage running to the shoreline; greenhouse, carriage house and stable, chapel, and manager's farmhouse were presided over by the great house.

A summer scene in such a setting would be redolent to the senses: the colorful chintzes of the main sitting room where young children were not allowed, the fragrance of clovered meadows mixed with honeysuckle, the chirp and buzz of birds and crickets, the delicious feel of sea-breezes from the Sound wafted through the large open piazza (so-called, but actually an enormous porch open to the water view) where the family breakfasted.

The women dressed in pastels, the cologned men wore summer white with blue cornflowers in their buttonholes and shoes shined to a mahogany finish; they sat to breakfast at a table spread with white damask, a great array of floral china, sweet peas in a Dresden bowl, and a great coffee urn from which the lady of the house poured.

Down from the homes and fields was the beach area with bathhouses and a big dock extending out into the water. The sand was white and brilliant; there were rocks at the end of the Chapin property where crabs could be uncovered or where one could stretch out basking in the sun, and little shallow pools among the rocks and stones for wading. Passenger boats and barges, and the graceful veering of sailboats were visible on the horizon as they steamed out of New London Harbor.

The Miller twins, just three years younger than Marguerite, recalled the Chapins coming down from their house to the beach, towels across their arms, to bathe: "Mr. Lindley Chapin, such a very decorative gentleman with his wonderful dark beard and the turquoise rings upon his fingers and such a high-pitched voice and almost always laughing. And there were the two little girls, Katherine and Cornelia, dressed in pretty ruffled frocks. And the young boy, Paul. And there was Marguerite . . . oh, so very handsome with her long dark curls and her perfectly beautiful dresses.

. . . She had a donkey and a donkey cart. We'd rather be Marguerite Chapin than anybody on the earth."[2]

Who indeed would not be Miss Chapin then? Yet all that had seemed beauty, ease, and elegance in Marguerite's young life was not so after her father died so prematurely and she was alone. Nine years separated Marguerite from her nearest half-sibling. But there were other, greater separations: she was Catholic and went to mass in the chapel with the Irish help while the second Mrs. Chapin and her brood went off by carriage to Protestant service; this, a reminiscing Marguerite later related to Eugene Walter, caused her deep feelings of estrangement. She emphasized, he noted, not so much sadness in her childhood as the feeling of difference and alienation from a stepmother she detested.

Marguerite was Lelia Gibert's daughter and she was different from her father's new brood; she looked to Europe, had a great desire to be on her own, and, at the beginning of the twentieth century when she was twenty-one and had come into her inheritance, was an attractive young woman of independent means who could do just that. She became the quintessential Jamesian heroine or, in the phrase the *New York Times* coined for her, the "original bachelor girl."[3]

Lovely looking, Marguerite Chapin also had a pleasing voice and a great taste for music. In 1902, with a Canadian *dame de compagnie* with whom she spoke French, she sailed for France to study singing in Paris. She never returned to the states. For years she attended the classes of tenor Jean de Reszke, whom she had very likely heard when he sang at the Metropolitan Opera in the 1890s. By her own account Marguerite was the *benjamine*—the pet—of her teacher's classes. She described him to Eugene Walter as a darling person and his wife so lively. They had a lovely home with a little theater where they gave marvelous musical parties— everybody was there —writers and painters and all.

Since the lovely young heiress did not marry until she was thirty-one—unusual in that day—how did she pass a whole decade in addition to studying voice? She had an apartment at 110 Rue de l'Université, she traveled, she took in the culture, she looked up her Gibert relatives who furnished her with introductions, she commissioned work from leading artists, among which is a five-panel screen painted by Bonnard that is now in Washington's National Gallery of Art, she read, she learned. Yet missing from the large canvas are any details of her daily life—the animating particulars that taken together give texture and color and life to a person.

I see her obliquely, as in one of the three paintings Vuillard did of her—"Interior with a Lady and a Dog" that now hangs in the Fitzwilliam Museum in Cambridge, England. Her countenance is all but invisible as she leans down toward the little dog at her feet; it is the terrier who regards the viewer, the lady does not. Vuillard's 1910 impressionist painting, an exemplar of his "Intimist" style, captures Marguerite at age thirty within a small angle of her cozy domestic environment, enough of her possessions around to convey something of her personality; and yet the turn of the head downward, the avoidance of frontal glance is, perhaps, the most indicative thing about her. She is seated on the fender before a fireplace whose mantle is decked with small objects; she is adjacent to laden bookcases in front of which a comfortable armchair, prominent in the painting, indicates that here the lady settles herself to read the many tomes within reach. The scene is Marguerite's Paris flat a year or so before her marriage. Almost fifty years later she described that painting in a letter she was dashing off in a fearful hurry to Eugene Walter, to whose curiosity we owe these details: "it is green on the whole and I am sitting in front of the fire playing with a fox terrier. Bonnard also did a portrait about the same time but I don't know where that is."

Other semi-glimpses of Miss Chapin come from photographs of the first years of the century reproduced in an elegant celebratory catalogue, *Hommage à Commerce*, which accompanied a retrospective exhibit in her honor in Rome in 1958; there she is in Switzerland, a dark-haired, slim beauty and very dashing in a huge hat swathed in veiling which ties under her chin and hangs down to her waist keeping much of her from view. Another photo catches her seated at an open window looking out, her head turned so that only a crown of luxuriant, piled up hair is visible—not her features; one hand rests in her lap holding a flower; her slim figure, in its full Edwardian garb, tilts slightly toward the view as if an Isabel Archer were ever so gently straining toward the wonders not yet disclosed to her; view and viewer are hidden, yet what is suggested in that tantalizing photo is highly romantic, significant.

Iris Origo, a close friend of Marguerite's, composed a tribute to her after her death in 1963 that appeared in the *Atlantic Monthly* and referred to those photographs as the combined "portrait of a lady": the young and undaunted Marguerite Chapin discovering Europe. Origo inferred a suggestion of "alertness and restraint . . . vagueness and tenacity . . . ruthlessness and romanticism."[4] An interesting note. Where did ruthlessness fit in, I wondered. Perhaps aimed against herself, in what Marguerite resolutely repressed?

Miss Chapin, the bachelor girl, the woman of independent means, lived well within the bounds of propriety during those Paris years. Although she performed in Jean de Rezske's private salon-theater, she avoided a public career in the limelight and seemed not to have ambitions for herself as an artist. Marguerite preferred to stay in the wings, "the Serge Diaghilev of literature" as her nephew Schuyler Chapin, himself distinguished in the arts and past commissioner of New York City's Department of Cultural Affairs, wrote in his reminiscences.[5]

Yes, it has a Jamesian ring to it—the lovely young American heiress from puritan New England stock but with an artistic bent—will she, or will she not marry, and who will it be? Marguerite gave the ever-attendant Eugene Walter a witty account of her meeting with Roffredo Caetani: she was at the opera with Romanian Prince Emmanuel Bibesco who, having pressed his courtship to no avail and becoming convinced that she had no interest in him, nor perhaps in any marriage at all, finally said, "I'll find someone for you to marry. You should marry. I know just the person for you even though he's decided not to marry."

"Who's that?" said Marguerite.

"Prince Caetani, the composer," replied the defeated suitor.

For two such handsome people as Marguerite and Roffredo, so immersed in the musical arts and so cavalierly disinterested in marriage, it was a perfect match. "We became engaged in about a minute—just like that," Marguerite said of their first meeting.

He was the scion of one of the most ancient families of Rome—a family whose early tombs lay in the Vatican grottoes close to St. Peter's; a family which included warlords, two popes, cardinals, ambassadors, learned scholars, authors, linguists, historians, and ministers who were the very "sinew of the state."

Roffredo Caetani, born 1871, the year after his grandfather Michelangelo Caetani had convinced the first king of Italy to leave Florence and make Rome his capital, had a Polish countess for his grandmother and Franz Liszt as his godfather, saddling him with the persistent rumor that it was Liszt who was actually his father and from whom he derived his musical gifts. Margaret Terry Chanler, daughter of the expatriate American painter Luther Terry, grew up in Rome and knew the Caetanis. She described them in her memoir *Roman Spring* as a great family who over the centuries had maintained a tradition for learning and accomplishment that put them in a class by themselves. In the mid-nineteenth century, an American visitor to Rome, George Ticknor, wrote home to describe an enjoyable dinner with Don Michelangelo, the then Duke of Sermoneta and a brilliant scholar: "The service was silver, as in most great Roman houses, and the dinner recherché after the Paris fashion. But it was really a dinner for talk, and this particular was very brilliant . . . Sermoneta [was] admirable. I have not been present at so agreeable and brilliant a dinner in Europe. Don't you think the Italians are improving?"[6]

In a note written in English by Roffredo in 1905, he thanks the director of the Boston Philharmonic Concerts for presenting his symphony to the Boston public in a recent performance, and was sorry that two other performances in Paris and Brussels kept him from being present. Roffredo the composer further stated that in his country almost nobody but himself was composing anything but songs and operas and he was, therefore, highly flattered that the Boston Philharmonic should have presented this "Italian exception."[7]

He was, indeed, an "Italian exception" to have attracted the attention of Miss Chapin. He was also forty, of fine bearing and distinction, stunningly attractive, and exquisitely attentive. He frequented music circles in Paris and may have already heard of the musical Miss Chapin. A mirror story to hers is that Roffredo himself was smitten when he glimpsed Marguerite at the Opera with her chaperone (the critical scene is always the Opera) and decided then and there he would marry her.

They were married in 1911, London chosen as neutral ground between their two homelands. Marguerite had no compelling reason to return to the states though the states did not forget her: "U.S. Heiress Becomes Bride of Italian Prince in Brilliant Ceremony" trumpeted a headline in the *New York Herald*. Her accompanying photograph was captioned Princess di Bassiano and shows her in 3/4 profile, head held high on a long, graceful neck, her hair luxuriant and dark, her glance regal and proud. She was married in the presence of high society and of the Diplomatic

Corps attired in full regalia in the Spanish chapel of St. James's Palace. "The bride, who is unusually pretty, was given away by her uncle," the paper reported, in a service which "attracted more than usual attention musically because the wedding march was composed for the occasion by Prince di Bassiano, who is an accomplished musician."[8]

It is certainly a romantic story—but I can't help visualizing from what a bleak rock pile Marguerite's title derived. I happen to know the hilltop hamlet of Bassiano some forty miles south of Rome since I had gone there to visit the birthplace of Aldus Manutius, the esteemed Renaissance publisher-scholar who created the renowned Aldine editions in Venice and became the subject of a book of mine. Bassiano is a forlorn and isolated place of dismal, huddled grey buildings and, except for Aldus (who was not remembered until 1965 when his bust was finally put up outside the walls), renowned for nothing. Now, along with Aldus, I can associate that no-place place with Marguerite Caetani's being its princess; she was to live splendidly in Villa Romaine at Versailles, at Palazzo Caetani in Rome, and in the grand romanticism of Ninfa, and yet the title by which she was most known came from a rocky hamlet of under two thousand inhabitants. Not much of a living, one would imagine. Fortunately, as in Henry James's novels, there was the New World fortune to attach to the Old World title.

Actually, for a millennium and more the Caetani history, as the oldest and most weighty of the Roman princely families, has been inextricably tied up with that of Rome itself. As if in a last glorious outburst before the extinction of the line in this century, the New York papers were often filled with admiring accounts of the contemporary Caetanis—Don Onorato, Roffredo's father, was a noted archeologist, mayor of Rome, and former Minister of Foreign Affairs who, as a young man had accompanied his famous father Michelangelo Caetani, the only liberal among Rome's nobility, to give King Victor Emmaunuel II in Florence the result of the plebiscite of the Roman people declaring their adhesion to the new kingdom of Italy.[9] The legend is that Pope Pius IX, infuriated, pronounced a malediction: within two generations the Caetani line would be extinct.

It seemed unlikely. Don Onorato had married a strapping Englishwoman, Ada Bootle-Wilbraham, and from their marriage were born five sons, Leone, Roffredo, Livio, Gelasio, and Michelangelo, and a daughter, Giovanella, named for Giovanella Caetani, who was the mother of Renaissance Pope Paul III. That family group is photographed in 1902; the brothers, already accomplished in several fields, are handsome, tall, and stalwart. It is impossible to imagine, seeing them grouped in their youth that, given such stock, seemingly superbly endowed to carry forward the House for another millennium, the family line would in fact be extinguished as the Pope was said to have forecast.

Roffredo and Marguerite, known as Prince et Princesse de Bassiano, first lived in Versailles where they brought up their two children, a daughter, Lelia, born in 1913 and a son, Camillo, born in 1916. By the 1920s, the great period of Bohemian Paris, the time of Picasso and Stein and Joyce and Eliot and the postwar ferment of creative excitement in the arts, their Villa Romaine was a center for the literary-artistic world of Paris. The Italian poet Giuseppe Ungaretti, in Paris as a journalist, was a contributor to Marguerite's new journal *Commerce* and likened its openness to the hospitality of Villa Romaine, "a true Italian home on French soil, open to anyone regardless of nationality." And Marguerite, too, recalled her gatherings as more of an open house than a pretentious salon. With her easy American manner and friendliness, Marguerite set the openly hospitable tone at Villa Romaine for all the creative people she liked having around her, feeding them well over sparkling talk in a relaxed setting.

"All the time we lived in Versailles," she told Eugene Walter, "we used to have Sunday luncheons that went on and on—always at least thirty to a table; afterwards we talked or played charades with writers, musicians, artists of all sorts—Joyce, Stravinsky, Paul Valéry, Gide, Bracque, Colette, Picasso, Claudel, Valery Larbaud." Eventually Marguerite and her closest Sunday friends began to meet as a smaller group in a Paris restaurant. From the spirited talk and exchange of ideas at these gatherings came the genial idea of preserving that *commerce des idées* in a review. Should the ideas exchanged in conversation take the written form of a series of letters to each other? No, thought St. John Perse, a future Nobel laureate, why not a review? It was he who suggested the title *Commerce* and it was Marguerite who financed it.

Marguerite was no salon-keeper of the type described by her friend, the editor Léon-Paul Fargue (*"des salonnardes charmantes, menteuses et trompeuses comme toutes les autres"*), driven by the snobbery of gathering a high elite about her. She did not fabricate a notoriety about herself and become an eccentric in the style of Stein and Toklas, or Natalie Barney whose Fridays were sometimes enlivened by concerts. Barney, who did publish her memoirs, mentions being summoned to lunch at Versailles by Marguerite to discuss the idea of subscribing an annual sum for Paul Valéry. Barney remarks rather tartly that until she herself thought of subsidizing authors of merit and gathering them together at her Fridays, "Princess B.," once completely devoted to the plastic arts, had amused herself only slightly with literature. In fact, before her involvement with *Commerce*, Marguerite had formed with an American friend, Alice Garrett, a group called "Les Amis de l'Art Contemporaine," showing young and old painters together, even though she had some reservations about it since, she said, Alice liked to make it more tea-party than she could take.

Commerce first appeared in fall 1924, a handsome limited edition of 1,600 numbered copies published at first by Adrienne Monnier at her bookshop in the Rue de L'Odeon. Paul Valéry, Valery Larbaud, and Léon-Paul Fargue were its directors. And as Sylvia Beach, the American bookstore proprietor of Shakespeare & Co. also on the Rue de L'Odeon, remembered in her eponymous memoir, she made an exception for *Commerce* to her rule of having only English-language reviews in her store since, she explained, it belonged to an American—"the Princess Bassiano, or, as she prefers to be called, Marguerite Caetani."

Paris was a hotbed of expatriate reviews and presses in the 1920s, all of them more noted in America than was Marguerite Caetani's *Commerce*. Though some American and English writers (in French translation) were published in the issues she called *cahiers*, the main focus and emphasis was European. At the same time in Paris, Robert McAlmon's *Contact Editions* published Hemingway; Harry and Caresse Crosby's Black Sun Press went in for esoterica and erotica; *The Little Review* had Ezra Pound as its Paris editor; and then there were the experimental *transition* and Ford Maddox Ford's *transatlantic review* among others.

The first issue of *Commerce* showcased an excerpt of Joyce's *Ulysses* (the Telemachus episode and parts of Ithaca and Penelope), translated into French by Valery Larbaud and Auguste Morel with Sylvia Beach's help. It set the tone, in a French review, of an interest in other literatures. It also illuminated a somewhat idiosyncratic editorial policy in regard to how other literatures would be presented: T. S. Eliot's "The Hollow Men," followed by other poems, appeared both in the original English and in French translation as did texts by Thomas Hardy, Roy Campbell, Archibald MacLeish, and Edith Sitwell; other English-language authors, among them Virginia Woolf, Hawthorne, Faulkner, Liam O'Flaherty, Edgar Allan Poe, and Joyce appeared in French translation and not in the original language. The very last issue featured

Faulkner's macabre story, "A Rose for Emily," the first of his work to be translated.

Joyce had considered the fragments of *Ulysses* that *Commerce* wanted to publish too few, and more were added. Writing to Harriet Shaw Weaver about his imminent appearance in what he called a *revue de luxe*, Joyce reported that "the princess di Bassiano objected to some of the passages," but then allowed him to overrule her. Joyce was intensely gratified by his inclusion in her review and added to Weaver, "This gem now blazes brightly in my crown." Joyce also insisted that the accents added to the French translation by the printer ("like so many hairpins") be removed from Molly Bloom's monologue. To effect this, he telegraphed for help to editor Larbaud who was in Italy and got a bilingual reply that pleased him: "*Joyce a raison Joyce ha ragione.*"

At the luncheon given by Marguerite at Villa Romaine to celebrate both the founding of *Commerce* and the publication in its first issue of the *Ulysses* selections, Joyce was an honored guest.[10] He had hardly been seated at the table when his hostess's big dog entered and put his paws on Joyce's shoulders. The princess laughed with delight; then, when she understood Joyce was not amused, had the dog removed. Joyce hated dogs, and according to what the Irish writer Michael Sayers once told me, actually kept stones in his pocket to throw at any he met on his walks. Marguerite, the dog-lover, said that her pet was harmless, although she allowed that once it had chased a plumber out the window. "I had to buy the man a new pair of trousers," she laughed. Sylvia Beach, who recounted this incident, says that Joyce shuddered and whispered to Beach, "She's going to have to do the same thing for me."[11]

Later, that summer of 1924, Joyce, impatient for the appearance of the first issue, wrote Sylvia Beach: "What is wrong about *Commerce*? Has that dog, who is so fond of raw posteriors, eaten the first batch?" In a later letter Joyce wondered "why Mr. Eliot had to fly over here to see what Shaun calls the proprietress," a reference to Marguerite. Richard Ellmann, the Joyce authority, didn't wonder; he footnoted Joyce's statement with a bold but erroneous explanation that "Princess di Bassiano was financing Eliot's review the *Criterion*." Ellmann sometimes got his women characters mixed up; perhaps he thought it only natural that Marguerite would bankroll T. S. Eliot, since he was a distant relative, but the *Criterion*'s actual "proprietress" was Viscountess Rothermere. Decades later, perhaps as a back reference, a *New Yorker* review of *Botteghe Oscure* stated that "if Marguerite Caetani did start as a patron, she is now the proprietress of something that shows every sign of becoming a going concern."

Archibald MacLeish, who would become a long and loyal friend of Marguerite's, was one of the few Americans in Paris who took the trouble to read French literature, and it was through this common interest that he met her not long after *Commerce* was started. In the spring of 1925, Archie was delighted that she liked all the things he sent her and a group of his poems appeared in the publication. Typically, as she would later do when running *Botteghe Oscure*, once she found a good poet and a loyal friend she invited him home and pressed him into advisory service.

Through a MacLeish contact, Marguerite attempted to get *Commerce* distributed in Boston, and then got Archie himself to act as a kind of scout for her. MacLeish solicited material from Elinor Wylie, E. E. Cummings, John Dos Passos, and Ernest Hemingway on her behalf. For Hemingway, who sent two stories, things did not go well. The stories were rejected and Archie had to write a disclaimer to any part of that decision: "I do no editorial work for any man including Bassiano. Anything you want to publish I receive and send on . . . Bassiano understands that perfectly."[12] Hemingway still burned, and again MacLeish said he was neither Pappy's agent nor Bassiano's manuscript reader "but just a poor guy who had agreed to get a story from a promising young Author."

The review was very well thought of and Marguerite had effectively become one of the beautiful people of those *années folles*. Nevertheless, she remained curiously unremarked upon even by her close associates in their written reminiscences of those times. Janet Flanner, who signed decades of "Letters from Paris" to the *New Yorker* as Gênet, was well acquainted with Marguerite. In Janet Flanner's *World*, a collection of her *New Yorker* pieces, she says that Marguerite was much revered by French writers and that André Gide often mentioned the Princesse in his journals.

In fact, in four volumes he mentioned her only twice and that in a brief, perfunctory way that is rather chilling: "Lunched the 26th at Versailles at the Princesse de Bassiano's," Gide notes on May 28, 1921, "her auto with Mme Mühlfeld and Paul Valéry already in it came to pick me up. An hour's reading or piano-practice is pleasanter to me than the most sumptuous dinner in the world; this one was exquisite moreover; nothing to say about the conversation." Eight years later the notation is again that the Princesse's motor came to pick him up for a day at Versailles; this time, he noted, he talked with much greater facility than ordinarily. But what the Princesse said, or wore, how she looked, moved, and behaved, he never noted. So, too, Alice Toklas in Rome in the 1950s reports being picked up by the Princess's car for dinner with her—and nothing more.

Of all those luminaries present in Paris in the 1920s, Sylvia Beach in *Shakespeare & Co.* has the most generous recall of Marguerite. Describing George Antheil's *Ballet Mécanique*, the performance of which at the Theatre des Champs Elysées on June 19, 1925, was partially subsidized by Natalie Barney and was one of the *de rigueur* events of the epoch, Beach wrote, "The entire 'Crowd' turned up and packed the big theater. . . . There were the

Joyces in a box. There was our rarely seen T. S. Eliot, so handsome and so elegantly attired, and with him was Princess Bassiano."[13]

Also present was Antheil's good friend Ezra Pound.[14] Being so immersed in the arts, Marguerite could not have avoided being aware of Pound in Paris. If she did not have at least a nodding acquaintance with Pound, her cousin Tom Eliot more than did. In any case, Marguerite would have noticed Ezra that night: the performance with its nine pianos, electric bells, xylophones, loud-speakers, whistles, and a whirring aeroplane propeller sparked a riot when they all started to play and Pound was said by witnesses to have had a heroic part in shouting down the demonstrators so that Antheil's work could continue.

Was Marguerite present a few days later at the Salle Pleyel when Pound's opera *Le Testament* was given its first performance?

It's more than likely that Pound and the Princess had to have crossed paths in Paris during his residence there from 1921 to 1924 when he was involved with editing the *Little Review* and fre-quenting Sylvia Beach's bookstore where everyone met. It was, after all, Pound who got Beach to undertake the publication of the complete *Ulysses*, and he surely knew that an excerpt had appeared in Marguerite's *Commerce*. And yet Pound's copious letters and memoirs make no mention of his countrywoman, not in Paris nor later in Italy.

This was the disconcerting pattern among the writers who knew or benefited from Princess Caetani: at most they mention a pleasant occasion, nice surroundings, good food but leave no trace of the woman in their letters, recollections, diaries, and journals. At Marguerite's death, her half sister Cornelia Chapin recalled how much Marguerite had meant to her in her early days abroad after her own mother had died. Cornelia still remembered how Marguerite's French friends were so amazed at her calm manag-ing of affairs—musical, literary, artistic. But Cornelia's most vivid memory was what a stunning pair Marguerite and Roffredo were: "It was thrilling to go about with them."[15]

By the 1930s, political and economic storm clouds were gathering in Europe and the depression in the United States sharply reduced Marguerite's income. She wrote to Larbaud of her financial burden with *Commerce*: "*Je veux bien et je tien à coeur de faire tout ce que je peux en diminuant toutes mes autres despenses au minimum . . . mais on est frappé de tous les côtes en ce moment.*" Despite her economies, she was forced to give up the review, which ceased publication in 1932, the year Roffredo and Marguerite closed Villa Romaine to return to Italy. She did keep an apartment at 4 rue du Cirque in Paris with its Vuillard panels in the charming, informal drawing room where she received her many callers on her annual returns, summer through fall.

Sylvia Beach, for one, noted the departure: "Marguerite Caetani was much admired by her French writer friends for her taste, intelligence, tact, and benevolence. They were quite jealous of Rome when it snatched her from Paris."

Don Leone, Roffredo's elder brother, had become a noted Arabist who was engaged in the monumental work of writing *The Annals of Islam*, nine centuries of history in ten volumes. He succeeded his father, "one of the last representative patrician types" of Italian nobility, commented the English ambassador Sir James Rennell Rodd when Don Onorato died in September 1917.[16] Don Leone's union with Princess Vittoria Colonna was not a happy one and from it was born just one child, a mentally infirm son, Onorato, who would only temporarily succeed to his father's title.

Disaffected with the fascist regime and also with a failed marriage, Don Leone moved to British Columbia in 1925 where he took up residence and became a British subject. When he died on Christmas Day, 1935, Roffredo and Marguerite became the heads of the Caetani clan. They were already established in Rome at Palazzo Caetani, and there ensues, as in her early years abroad, another decade of silence. What could it have been like, in Rome, at the height of the fascist regime? One small allusion to what might have occupied Marguerite is found in a letter to her sister Katherine when she mentions providing lavender to perfume manufacturers. It was known, too, that she had introduced peach trees from American stock at Ninfa to produce income for maintaining the vast gardens. Her children grew to adulthood and while Lelia showed interest in painting, Camillo's talents are not known. He was at Harvard for a year just before the Second World War broke out and is remembered by his American relatives as a dashing, handsome blade as were all the Caetani men. He loved being in the states and visited his Chapin relatives in New York and the Biddles in Philadelphia. According to his aunt Katherine, he was extremely fond of his uncle Francis Biddle to whom he emphasized his love of America by saying he'd rather drive a cab in New York than return to his title and heritage. It is said by more than a few that during his year at Harvard a love affair with a Boston socialite produced a child he never officially recognized. Was Camillo brusquely whisked back to the family seat without finishing at Harvard to avoid scandal as well as to fulfill military duty? In the end, duty and family prevailed and Camillo was back in Rome at the end of 1939.

Then came the emotionally trying war years when Marguerite, American by birth, but Italian by marriage and with Italian children, must have been sorely tested. As Harold Acton, the elder of the Anglo-Florentine expatriate world put it, their world became despondent and divided, deeply troubled about their Italian friends or family connections who loathed the Axis powers yet were obliged to do their patriotic duty. This was the dilemma of divided loyalties experienced and recorded by Iris Origo in her *War in Val d'Orcia*, and by Vittoria Colonna, Marguerite's supremely chatty and socializing sister-in-law, in her second book, *Sparkle, Distant World*. The Caetanis had been leaders of Italian government since the country's unification in 1870; for them the question of loyalty was to Italy their country, not to the regime of Il Duce.

Vittoria does not tell quite all in her two books of memoirs, but she does recount her staggering social life among kings and kaisers and such, gives the history of the House of Caetani, and an impression of what it was like to live in the palace on the Street of Dark Shops ("gloomy . . . melancholy . . . grim . . . forbidding . . . stingy heating . . . separate bedrooms . . . late meals"), and what it was like in the period of the fascist regime and its downfall when so many of Rome's aristocrats had to go in hiding from the Germans.

In contrast to gad-about Vittoria with her awesome progresses through Europe, America, Africa, and Asia Minor, Marguerite seemed content to reside in the big, square, graceless Palazzo Caetani where the family name is cut in huge capitals over the portal. The years from 1932 on were years of domesticity, with children and the Ninfa garden to attend to, interspersed with quiet visits to Switzerland or France. Whereas Vittoria mentions her various encounters with Il Duce and her fascinated impression of him despite her disdain for his entourage, Marguerite was cold to Vittoria and refused to speak to an openly pro-fascist sister-in-law, Donna Cora. Marguerite's admiration was for Don Leone whom she esteemed as a great scholar and pitied as a man craving affection; she was closer to him than to any of her other in-laws. According to Schuyler Chapin, Marguerite was known to have anti-fascist views, something that must have provided great tension in the family given her brother-in-law Gelasio's very pro-Duce stand and the Caetani tradition of being foremost in doing their duty so that her own son was fighting for the regime.

Marguerite Caetani, the champion of writers, left no published writing of her own. Missing are her thoughts on the arts and literature, or even diary notes replete with famous names and inside glimpses of artistic and social life in Europe between the wars along with her own experience of the wars. In those years, if you weren't fascist, you had no public life; instead of a journal, Marguerite left questions to ponder: did she speak openly as an anti-fascist or keep her views to herself, and what did that mean in a family awash in internal as well as political feuds between old-line liberals, fascist sympathizers, and a socialist deputy to Parliament? Did she meet Ezra Pound during his long residence in Italy from 1925 to 1945, and how did she view his open support of fascism?

The cruel deceptions and betrayals with which Italian officers and troops were thrown into the ignominious invasion of Albania, a campaign they never understood and for which they were ill-equipped, without adequate clothing, supplies, or weapons, was part of a cynical plan meant to provoke war with Greece. Their slaughter was assured and was devastatingly reported by American war correspondent John T. Whitaker, who called Mussolini's attack on Albania one of the most brutal and cynical aggressions in history. In his 1943 book about the war, *We Cannot Escape History*, Whitaker tells of his last meeting with his dearest Italian friend, Camillo Caetani:

> On his last night in Rome, before going off to join his regiment, Prince Caetani came to my house for a cocktail.
>
> "Hating Fascism and your German ally, how can you go off to fight?"
>
> "It's a purely personal matter with me. I have come to hate Fascism, yes. These Fascists have made me ashamed of every drop of Italian blood in my veins. But I have got to go. I have got to prove to myself that under fire I will behave like a Caetani."
>
> Camillo of the laughing eyes and quick wit did act like a man. He showed the lion-like courage of the uncle who beat an Austrian army in 1917. But his fascist soldiers let him

bleed to death in no man's land. Not one had the courage to crawl out and drag in the wounded tenente. I know. I read his colonel's report in the Italian War Office.

It was a doubly unnecessary death had there been any organized medical service with the Italian army. Camillo's relatives still speak of the "mysterious circumstances" of his death. It's been said that Marguerite asked her brother-in-law, Francis Biddle, to investigate Camillo's death through U.S. secret services. Did she also try to uncover the story of Camillo's child, to ascertain if she had, in fact, an American grandchild? Why did she never return to the United States?

These are heavy questions. The posing of them renders ever more complex, more profound, and more transcendent the woman who avoided the foreground, the factual daily record, and any figuring or precise accounting in order to keep to the realm of some remote, ideal world. Poetry was more real to her than society; shadings and suggestion more agreeable than blunt full exposure. Perforce she kept no diary: the vanity of documenting herself in order to ensure her prominence and position was not her way. She honored and believed in the Artist.

These lines from Theodore Roethke, the American poet she most esteemed, could have been written for her:

Too much reality can be a dazzle, a surfeit;
    too close immediacy an exhaustion.

Another of her poets, the Austrian Hugo von Hofmannsthal, responded thus to her notable charm: "It is an exquisite pleasure to think of you. You surround yourself with poets and artists, and the air around you remains very pure and very clear, with no shadow of snobbishness. You talk to dogs as one should talk to dogs, you talk to plants as it is fitting to talk to plants, you talk to poets as one should talk to poets—and you remain yourself, of an unfailing grace. You are admirable."[17]

Every life has a plot structure or narrative and beneath it, if one probes—as at a piñata, trying for the contact to spill out the secret contents—is the underlying myth that informs and shapes that life. Every life has its interest, depth, color, highlight of conflict along with the grey tones of banality, commonplaceness. Some reveal the composition in too-bright detail; others keep it in penumbra as did Marguerite Caetani.

The decade of her life when she lived in a fascist society so alien to her heritage and so devastating in her personal life is when one can sympathize most deeply with the dilemma of her divided loyalties. She must have recoiled from Pound's treasonous broadcasts from Rome in those years. Pound's mad allegiance to fascism and his anti-Semitism is too well documented to be disputed. His letters addressed to Il Duce, signed "with devoted homage," were recovered by American forces in Italy in 1945.[18] Attached to his correspondence to Mussolini were memos from Italian officials stating that Pound's books clearly demonstrated a friendly feeling for fascism.

Pound even tried to weave a tenuous connection with Iris Origo through references to her uncle, Bronson Cutting, a U.S. senator. In 1934, Pound mentioned him when he wrote Mussolini: "Two faint glimmers of hope exist in the United States Senate. I haven't yet received the Congressional Record containing Cutting's speech but it seems that he is beginning to see the light." Both uncle and niece would have been horrified at the distorted interpretation made by Pound of the senator's words in a speech in Congress on January 27 in regard to an amendment to the Gold Reserve Act of 1934. Pound's arguments on the monetary system were not only muddled in themselves, they were written in an "incomprehensible" Italian, as the official noted when he sent it on to Mussolini adding that it was clear that the author (Pound) was mentally unbalanced.

There had to have been many complex strands of conflicted feelings and ambiguity during that period of Marguerite's silence: her brother-in-law, the handsome Prince Gelasio, was one of the first Roman nobles in December 1920 to enroll himself among the original Fascisti. He arrived in the United States in late 1922 as Italy's ambassador and, as reported in the *New York Times*, addressed admirers at the pier by identifying Fascismo with "a patriotic movement" to sweep Italy clean of Bolshevism, anarchy, and "all the old dusty trash which hindered the work of redemption and reconstruction." He identified Mussolini as "a remarkable man who has proved part of what he is capable of doing and not for Italy alone, but for the good of Europe. He is backed by all there is best in the country."[19]

Gelasio Caetani's early sympathies for the fascist regime may have worn thin. He was a compelling figure, a strikingly handsome man of versatile abilities who never married and was remembered for his legendary feats in war and peace in an extensive obituary in the *New York Times* when he died in 1934 at age fifty-seven. He was not only a diplomat of repute and a brilliant engineer who showed the fascist government how to reclaim the Pontine Marshes (large tracts of which, including Ninfa, belonged to the Caetani), but he was also a devoted historian of his illustrious family, the restorer of Ninfa and their Castle at Sermoneta. Gelasio, who had been given Ninfa as his share of the ducal properties when the huge holding was broken up by his brother Leone, left it in his will to his nephew Camillo, confident that the title would be carried on by that last male descendant of the Caetanis.

Marguerite had described as "sort of anti-fascist" Roffredo's opera *The Sunny Isle*, which was successfully produced in German in Basel in 1950. Incredibly, it had opened in Rome in 1943 during the peak of the war as *L'isola del sole*. Described by Roffredo as a "musical novelette" of lovers finding happiness on the Isle of Capri, it must have been cleverly disguised to have had any sort of anti-fascist message get past the censor. Roffredo was the librettist as well as the composer and might have managed some undetectable subtleties. Or perhaps the title alone and love story plot was enough to make it seem innocuous. Still, the idea of the opera is almost bizarre given the war, the death of Camillo, the privations and persecutions all around them. What did Marguerite mean by "sort of anti-fascist"? The reviewer of the Basel production evidently saw nothing in it but what he describes as exciting and grotesque scenes in the first two acts reminiscent of Italian comic opera along with "great melodic pictures in the epilogue."[20]

As was the case for Iris Origo, whose background and marriage to an Italian noble closely paralleled Marguerite's, they stood with their Italian husbands, while suffering the internal contest between loyalty to the country of birth and heritage, or to the adopted land of their marriage and their children. Vittoria Colonna in 1938 wrote in her diary: "I suppose England and Italy will be on opposite sides. Well, that would be the end of my life; I couldn't bear it."[21] As an Italian she owed loyalty to her country but, with English blood, she felt that all her heart went out to the England she loved so well. She fully documents her wretchedness at such conflicted feelings. Marguerite, who described her sister-in-law to Francis Biddle as "a horrible fascist," does not record hers. Vittoria also chronicled the ceremony at which she, along with the Queen and other members of court, at Mussolini's behest, dropped their gold wedding rings into an urn to be melted down for the war effort. Iris Origo had contributed hers; my surmise is that Marguerite did not. Vittoria notes in her diary the day U.S. troops entered Rome: "As an American, Marguerite was wild with joy."[22]

Even before the war the great and illustrious *Domus Caietana* had become a house divided against itself. Vittoria, revealing all, tells how the old duke had never forgiven her husband Leone, his eldest son, his socialist politics. Though at the old duke's death, Leone inherited the title and became head of the family, the will favored the second son, Roffredo, who was his mother's favorite. "Violent quarrels broke out in the family, between the Dowager Duchess, my husband, his three brothers and his sister, that were quite medieval in their fierceness," Vittoria noted.

At her marriage, when she became part of the Caetani family, Vittoria found them, as she put it, on a very original footing: "They all lived in the same house, but most of them were not on speaking terms; however, they all kissed whenever they met." Both Leone and Vittoria disliked the gloomy Palazzo Caetani where, especially in winter, one groped one's way through the dim rooms. They bought Palazzo Orsini for their residence and left the family palace to Roffredo and Marguerite. Although some of the interior gloom was lifted when the shops were razed and a broadened Via delle Botteghe Oscure let in more light, still in the early 1950s when the young American poet James Merrill, whose work appeared in *Botteghe Oscure*, was invited to a dinner party there, he found it "hard, in the talk-filled dimness, either to hear or to see as much as I would have liked."[23]

If Marguerite and Roffredo had no use for fascism, they nonetheless had displayed the conduct that went with their rank and privilege by not deserting their country and by staying with the working people who were their dependents. During the difficult period of the invasion, the Caetanis shepherded into the walled castle and courtyard of Sermoneta whole farm families, livestock, chickens, and all—like a kermess in a Dutch painting. I happened to meet, during my visit to Ninfa, a school teacher who, as a boy, had been one of those refugees. He described the fierce hunger they all endured when, as he said, there was nothing to eat, not even grass. And in Rome, in Palazzo Caetani, Roffredo and Marguerite sheltered two escaped Polish noblewomen related to him through his grandmother, along with Vittoria Colonna and her English maid against whom the German occupying forces had put out warrants of arrest for her being, as Vittoria put it, a member "of the educated and cultured classes." Harold Acton's American mother was arrested by the fascist police and held in prison as were other English and Americans who had lived for decades in Italy.

In early December 1940, Marguerite had written her sister Katherine in Washington that Camillo was seeing action in Albania "right in the thick of it."[24] Circumspectly (because of censorship) but ominously she adds, "Now I hope soon he may have a leave—Oh, if I could talk with you an hour, what I could tell you!" Some think that because Marguerite had access to American diplomats in Rome and was in touch during the war years with her highly placed brother-in-law Attorney General Biddle in Washington, she drew Il Duce's enmity and for this Camillo was deliberately ordered into "the thick of it."[25] On January 2, 1941, Camillo was reported missing; ten days later his death was confirmed. The terrible fact of Camillo's death (he was found with a letter from Marguerite at his side) devastated his family.[26] Marguerite's heartrending sorrow found expression in letters to her sisters. She wrote Katherine that only to her and Cornelia could she disclose the depth of the dark, lonely hole in her heart, cry all her tears, and express all the bitter feelings she felt.

While in Nuremberg as a judge for the Nazi war criminal trials, Francis Biddle visited the Caetanis in Rome. In letters home to Katherine he described Roffredo as old, stooped, and very suppressed, Lelia suffering from jaundice, while Marguerite was "handsome and well, very affectionate." But in his memoirs Biddle describes Marguerite as "shut in on herself" after her son's death. Again to his wife: "[She] doesn't want to be alone with me, and I suspect, with anyone. She draws in on herself and faces no intimacy." She asked him almost nothing about her American family after the first meeting and began to seem to him profoundly lonely. When he was leaving to return to Nuremberg, she said she was sorry there had been little chance for them to be alone together—yet, Biddle noted, she had asked people for every lunch, every tea, every dinner! As he wrote Katherine, "Her idea of intimacy is having small dinners."

After Camillo's death, Marguerite was never heard to mention him again and no photos of him were ever in view in her homes. Roffredo wrote a note to a Chapin nephew in New York thanking him for his words of sympathy and saying that the misfortune had ruined their lives since all hopes had been centered on their only boy. "You have been much in my thoughts," T. S. Eliot had written to Marguerite on Camillo's death, "and I knew that your loss would not become easier. I do not pretend that such a loss ever does; only in time perhaps it is simply like learning to live without one's eyesight, or crippled. One just makes do and carries on the rest of life. I don't even maintain that faith makes loss easier; it just, if I may say so, improves the quality of the suffering and makes it sometimes fruitful instead of useless."[27] Marguerite was a believer, as intensely as was Eliot, which was why he could write her in such terms, and her suffering was fruitful.

Life went on. Marguerite kept busy distributing children's food to their peasants from American Relief to Italy; she kept in touch with her sisters to whom she expresses great affection and to whom she remained deeply devoted, longing for their letters and company as well as things in short supply: nasal jelly, tooth powder, coffee, sugar, Pond's cold cream, chocolate tablets with vitamins, cotton stockings, hot-water bottles, oil colors for Lelia, and, above all, literature. The Biddles came to visit and among Katherine's papers is the program for a concert organized at the Castle of Sermoneta by Roffredo. Marguerite went to Paris for her sister

Cornelia's sculpture exhibit. They all sent mutual friends back and forth to each other.

The glittering characters from the 1920s had become less than fabled beings leading enchanted lives—there is loss and pain, the shattering of dreams for the future, regret and disillusionment. But Marguerite had stamina. Scornful of Rome society with its tiaras and feather adornments, she stuck to her tweed suits, prim white blouse, and sensible shoes. She was determined, impulsive but once her mind was made up there was no turning back.

In the war's aftermath she rebounded from her personal tragedies imbued with a noble mission and conviction: she wanted to raise Italy in world opinion from the ignominy of the fascist period, to showcase Italian writers who had been silenced during the regime, and to do so in an international review. Soon she wrote Katherine of being tempted to try a sort of *Commerce* again, but this time prose and poetry in French, Italian, and English; she was suffocated, she said, by the "dry-as-dust" existing publications which were all politics, criticism, or history. She longed for "some light and air and a bit of phantasy." Not only would she help restore Italian letters but also help to insure the open communications between nations and the good will that would avoid future conflict through cultural exchange. The literature in her review would be international in scope and would, above all, represent the young, untried, obscure writer. *Botteghe Oscure* would be dedicated to the proposition that literature—as all Art—exists in a world beyond political imperatives, narrow nationalism, and boundaries.

As for Ezra Pound's clash with Marguerite's American family, it was ironic circumstance that Katherine Biddle was on the Library of Congress advisory panel of the Fellows in American Literature in 1949 when they awarded Ezra Pound the first Bollingen Prize (renamed by him the Bubble-Gum Award) while he was confined to the mental hospital of St. Elizabeth's in Washington.

Pound biographer Humphrey Carpenter reported that Katherine was furious that Ezra should be considered at all, and talked to her husband who felt similarly and wrote to the Librarian of Congress, Luther H. Evans, that he "recommended strongly against the decision."

Francis Biddle's *In Brief Authority* gives this account: "The Fellows decided to honor Ezra Pound with the award for *The Pisan Cantos*, which had recently been published. But since several could not attend the meeting—Katherine and I were in Rome—it was decided to take a vote by mail. Katherine voted with one other of her associates against the award."[28] Katherine and fellow poet Karl Shapiro voted for William Carlos Williams, the others voted for Pound and one abstained.

Pound himself was so deluded as to tell Archibald MacLeish that had Katherine Chapin not been married to Francis Biddle, she might have supported him. In a letter to MacLeish, referring to a recent visit to St. Elizabeth's by the Attorney General's brother George whom he had known in Italy, Pound wrote, "Geo Biddle said his sis-in-law was afraid to come in [to St. Elizabeth's] cause she thought I wd/ be so rude about her legitime."[29] The reasoning is so bizarre, it can only be understood in light of Pound's whole history of believing that even his treason was not treason. Eventually Marguerite would get in her own memorable last word on *il miglior fabbro*.

Marguerite had kept rank and remained a loyal Caetani, still devoted in her way and in her separate quarters to Roffredo, their courtesy and common interests in the arts holding together a marriage that had become ever more distant. There are almost no details of their life together; she is said to have much earlier "closed out" Roffredo from her emotional life when his affairs with other women became flagrant. One can sense in Marguerite the rigor of a Catholic believer made even more intransigent by New World puritanism. Tolerating infidelities was the way things were done in

Italy where the talent for staying married, come what may, and especially for those of a high social standing, prevailed in that period before divorce. The woman who was shocked by Joyce but let the artist overrule her does not give way in private matters. She makes one of her rare mentions of Roffredo in an early letter to Theodore Roethke when she explains she's been terribly busy as she helped her husband in the preparation and organization of an old castle as a summer colony for poor children of Rome. Yet she remained always appreciative of Roffredo's music, approaching Samuel Barber in the late 1950s about having her husband's opera *Hypatia*—"a most beautiful work"—produced in the states, it not having been seen since Weimar in 1926.

And she had a consuming new interest—her *Botteghe Oscure*. When she said that she wanted to launch it in several languages, everyone, including cousin Tom Eliot who was experienced in editing a journal, "sat on her" and said she was mad—it was quite difficult enough to make a go of a single-language journal. Two other women had founded literary reviews in Italy in the immediate postwar years; Elena Croce Craveri, daughter of the eminent philosopher Benedetto Croce, started *Arethusa* in Naples and novelist Alba De Cespedes launched *Mercurio* in Rome. Both were well received; both perished for lack of funding in that difficult time.

Marguerite was willful and determined and also rich enough to make *Botteghe Oscure* happen. The first issue, Spring 1948, was an all-Italian issue. It included Eugenio Montale's marvelous poem "L'Anguilla" (which Robert Lowell snaked into his version, "The Eel"), poems by Sandro Penna and Attilio Bertolucci, and stories by Guglielmo Petroni and Giorgio Bassani who became Marguerite's Italian editor. That initial issue was the only one published in Naples because, as Bassani was to recall, its publisher, Riccardo Ricciardi, entrusted its hand-setting and printing to an establishment that used inexperienced war orphans (ten to fifteen year old ex-*sciuscià*, shoeshine boys, more suitable for a Rossellini film than for composing a literary review). That issue was filled with errors and was redone in 1949 in Rome by the printer Luigi De Luca, who became Marguerite's mainstay from then on.

The new review was in the form of an octavo volume of several hundred pages and, in the plain style of its predecessor *Commerce*, rather severe in look with its plain beige cover, brown Roman lettering, and Roman numerals for issue numbers. It sold in 1948 for 500 lire, in 1949 for 700 lire, and in England at 8 shillings the copy. Each issue of the biannual publication was called a *quaderno*, after the French cahier. The inside-back cover advised it would come out twice a year, spring and fall, and that submissions could be sent to the editorial office at 32 Via Botteghe Oscure; half of the review would be reserved for Italian literature and the other half dedicated to foreign literature in its original language, but heavily weighted to work in English. Without an English-language market, Marguerite realized early on when she made great efforts to obtain distribution in the United States, readership and influence would be too limited.

The publication had no advertisements, announcements, illustrations, or even, at first, contributors' notes. Not until 1950 did Marguerite Caetani's name appear as publisher, followed by that of editor Giorgio Bassani. In 1951, Marguerite wrote her sister Katherine that she was working like three devils on *Botteghe* "which swells and swells in spite of me." Eventually an issue would billow to almost five hundred pages and its top circulation would approach 5,000 copies.

Following her first issue, Marguerite wrote to Theodore Roethke, whose first book of poetry she admired enormously, explaining *Botteghe Oscure* as an Italian review but each number having important foreign contributors and many previously unpublished works as well. The review was to circulate outside Italy in Switzerland, France, England, and the U.S. and was mainly to help young writers, especially poets, get known outside their country. She was happy to have his contribution and was touched by his desire to help with the review since it was run almost entirely by her and young Bassani with a bookshop as general agent. "The review is a great success in Italy," she exulted, "they've never had anything quite like it before."

"I do hope for the great honor and joy of having your name . . . in this coming number," she wrote E. E. Cummings early on and indeed got him for *Botteghe Oscure* II. Thanking him for his delightful poems she hoped her check (sent prepublication, and probably for a generous $300.00, the sum she sent Theodore Roethke for "Give Way Ye Gates" at a time when the big glossies like *Harper's Bazaar* offered only $75 a poem) was sufficient. She was always afraid it wouldn't be, "especially with celebrities."

Please, she implored Robert Lowell and others, send your poems! and send advice and the names of young, unknown poets, all of which would be precious to her. At the same time she warned that she was terribly anti-critics and -criticism.

The second issue, in addition to Italian writers, featured English language contributors including W. H. Auden, Kathleen Raine, Walter de la Mare, C. Day Lewis, Hayden Carruth, Leonie Adams, Mariannne Moore, William Carlos Williams, and Edith Sitwell. The copyright page carried a notice of gratitude to the foreign poets and writers who, with their collaboration, had effectively shown their understanding and adherence to the principles guiding the review. Word of mouth was its early publicity.

In the case of young Alfred Chester whose writing first appeared in *Botteghe Oscure*, according to his friend Edward Field, Marguerite "was able to get him a Guggenheim Fellowship by arranging for Lionel Trilling and other famous writers to sponsor his application." When Trilling's letter of recommendation was not strong enough, Caetani returned it and demanded "more enthusiastic sponsorship."[30]

Marguerite wrote to Carson McCullers and invited her to visit, entertaining McCullers and her husband in Rome and at Ninfa. She welcomed her writers wherever she was—at the palace in Rome, her Paris flat, or in the country at Ninfa and once complained she couldn't understand why they would bypass her (including Ted Roethke on his honeymoon) to follow Truman Capote and troop off to Ischia instead. Gracious as a hostess, Marguerite in her correspondence was always in a hurry—"in a pitiful hurry"—but she always sent her love. It is precisely in the routine correspondence concerning *Botteghe Oscure* that she emerges as a warm-hearted and generous backer of the writers—but especially the poets!—whom she adores. Kinsman Eliot did call on her in Rome with his new bride Valerie. At tea, when he dropped a canapé, retrieved it, and was about to pop it in his mouth, Marguerite was treated to the sight of Valerie lightly slapping his hand and saying, "Tommy, not off the floor!"[31]

E. E. Cummings came to Rome in 1951 and on his departure, Marguerite wrote him to suggest a cure for his arthritis and to thank him for the gift he had made her of Ezra Pound's *Collected Letters* (1950). "How generous of you to let Ezra share your travels!" Cummings responded (mockingly?) to her when she wrote that the book would accompany her to Lausanne. Pound, when asked in a prewar interview who were some of the day's great poets said he would name only one—E. E. Cummings. Cummings, in turn, was one of Pound's staunchest supporters.

She took the occasion of her reply to Cummings to mock in her own way. She enjoyed Pound's *Letters* in great part, she said, because she, too, was engaged in editing a little review, but found that she also understood still better why she never cared much about Pound as a poet since "a poet for me is a being so high so apart that a sort of miscellaneous creature like that . . . well you know what I mean if anyone does." Cummings surely knew what she meant: the most devastating thing that Marguerite could have said was not that Pound was a fascist and traitor, but too miscellaneous a creature to reach the heights as a real poet.

Cummings had contributed monetarily to Pound's defense and may not have known of Marguerite's loss of a son in the war. And other, more complex factors are involved: there was not only Pound's treachery during the war, but also his attack on the very system, capitalism, which had given her the wherewithal for Europe, for indulging her penchant for the arts, for founding and supporting two costly prestige reviews. In attacking the monetary system of their *bien-être*, he attacked the very heart of the Caetani, the Chapins, the Biddles.

At the start, Marguerite's English connections rallied rather more heartily to her new publication than did her American compatriots. Reviews of *Quaderno* II and III appeared in the *Times Literary Supplement* for August 19, 1949. As a bi-annual anthology of prose and verse, it was ranked with the best of valuable international periodicals. And it was noted that *Botteghe Oscure* did not reveal its publisher's or editor's names, only that its own name was taken from the street where it was edited. Thus a certain mystique was created: whence did this ungainly but packed magazine originate? Who was behind it?

It becomes clear that when *Botteghe Oscure* was anonymous, it received more lavish praise, for once Marguerite was revealed as patron-publisher with a strong editing role, reviews became crankier. By 1955 an ad for *Botteghe Oscure* appears in the *Times Literary Supplement* with the caption "Edited by Marguerite Caetani," and accompanied by lavish blurbs of endorsement. But alongside this ad a review begins, "Swollen with spoil from the Continent and the New World, *Botteghe Oscure* looms strangely on the English literary scene."

Botteghe Oscure had started on a high note of editorial purpose: to supply a wide variety of work to an international readership. The line-up of famous names continued: Edith Sitwell, W. H.

Auden, Paul Valéry, Vasco Pratolini, Umberto Saba, Tennessee Williams, William Carlos Williams, Stephen Spender, Elsa Morante, Natalia Ginzburg, and Mariane Moore. And so it went—not an issue without some established splendor to add weight to the unknowns in whom Marguerite took especial delight. But with *Quaderno* X, Fall 1952, there is a caveat from the *TLS*: the issue does not merit unreserved praise; there are too many contributors who display immaturity in values and discipline, and "there is a limit to the amount of private fantasies" in which authors can self-indulge. The reviewer notes that the emotional maturity of contemporary Italian writers such as Calvino or Bassani was missed in many of the English and American writers. However, by publishing *Botteghe Oscure* Marguerite Caetani had done more than Mussolini to elevate Rome to the world stage.

In the United States, poet Louise Bogan, writing in the *New Yorker* issue of September 19, 1953, gave a judicious, balanced account of how *Botteghe Oscure* had become an important factor in the total cultural picture. Its chief value, she felt, was its quiet and steady pressure against any tendency toward provincialism in either European or American writers.

Through the years of *Botteghe Oscure*'s existence, Marguerite was always enormously touched and grateful when people like Theodore Roethke, Stanley Young, or Niccolò Tucci helped her out. For Eugene Walter's help she was constantly beholden. And if, as Roethke wrote her, he was bucked up by his appearance in her review, she replied that she was even more so at the privilege of having him there.

She was to become, according to George Plimpton, who was among the callers at rue du Cirque in the 1950s when he was starting his own *Paris Review, l'esprit* of that time. Often she was to summon Eugene Walter by *pneumatique* to meet Carson McCullers, or Alfred Chester, or whatever writer was passing through Paris while she was there. Yet, for the most part her writers are silent about her. Delmore Schwartz, did mention how Princess Caetani's acceptance of an excerpt from his wife Elizabeth Pollett's novel saved their lives after two parking fines halved their weekly income; and he recorded in his notebook a cryptic scenario of a projected "Pajamas Opera" in which he assigned Marguerite a peculiarly weighted role—"choice of man versus career. Pathetic answer." How to decipher that cryptic notation?

Apart from solicitations and appreciative comments on their work, Marguerite herself does not have too much to say about the literati. When she does, it is a brief aside in her hurried business correspondence to Eugene Walter: she's terrified Carolyn Kizer might turn up in Rome with her beau; it's such a bore Roger Straus and wife are coming to Rome since they're both so disgustingly rich; Carson McCullers is a pathetic figure who must feel great guilt over her husband's suicide since she was the one who left him; Ted Roethke is the greatest contemporary poet in America—but so wild!

In 1950, James Laughlin, publisher of New Directions, became Marguerite's distributor in the United States for the *Anthology of New Italian Writers* culled from the first five issues of *Botteghe Oscure*. He was well aware how difficult, almost impossible it was to get a good book distributor to take on a magazine, especially if it was eccentric in format and presented problems of importation through customs.

The problem of a U.S. distributor for *Botteghe Oscure* was always a great strain for Marguerite and took up enormous energy and time as she penned dozens of letters, trying even to secure advice from her American writers. "How I long to discharge my decisions onto you," she informs poor Lowell, and on New Year's Eve of 1951 she writes him that she will try Farrar, Straus, although she is horrified that Roger Straus wants to put a price of $2 per copy on the review. "Is he dotty?" she wonders.

Farrar, Straus distributed *Botteghe Oscure* from Spring 1953 through Fall 1955. It proved to be an unhappy alliance on both sides: Marguerite wanted to do it her way but Roger Straus, writing about the problems of handling *Botteghe Oscure* to Frances Steloff of the Gotham Book Mart in New York where it was stocked, was puzzled by Marguerite's demands and felt that the time and energy and detail that would be necessary to meet them would be absolutely killing.

Frances Steloff, who was of Marguerite's generation and literary persuasion, took a less commercial view to stocking the review; Steloff, like Sylvia Beach before her, believed in little reviews and was a punctual and precise merchandiser in her correspondence with Marguerite, whom she addressed as Lady Caetani. Steloff's first order of *Botteghe Oscure* was for twenty-five copies; then one hundred which grew to be three hundred. In time Farrar, Straus was distributing one thousand copies to the book trade at the then high price of $2.50 a copy.

Marguerite was unhappy with Roger Straus, at that time considered the cockiest young publisher in town as he drove his open Mercedes convertible to shabby-chic quarters on Union Square. By 1955 she was asking Eugene if she shouldn't "chuck" Farrar, Straus. She had wanted them to do an anthology of prose, then later one of poetry whereas they wanted both in one volume of no more than 350 pages—a drastic reduction, in her mind, and, worse, a falsification since they would include only the big names without any of the young writers she had discovered. Exasperated, she let off steam to Frances Steloff, the faithful stocker of *Botteghe Oscure*: "I chucked the Anthology after all that work and worry as it would have had nothing of the letter or spirit of *Botteghe Oscure*. . . . I could have made a marvelous lawsuit!! . . . What propoganda for *Botteghe Oscure* . . . I would appear as the defender of the interests of the young and unknown etc. etc."

Marguerite continued to try all the leads that turned up and appealed in turn to Knopf, Viking, Doubleday, Scribners. Though she had once said she was afraid of small houses, she formed an agreement with Noonday Press which distributed Spring 1956 through Spring 1959; the last two issues were distributed through Wesleyan University Press.

It wasn't only distributors, writers could be problematic too. With the time and effort Dylan Thomas spent writing Marguerite long, contrite, self-flagellating letters of apology and repeated requests for money, he might well have given her the completed *Under Milk Wood* that he had persuaded her to pay for in its entirety with the promise that he'd finish part two rapidly. She received only part one, published in *Botteghe Oscure* IX, Spring 1952 as "Llareggub, A Piece for Radio Perhaps." When, after infinite patience and after all her payments, she asked an intermediary to implore Dylan to send her the rest, he sent back word that he'd rather let her down than himself. He then sold the remainder elsewhere. Still, Marguerite's faith in Dylan the poet never wavered and, grieving at his death in November 1953, she movingly commemorated him in the Spring 1954 issue of *Botteghe Oscure*.

James Agee's *gran rifiuto* was a noble and exceptional refusal to Marguerite's offers of financial support. He advised her to give her help where it would bring the best return, i.e., to a single person. "I wish I thought I could be helped," he wrote her. "My situation is that I have a wife and two children . . . I'm beyond the kind of help which for a single person can make so much of the difference."

Sometimes Marguerite got her own comeuppance. Quite ingenuously she had written Cummings that though she loved five of his seven submitted poems, two "I don't love so much and I thought perhaps you might not mind if I only printed those I love very much and perhaps before Feb. 15 you might have an inspiration to write two others equally lovely." Cummings replied that feeling as he did that his seven poems constituted "one shallwesay nation indivisible," he had no choice but to remove them all from her consideration and return "the more than generous largess" she had paid him. She instantly replied begging him to forgive her frightful faux pas and to allow her the privilege of reparation.

Marguerite Caetani was not a remote patron-in-the-skies. She worked nine to ten hours a day on *Botteghe Oscure* reading manuscripts, doing correspondence, proofs, arrangements, paying bills. She had no office, no secretary; all her correspondence was written by hand, in a hurry, and with no copies made. She corresponded constantly—on Easter Sunday, Christmas Day, or New Year's Eve. Occasionally, with unabashed self-deprecation, she'd call herself a pig for not having written sooner, or *stupidissima* for forgetting to mention something. Understandably, she forgot details or repeated herself, was uncertain of paid-up subscriptions, accounts, who'd received copies or not, if her editors had been paid or not. For a whole year she forgot to pay the faithful Eugene who, being a true Southern gentleman, didn't remind her but managed to survive barely on his book royalties until someone mentioned to her that he was having a hard time paying the rent.

She had her own editing style and reservations which must have been apparent to Roethke quite early, for he hopes words like "bitch" or references to "Lesbianism" won't offend her; she rejects a poem of his about T. S. Eliot and later another from a young poet, Richard Selig, although she finds it excellent and returns it with regret. But Eliot is a distant cousin, she explains, and what's more important, a friend. Likewise, some passages of Roethke's prose piece "The Last Class" are left out because they mention friends. Roethke's "Song for the Squeeze-Box" was rejected with what he called "pious horror by the Princess" and he speculated on the reason with William Carlos Williams's wife Flossie: "Maybe it's too coarse; maybe money's a sacred subject, I don't know."[32] Indeed, each of the ten stanzas ends with the word "money," as in getting rid of it or drinking it up.

Despite Eliot's warning, Marguerite had found the way to publish as she wished. She managed because of the hard work and devotion of her minimal staff, Eugene in Paris then Rome ("your interest and enthusiasm seem too good to be true," she wrote him); Giorgio Bassani, her Italian editor who made all the choices of Italian authors; the meticulous attentiveness of her excellent printer Luigi De Luca; and the help of friends. Elena Croce Craveri brought to Bassani's attention a manuscript from an unknown in Sicily that turned out to be Lampedusa's *The Leopard* and first saw print with Chapter One published in *Botteghe Oscure* XXI.

Marguerite could be difficult; she begged "Dearest Ted" to find her new poets and when he had his students Carolyn Kizer and James Wright send her their work, she found the former "slightly exuberant" for her taste and the latter "not quite quite" although he soon became first-rate when he evinced a strong interest in translating René Char of whom Marguerite was the great champion. She was jealous of her prerogatives and wanted everything first, always lamenting when she saw one of Roethke's or Lowell's poems appear elsewhere. She chided when they failed to keep in touch: "silence . . . silence . . . silence," she wrote to Roethke of his longueurs between letters.

He, on his part, when he sent poems to Jackson Mathews rather than to her, wrote, "But please, for Jesus' sake, don't mention to Marguerite." She was generous, but with that went her sense of privilege, of being entitled to demand what she wanted. She didn't like her poets being reprinted in anthologies and neglecting to mention having first appeared in *Botteghe Oscure*. She wrote hastily to Elizabeth Hardwick to implore her not to let a poem of Lowell's appear in *Partisan Review* before it came out in *Botteghe Oscure*. As she said, it was the best "propaganda" for *Botteghe* to be associated with great poets and be disseminated far and wide.

Once again, as in her *Commerce* days, a story from Hemingway was rejected; and she told Robert Lowell she didn't like a story from Nabokov because it was "all full of quips and quirks and tricks!" adding that she also refused a story from Moravia because it was the same old Communists and sex all over again.

For all the headaches of editing a multi-lingual review, Marguerite was in her glory doing it; her very happiest moment, she told George Plimpton, was hearing the thump outside her door that meant a delivery of manuscripts and the possibility of finding in them a major new talent. She was flooded with submissions, especially from America, and had to make a rule that no one could appear two times running, a rule she ignored for her favorites. The ones she rejected, she told Eugene, Plimpton might like for his *Paris Review* which she said was "falling low"—it had published Gênet.

Two images of Marguerite emerge in the last part of her life as she gave herself over to the two enterprises she loved best: *Botteghe Oscure* and her country place, Ninfa. Like its name, which means nymph, Ninfa is a romance in itself. Perhaps in Roman times a temple had been erected there to a woodland nymph, possibly near the still standing Roman bridge. What's known is that a settlement named Ninfa began to grow in importance after the eighth century because its location on a main roadway leading south allowed it to levy tolls and made it a strategic site. By the twelfth century it was ringed with a double circle of walls and filled with homes, artisan shops, streets filled with commerce, a municipal building, and churches including S. Maria Maggiore, where Alexander III was crowned pope, and whose ruins remain. Ninfa became a Caetani holding in 1297 but by the next century warfare had culminated in the town's destruction. Malaria decimated the few remaining inhabitants, and the place was abandoned and left to fall into ruin.

For the Caetanis of the nineteenth century, the site had become a place for family picnics where Roffredo's English mother typically began planting rose cuttings among the ruins. It was Gelasio who, in 1921, started reclaiming the area and restored the Palazzo Comunale, making that old municipal building into the family's country residence. The Great Room, adorned with the Caetani coat of arms, is where Marguerite concentrated all aspects of her life: it was her work room, living room, reception room, dining room, and rest room. It is homey and comfortable with many deep couches and lounge chairs. The piano of Franz Liszt, Roffredo's godfather, is there but no television or telephone contaminates the calm. On the walls, somber portraits of cardinals and dignitaries contrast with the delicate landscape watercolors done by Lelia. Scattered about are books, photos of visitors like the Queen Mother of England, and a photo album with notations by Lelia's husband, Hubert Howard, showing a smiling Marguerite in sturdy country clothing and walking shoes, and a girlish Lelia arm-in-arm with her mother. Another photo shows a *Botteghe Oscure* group seated around a table in the courtyard in a rare take of the staff for a publicity shot.

At Ninfa, with tables set out among the greenery, Marguerite continued the Sunday lunches begun at Versailles decades earlier. The perfect connecting symbol between Marguerite's role as literary patron and her passion for gardening was the oft-described garden basket full of submitted manuscripts that so many guests at Ninfa remember seeing near her, always at hand. Writers passing through Rome were invited out. Eugene Walter once brought a young Gore Vidal who came, saw, and declared it all too literary—he had by then already written a best seller; it was markets, not literati, that interested him.

Marguerite was most happy at Ninfa and regularly left Rome for four-day weekends in the country. With a passion shared by her daughter Lelia, she dug, sowed, and transplanted, continuing the old duchess's garden, and fashioning Ninfa into Italy's premier romantic landscape. At Ninfa, roses clamber up medieval towers, wondrous freshets of calla lilies bloom along the streams, wisteria twines across an old Roman bridge, and corners of New England birch and American redbud set off the remains of old chapels. Miles Chapin, Marguerite's grand-nephew, describing Ninfa in an issue of *Garden Design* magazine, wrote, "Everything is meticulously planned to look completely unplanned . . . as if 10,000 different species of flora had simply landed there and sorted themselves out."

Marguerite and her daughter were extremely close. Marguerite was proud of Lelia's career as a painter and always, in her correspondence, mentioned her shows and promoted her. The *New York Times* reported on Donna Lelia Caetani's one-woman show at the Hugo Gallery in New York in 1954 noting the "appreciable lyricism and poetic grace" in landscapes which put one "profoundly in touch with her ancestral mountains, valleys and vineyards near Sermoneta and Ninfa." It was attractive work but nonetheless weaknesses (a childishness that Francis Biddle had noted a decade earlier) were evident: "a certain gaucherie in drawing . . . and a kind of listless brushwork that is insufficiently expressive to lend her work the degree of vivid actuality that it aims at." The work seems to mirror the few details ascertainable about Lelia. She was very attached to her mother and did not marry until her late thirties. Her handwriting shows a childish, uncertain script that slants both ways and is neither the Italianate hand nor the American. A visitor recalled her child-like demeanor contrasting with the awareness of her titled position, and described the servants at the Castle of Sermoneta kneeling on the courtyard cobblestones and kissing the hem of Lelia's dress, an adulation she received quite naturally. At Sermoneta, Francis Biddle observed the peasants paying their respects to Prince Roffredo and asking after *la bambina*—Lelia in her thirties.

Marguerite and Lelia often gardened together, rising early and dressing in their drabs, doing heavy duty work except in the hot weather when they left their paradise and traveled together to Switzerland, France, and England every July through September. "My daughter and I are very earthy gardeners," Marguerite wrote Roethke, "so you see one of the many reasons I love your poetry." She keeps mentioning the beauty of Ninfa, wishing she could entice him over for a visit. Especially with Roethke she seemed to find echoes of her own voice, her own longings. He was a poet attuned to the rhythms of the natural world and in his long, lyrical sequence "The Lost Son" (echoing losses from childhood which Marguerite could identify in her own life), with its images of greenhouses, plants, soil, and empathy for all animate life, he particularly spoke to her in her green kingdom at Ninfa.

Writing Eugene in December, she gave him a catalogue of what was in bloom at Ninfa: "In the garden are any amount of roses, a beautiful kind of mimosa with grey leaves . . . some winter tree-heather, berberis and cotoneaster . . . camellias and odds and ends in the rock garden . . . also winter narcissus and quite a lot of plants with berries." Eugene answered with seed packets of four o'clocks and cosmos. "It's a beautiful spring day in the garden," she wrote Lowell from Ninfa on the 4th of January 1951. And references to Ninfa continued to crop up in her business matters with Eugene: "What are they called those imitation owls we have at Ninfa that squeak all day and night, too?"

But was there, as in all enchanted gardens, a curse? Did Lelia, like Rappaccini's daughter in the Hawthorne tale, fall prey to the lush surroundings? She married Hubert Howard in 1951 in her late-thirties but remained childless. The garden had been her private paradise and Kathleen Raine's poem "Ninfa Revisited" imagines Lelia as custodian of a Garden of Eden protecting it against "crowds that envy and destroy." Charles Quest-Reston pointed out in his chapter on Ninfa in *The English Garden Abroad*, that Giorgio

Bassani wrote his *Garden of the Finzi-Contini* at Ninfa and based certain elements of the secretive, isolated, private world of the Finzi-Contini on that of the Caetani realm. Both Bassani's fictional characters and the Caetanis "faced extinction despite the opulence of their house and garden."

When it was clear there would be no heirs from Lelia, Marguerite successfully petitioned the Italian Parliament so that no other claimants to the title and inheritance of the dukedom of the Caetani di Sermoneta would be recognized. This act excluded the son of Marguerite's niece Topazia Caetani who had married the eminent conductor Igor Markevitch, Lelia's one-time rejected suitor. With Lelia's death in 1977, the direct Caetani of Sermoneta line was extinguished; Sveva Caetani of Sermoneta, Don Leone's illegitimate daughter, died in Canada in 1994. The Caetani name and holdings exist now in two Foundations, one named for Camillo and the other for Roffredo, the last duke.

In her Italian years Marguerite came into her own. Having taken direct charge of her new literary journal, she made *Botteghe Oscure* more an expression of her personal tastes and more generously open to new, young writers than *Commerce* had been. She finally became known in her homeland as she launched American writers.

The end of the Second World War witnessed a new interest in Italian style, cinema, design, cars, food—and thanks to Marguerite, a new acquaintance with the literature. By producing an Italian-titled review in Italy, and always including Italian writers, she gave contemporary Italian literature a foothold, a cachet, a weight in the world. She was truly *l'animatrice*, as Giorgio Bassani referred to her, the leading spirit of postwar literary revival in Italy.

As *Botteghe Oscure* grew in esteem and elicited attention in American magazines from *Vogue* (whose illustration of her, Marguerite complained, made her look like a Holbein bishop) to *TIME* (which headlined her review "Highbrow Refuge"), she was intensely gratified. In 1954, she was awarded the Legion d'Honneur by the French Embassy in Rome. In 1958, she was recognized by both France and Italy as having been an extraordinary presence in the literary ferment of two postwar generations. The exhibit *Hommage à Commerce* was organized by the French Ambassador in Rome and paid tribute not only to that review but to *Botteghe Oscure* as well. The exhibit was a full retrospective crammed with letters, photos, drawings, and other memorabilia of all the illustrious with whom Marguerite had contact.

The commemoration came just at the right time. Shortly after, Marguerite was attending to a failing Roffredo who could not be left alone. Even before his final illness, there were indications of Marguerite's own decline: demonstrating failing judgment, she sacked Eugene Walter. He continued to prize the memory of his association with the "Great Lady" and attributed his dismissal to Elsa Dallolio's personal dislike of him and the suggestion she made to Marguerite that he was leading "a double life" in regard to *Botteghe* by working with other reviews. Yet Giorgio Bassani was at the same time dividing himself between *Botteghe Oscure* and the new publishing firm started by Giacomo Feltrinelli whom Marguerite described as young and ignorant but with heaps of money. Marguerite kept Bassani and fired Eugene with the regal gesture to pay his passage back to America, an offer he refused.

Eugene suggested that Marguerite was already showing personality alteration and was under terrific pressure from her son-in-law to stop draining her fortune on the review. With Eugene gone, Florence Hammond, daughter of dear friends and a recent Radcliffe graduate, was invited by Marguerite in a hand-written note to be her assistant and help with reading manuscripts for *Botteghe Oscure*. Marguerite's eyesight was going, her hand-writing had grown shaky, there was Roffredo to look after, and she was approaching her eighties.

By the end of 1959, Marguerite no longer dashed off a hurried, hand-written letter on her blue, tissuey paper in reply to Ted Roethke but had Florence Hammond type a response on formal letterhead saying it was on behalf of Princess Caetani who was quite tired following her return from Paris, but do send a poem. But it was the shock of her irreplaceable printer's sudden death by decapitation in a car accident that precipitated the end. Marguerite took that horrendous event as a sign that *Botteghe Oscure*'s time had come.

The final issue, *Botteghe Oscure* XXV, came out in 1960 with a farewell note from Giorgio Bassani that paid full tribute to the invigorating American influence of its founder. Although so Europeanized, Marguerite had always kept her American citizenship (almost as a talisman, Bassani noted) and her American zeal and enthusiasm was very symbolically a generating force for the new growth rising out of war's desolation and decades of repression.

Robert Lowell told her she could be proud of her years of service, of bringing the many nations together, and of pepping up so many young poets. Indeed, Archibald MacLeish later noted in his introduction to the *Botteghe Oscure Index* (1964) that an astonishing 650 writers of 30 nationalities had passed through the journal's pages.

Roffredo, previously described by Marguerite in a letter to Roethke as pathetically old and helpless and with no memory, is remembered by Florence Hammond Phillips as a tall, elegant, exquisitely mannered old gentleman in a flowing cape who was escorted by a large female attendant to meals where he would look around wonderingly and murmur, "Poor Liszt!" Strangely, although his father's, his brothers', and his son's death were all communicated to the *New York Times* and written up, no obituary notice for Roffredo appeared in that paper when he died in 1961.

In August 1963, Roethke died suddenly, face down in a friend's swimming pool. Marguerite, who had remained young and vital through her constant contact with young and creative people, did not long survive her beloved poet whose very beautiful sequence, "Meditations of an Old Woman," could be identified with her. Did she recognize herself in Roethke's lines:

> I am benign in my own company.
> A shape without a shade, or almost none,
> I hum in pure vibration, like a saw . . .
> I live in air; the long light is my home . . .

The lady of the street of dark shops slipped gradually into her own darkness. In early December 1963, the day before she was to return to Rome from Ninfa where she had enjoyed the last of the autumnal garden, she was indisposed with a sore throat. Against a soaring fever, antibiotics ceased to have effect. For a week she lay ill, but quiet and peaceful. Then she expired. The funeral service was held in the country and she was brought to Rome to be laid to rest in Verano Cemetery where Roffredo and Camillo had preceded her in the Caetani mausoleum.

My husband, a contributor to *Botteghe Oscure*, never had occasion to meet Princess Caetani, nor did I, since our return to Italy came after her death. Still I can picture her at Ninfa seated in her garden as she appears in a last photo when she is an elderly woman. A tender smile is on her lips as she still avoids looking at the camera, her gaze, rather, going off into the distance of her earthly Ninfa paradise toward something only she could discern, toward her vision, personal and private, of *la Poesia, la bellezza*.

Though Yankee born and bred, Marguerite Caetani blended well with European cultural life as did her friend and future memorialist, Iris Origo. Both women had American roots, both married Italian aristocrats, and both left indelible imprints on cultural life—Marguerite as a publisher and promoter of writers, Iris as a writer in her own right.

Iris Origo, 1902–1988

Picture a 1458 Tuscan villa fronted by a terrace mossy with age and looking down from Fiesole's heights to Florence below, a city cradled between hills in the valley of the Arno river that flows through it. Built on foundations dating even earlier, when it was a stronghold, Villa Medici had been transformed by the great Florentine architect Michelozzo for Cosimo de'Medici into a "place for leisure pursuits."[1] It was thereafter most associated with Cosimo's grandson Lorenzo, known as Il Magnifico for the grandeur with which he illumined Florence. From the villa Lorenzo would ride off for the hunt in the Mugello valley; on spring and summer nights, banquets were held followed by the reading of poetry, by dancing, music, and courtships. Here humanism reached its fine flowering during Lorenzo's short but stellar lifetime, 1449–92, when his city was at the zenith of its glory.

Villa Medici was also the childhood home of the distinguished biographer Iris Origo, and recalling it she wrote, "no child could have had a more beautiful one."[2] She seems to have been destined from birth for it. Though born in the English Cotswold village of Birdlip on August 15, 1902, she was presciently named for a flower symbolic of Florence—the iris as fleurs-de-lis. Connected through her American father, Bayard Cutting, to the New York family whose fortune came from railroads, and through her mother to Lord Desart, an Anglo-Irish peer, Iris's childhood was divided between their several worlds—a Madison Avenue mansion, a Long Island estate, and the seventeenth-century manor house of Desart Court in Ireland.

The distancing of herself from her own life to the studying and writing of other lives may be a consequence of her own sense of unsure identity. Evident in her memoir, evocatively titled *Images and Shadows: Part of a Life*, are not only the images of the wondrous places she lived in and the celebrated who peopled her world, but also the shadows that never fully reveal her. One could ask: did she more securely anchor her own life by probing the lives of others?

"We know little about other people and it is gradually borne in on us how little more we know about ourselves. How then can we presume to become historians or biographers?" she asks in the introduction to *A Measure of Love*, her collection of five biographical sketches on both English and Italian subjects.[3] Origo's approach was to let her subjects speak for themselves. For she knew that as we sometimes are able to communicate more openly with strangers, we can also sometimes come closer to people of the past than to our own contemporaries. It was the fascination of achieved human understanding that made the writing of historical biography irresistible to her and made her a deeply intuitive interpreter of lives. What is revealed in Iris Origo's own story is how in a life of variant cultural influences, she made her choice to be who she became in Italy.

It was Iris's young father who cast the deepest image and longest shadow over her life although he disappeared from it when she was only a child of seven. Dying of tuberculosis at age thirty, he left his wife Sybil the strong wish (and the financial means to carry it out) that their child be brought up in Europe "free from all this national feeling which makes people so unhappy." His wish was granted; his widow acquired Villa Medici in 1911 and settled there with Iris in the hills outside Florence.

Lady Sybil Cuffe, fair-haired and petite, was twenty when she met the equally young Bayard Cutting who was in London as the secretary of the American ambassador Joseph Choate. Cutting, an outstanding student on leave from Harvard University and earmarked for a brilliant career, was the tall, slim, dark-haired elder son of an American millionaire. George Santayana, who had been Cutting's professor of philosophy at Harvard, recalls in his autobiography that at a faculty meeting with the president there came up the "question touching a degree to be granted out of course to an absent undergraduate, Bayard Cutting, who . . . had written a thesis on David Hume as a substitute for his unfinished work. I had read the thesis, and gave my opinion on it. The degree was granted."[4] Santayana's understated account barely hints at the brilliance and promise of young Cutting. At Groton, he was a legend remembered by painter George Biddle in *An American Artist's Story*: "the school got a half holiday every time that Bayard Cutting was awarded a John Harvard scholarship."

Given Bayard Cutting's youth at his marriage and the unfulfilled potential of a life cut so short, Santayana was to recall his past student with melancholy poignancy when Cutting's daughter Iris (by that time Marchesa Origo) asked him to write a foreword to her first book. It must have seemed natural to contact her father's old teacher, for Santayana had prestige as an author and, as she, was living in Italy. In sad coincidence, the Origos had just lost a seven-year old son named Gianni, their then only child. Given the circumstances, Santayana's memory of Bayard Cutting, his marriage, and child, has an elegiac ring: "It is a strange sadness that hangs for me now over all that history. An international Intelligentsia adrift amid unsuspected currents and wrecked one by one on the reefs of El Dorado."[5]

Lady Sybil, quick-minded and of a willful temperament, would not have concurred about having been left adrift or wrecked. Following her husband's death, she settled at Villa Medici and went on to two more marriages. She succeeded better with managing property than she did with marriage, friendships, or closeness to her only child in that child's recollection.

Just downhill from Villa Medici is Villa Diana, given to the Renaissance poet Poliziano by his patron Lorenzo. In the contemporary period it has been the home of several tenants, among them author-journalist Alan Moorehead who lived there just after World War II and described his surroundings: "Everything about the countryside is old. . . . These paths were made and these terraces were cultivated in just this way before the Romans arrived, perhaps even before Fiesole was a great Etruscan city in the third century B.C. and Florence was nothing."[6]

By the beginning of the twentieth century, Florence was the most Anglo-American city on the continent. In the vanguard of motorization was the indefatigable Edith Wharton collecting material for her book on Italian villas in what she called her "buccaneering raids" on Tuscany. In 1903, she had made the trip to Villa Caprarola in the automobile of the American Ambassador to Rome when such vehicles were still notorious and few; they went the distance of one hundred miles in an afternoon tearing through the Campagna, "over humps and bumps, through ditches and across gutters, wind-swept, dust-enveloped."[7] She found it blissful and swore then and there to make enough money from her writing to buy a motor, which she did.

Not only were the hills around Florence jammed with foreign residents, but also the so-called "untrodden ways." Florence became known as the nesting place of dotty dames, American or English, who devoted themselves to Art while preserving their English or American habits. Franco Zeffirelli, who was brought up by an English woman in Florence, portrayed that pre–World War II circle in his film, *Tea with Mussolini*. But Kinta Beevor in her memoir of Tuscan life in the 1920s records Aldous Huxley passing through Florence and calling it "a third-rate provincial town, colonized by English Sodomites and middle-aged Lesbians."[8]

The drive to Villa Medici ascends uphill, first between high walls over which yellow banksia roses and a tangle of wisteria tumble, then through olive groves opening to an ever-wider view, and finally following a drive overshadowed by ilex to a terrace with paulownia trees scattering mauve flowers on the lawn. So irresistible is the setting that a guidebook calls attention to the villa's second gate where a bench beneath the cypresses invites one to sit and gaze at the panorama of all Florence. The villa itself is in traditional Tuscan style, its deep loggia looking due west toward the sun setting over the Arno valley. Redolent of history and humanism, this was Iris Origo's original villa home. In her marriage, she would go on to create with her Italian husband her next and permanent one.

The main structure of Villa Medici with its two deep loggias had remained the same as in Lorenzo's time but, as Iris Origo relates in *Images and Shadows*, in the eighteenth century the property passed into the hands of Horace Walpole's sister-in-law, Lady Orford, who introduced into the drawing rooms exquisite Chinese wallpapers designed especially for them. The paper was still gorgeous, though aging, when I visited Villa Medici several years ago, but the ambiance of the room had been drastically altered from Lady Sybil's day by the addition of a modern L-shaped grey leather couch and other contemporary furnishings. The villa was sold in 1950 when Iris Origo inherited it from her mother. Now, after two centuries of English ownership, it once again has an Italian owner.

It has also a gentle but omnipresent air of decline. No longer the exquisitely maintained show-place of Lady Sybil, its fountains no longer splash jets skyward; the stairs between terraces are clogged with weeds. The wall backing a circular stone bench in what was once an outdoor sitting room now holds only broken remnants of statuary. Just beyond the open-air sitting area was a secluded woodsy strand that could have been the place Iris described as her hide-away when she wanted to be alone. Nearby, a purple plastic hose had been carelessly left lying on the ground. Where there was once a staff of five gardeners under a Head Gardener, only one remained. It's understandable—help is hard to get and expensive when it is found; things are not as they were in the expatriate heyday.

When the young Iris Cutting lived at Villa Medici, among neighbors who came to call were the Berensons—the debonair, impeccably-outfitted Bernard and his American Quaker wife Mary, a full-blown Valkyrie of a woman who dwarfed him. A handsome, full-bosomed young woman when she first met Berenson, Mary had become portly; upon meeting her, Leo Stein described her as "well past her prime, a large and blowsy blonde of at least forty-five," though she was then only thirty-six. Mary Berenson's first call on Sybil at Villa Medici was enthusiastic, but others became progressively less so and she eventually wrote to her sister Alys, wife of Bertrand Russell, that she was "fed up with Lady Sybil whose unceasing flow of chatter is more than I can bear."9

Edith Wharton was close to the Cutting family of New York and had spent time with Bayard and Sybil during her visit to Florence in 1903. She then had the couple spend a summer with her at The Mount, her home in the Berkshire Mountains. She mourned young Bayard's passing and became ever more rancorous toward Sybil, whom she saw as a predatory dolt bent on annexing her own men friends. She said Sybil was given to illness as a form of hysterical exhibitionism and was a humbug who spoke in unintelligible *glapissements*—yelps and screeches. It is ironic, or perhaps foreordained in those tight little interconnected social circles of Anglo-American literati, that it would be Lady Sybil's third husband, Percy Lubbock, who was chosen to write the early biography *Portrait of Edith Wharton* not long after the writer's death. It is a wittily sly portrayal of the woman, not her work, and includes the reminiscences of an unnamed young Englishwoman (whose circumstances and dates coincide perfectly with Sybil's) who contributes unflattering insights into the formidable Edith. Later, Sybil's daughter, Iris, would recall Wharton's return to America as the great woman of American letters when Yale gave her an honorary degree. Wharton, a close friend from youth of Iris's grandmother, stayed at the Cutting country place on Long Island while Iris was there to observe her, not as the terrifyingly autocratic woman she had encountered in Europe, but as "another Edith: mellow, benign—almost cozy . . . Edith coming home."[10]

Lady Sybil may well have learned of the care and keeping of a Tuscan villa from Wharton's popular 1903 work, *Italian Villas and Their Gardens*. Wharton deplored the Anglicization of traditional villa-gardens effected by the English when they colonized the hills above Florence and destroyed the Italianate terraces, olive groves, and vineyards only to introduce two features alien to Tuscan climate and soil—lawns and the shade-trees familiar to English landscapes. The English, wherever they went, tried to reconstitute the familiar home garden and sweeping lawn of their blessed isle. A childhood memory for Iris Origo was the ludicrous sight of Mrs. Keppel, King Edward VII's mistress, crying out to her Tuscan gardener, "*Bisogna begonia*!", emphasizing the words with taps of her parasol and using it to mark the precise spots in the beds where she said begonia were needed to recall her grounds at Sandringham. A few of the Tuscan nobles aped the foreign residents by altering their own grounds to accord with the fashions from England and France, but Lady Sybil's merit was to respect and conserve the traditional appearance of Villa Medici.

A contemporary of Iris, Sir Harold Acton, also of Anglo-American parentage and also brought up in a Renaissance villa, was born in Florence in 1904. Although they were neighbors and Acton, by defining himself a citizen of the world, closely embodied her own father's beliefs that true culture is universal, Origo curiously omitted him from her memoir, mentioning only an annual Christmas party at the Actons' where the tree was larger and the presents more expensive than anywhere else. But then she, too, was omitted from his own account of his life and times, *Memoirs of an Aesthete*. "Nearly all the old Florentine families had Anglo-Saxon ramifications," he wrote without naming names, "and a large proportion of Florentine palaces and villas were inhabited by Englishmen. . . . They took root among the vineyards and became part of the landscape." And in an unmistakable swipe at Berenson and his competitors, he notes "the Guelfs and Ghibellines had been replaced by rival schools of art-historians."[11]

Lady Sybil restored Villa Medici's formal garden to its original design and furnished the house with pieces from the antiquarians in Florence, relying on the help of a gifted young English architect, Cecil Pinsent, and his friend Geoffrey Scott, who was Bernard Berenson's secretary at the time. Eventually, though twenty years younger, Scott became her second husband. Previously, Lady Sybil had the Olympian advice and attentions of "B. B." himself, who found the attractive young widow an appealing divertissement in the bland world of Florentine society; as he put it, she had an attractive house at the distance of a pleasant walk.

As B. B. pursued a romantic attachment to Lady Sybil, he embittered his wife who recalled to him: "The thought that thee gave this withered chattering child the best of three years of thy life, and that Geoffrey is planning to give his entire life to her—casts over my spirit . . . the same kind of feeling that seasickness induces." Earlier in their involved romantic circlings, Mary Berenson tried to bind Geoffrey Scott to I Tatti first by her own attraction to him, then by steering him toward Nicky Mariano who would become B. B.'s secretary and his last great attachment. All this sexual rivalry indubitably had its effect on young Iris, who recounts that her childhood recollections of Bernard Berenson are extremely inhibited and that she could never feel at ease with him. Eventually, as a grown woman and accomplished writer, she did move with ease in his presence and took advantage of their long connection to plumb both his library and his mind for information. After his death in 1959, she wrote an affectionate tribute to him, and then a generous and reflective account of his life and character in her introduction to the diaries of his late years, *Sunset and Twilight*.

It is remarkable how that select circle of acquaintances traveled back and forth across Europe and in and out of each other's lives during those years of World War I; they focused on their love affairs and social positions or the waxing and waning of feuds and not much of the larger world. Acton had noted that during the First World War Florence had remained a city of ivory towers. The self-indulgence of the foreign colony made a distinct contrast to the noted Tuscan temperament of *grinta*, which combines discretion, frugality, shrewdness, scrupulousness, toughness, and laconic expression to give the Tuscan a kind of Spartan character quite in contrast with the pleasure-loving denizens of the villas on the hills.

The doings of her mother's circle are also in quite distinct contrast to the goings on of Iris Origo's adult life, to her partnership with her Italian husband in managing a working estate, and to her dedication as an author. She lived her humanistic ideal: the synthesis of active and contemplative life. Her own experience of war during World War II was the vastly different one of dealing with day-to-day survival when she and her family were caught on the front lines of battle between Germans and Allies, a period she recorded in her *War in Val D'Orcia: An Italian War Diary, 1943–4*.

With so much colorful material at hand in the celebrity lives all about her, Iris Origo might well have been a novelist; she became, instead, a distinguished biographer and historian. It was not the artistic Florence or the poetic one of Elizabeth Barrett Browning that attracted Origo: her deepest interest lay in retelling the lives of real people of the past.

Iris's childhood in Italy presented a unique but doubtlessly lonely life for a child who was overexposed to adult conversations on culture and art, and had a minimum of encounters with children her own age. In her wealthy home, Iris felt she passed a childhood poor in affections. She omits all mention of her collaboration with her mother's poetry anthology, *A Book of the Sea*, published in 1918 when Iris was sixteen. Yet Lady Sybil generously credits her daughter's help in "sharing the preparation of the book." Iris, instead, longed for the absent dead parent with whom she had felt such intense companionship and well-being in their brief time together. She became fascinated by the personages of her readings—the only ones to whom she felt close. Iris was schooled alone in Villa Medici with a parade of governesses until, as an adolescent, she was allowed to go by tram from Fiesole to Florence for private tutoring sessions with Professor Solone Monti, a classical scholar recommended to her mother by Bernard Berenson.

As a child and as an adolescent, Iris Origo sometimes felt bewildered in the transitions between three distinct cultural influences, three sets of codes and values. Only in her lessons with Professor Monti did she find an inner stability that formed her inclination to become a scholar and writer. With the learned Monti, who introduced her to the classical worlds of Homer and Virgil, she spent, she says, the happiest hours of her girlhood, perhaps the happiest ever known. Those years, from age twelve, with her *caro maestro* were the formative ones when she honed her love of poetry and the classical spirit. Professor Monti was a leading light in her life and to him she acknowledges the greatest debt: "I owe to him not only what he taught me then, but, in enthusiasm and method of approach, all that I have learned ever since."[12] Not a word, though, about her own mother's publications and their probable influence on her.

Iris also paid loving tribute to her grandfather, Lord Desart, described as a true gentleman whose viewpoint throughout his life was thoroughly English. It was to him that she turned with the problem of her divided loyalties when the question of her education caused a rift between Lady Sybil and her American grandparents. Iris and her mother were in the mid-Atlantic for a visit to the American family when the start of World War I was announced; landing in New York, Lady Sybil decided on immediate return to Europe against the wishes of the Cuttings who would have liked to take charge of Iris's education.

From then on, Iris grew up isolated in her "mother's ivory tower," in communication mainly with her English grandfather who remains, along with her Tuscan teacher, a luminary in her life. In her memoir she describes three very different, and very past, ways of life: the Tuscan, the British, and the American. All of them privileged. But given her solitary childhood, she was also in many ways the poor little rich girl who suffered deprivation of other kinds: rarely a playmate, a distracted mother, out-of-sorts governesses. A photograph in Kinta Beevor's memoir, *A Tuscan Childhood*, shows an exceptional occasion—a gathering of children for Lady Sybil's 1917 May Day party at Villa Medici just before they were served raisins in flaming brandy.

If Iris was enriched by the multiple strains in her life, the diverse backgrounds were also responsible for a sense of rootlessness and insecurity during her youth. "Extremely adaptable," she writes, "on the surface . . . I found no difficilty in 'fitting in' as I passed from my mother's Tuscan villa to the country house on Long Island or to Desart Court in County Kilkenny . . . the uprooting was followed by a re-adjustment of my manners and, to some extent, of my values . . . it was a question of . . . becoming each time . . . a slightly different person. However, even a child could then hardly fail to ask herself, 'But which, then, is me?'"

She spoke several languages by her teen-age and had already become aware that she was not the same person in Italian as she was in English. Her greatest affinity, as she felt her father's to be, was with the Latin world. He had an enlarged, enlightened view and interest in Mediterranean culture. Despite failing health, he had organized assistance to the city of Messina when it was devastated in 1908 by an earthquake claiming 40,000 lives; he reopened the United States consulate in the stricken city, directed the relief effort, and wrote a brilliant report to stimulate aid, a model still in use by the State Department. He wanted his daughter to be a world citizen, free from the nationalism that makes people so narrow. To that end, shortly before his death he wrote to his wife about their child: "Bring her up somewhere where she does not belong . . . I'd rather France or Italy than England, so that she can really be cosmopolitan, deep down."

It was a noble idea and it somehow worked, for Iris Origo would come to write that she is chary of generalizations about nations: "I believe in individuals, and in their relationship to one another." Thus her father's plan was successful in avoiding narrow nationalism, but, on the other hand, fraught with the obverse consequence of feeling split in allegiance.

Iris had not only the advantages, but also the constraints of her class: like young Harold Acton, moving between her family's different worlds, she became "adaptable." She longed for an Oxford education but, instead, was made to endure the social ritual of "coming out" not once, but thrice—in Florence, in London, and in New York. It was a ritual that she found silly and a useless waste of a few years of her life, and one that only accentuated her feeling of divided loyalties. Though she also loved England (a moving moment in her memoir finds her, a young bride, huddled against a clay mound in the desolate Orcia Valley where her new home was to be, longing for the green lawns and trees of England), and briefly thought she would marry an Englishman who replicated the qualities of her grandfather, her choice was finally Italy. But she had determined at an early age that if she stayed on in Italy it would only be if married to an Italian. She did not wish to live there as part of a foreign colony as her mother did.

Iris Cutting met the tall, dark, handsome Marchese Antonio Origo when she was not yet eighteen and he, ten years older, had escorted his sister to a debutante dance in Florence. He asked Iris to dance and she thought him "possessed of more than his fair share of charm." Though Iris was smitten, her mother, she records, found the Marchese "too good-looking and too grown-up for me." They began to see each other discreetly and never was there a more circumspect courtship. A dutiful daughter, Iris agreed to her mother's preengagement condition that she not be in touch with Antonio for six months. At the end they were resolved to marry. It was Iris's deliberate choice of an Italian life.

A few months before their marriage in 1924, filled with plans and hope, Antonio and she together, with the help of her several inheritances, had bought the run-down estate La Foce in the remote Val d'Orcia about 40 miles south of Siena with the shared dream of bringing it back to life. They had the inspired help of architect Cecil Pinsent, who started working to make the place habitable while she and Antonio were on their honeymoon.

She described the rural setting into which she settled: "We live on a large farm in southern Tuscany—twelve miles from the station and five from the nearest village. The country is wild and lonely: the climate harsh. Our house stands on a hillside, looking down over a wide and beautiful valley, beyond which rises Monte Amiata, wooded with chestnuts and beeches. Nearer by, on this side of the valley, lie slopes of cultivated land: wheat, olives and vines, but among them still stand some ridges of dust-coloured clay hillocks, the crete senesi—as bare and colourless as elephants' backs, as mountains of the moon."[13] In her country life, Iris Origo could daily find some connection to the past among the customs of the peasants, or even in seeing the great jars, identical to those unearthed from ancient sites, which were still used after the olive harvest to hold oil. The very settings and verbal patterns of her beloved Tuscany were rooted in a past stretching back to classical times. It was a kind of georgic ideal, derived from her education, to live a Virgilian existence on the land, making it bloom and bear fruit.

Even though both partners had extramarital love affairs, Iris and Antonio maintained a long and committed marriage as well as a working partnership in reclaiming and managing almost eight thousand acres at La Foce. Fifteen years of intense dedication saw the establishment of fifty-seven separate farms of about a hundred acres each radiating out from the central hub of the estate—the hilltop villa with its administration center and granaries from which all was managed. Nearby were the other central buildings in this self-contained community housing some six hundred souls: a school for the farm children as well as for adult classes, a nursery school, clinic, a workers' meeting place, blacksmith and carpentry shops.

La Foce—set in an ancient landscape known to Etruscans, Roman legions, medieval warlords, and invading foreign kings—was so-called from being at a crossroad. In the 1920s the estate was run-down and unproductive, in an area that was a far cry from the poster-pretty views of a Tuscany with cypresses on hilltops and wheat fields dotted with red poppies. Nor was it the backdrop of gentle tree-dotted hills so familiar in the paintings of Giotto. What the Origos found was more like a moon landscape than a terrestrial one. They restored the sixteenth-century villa, laid terraces and gardens, rebuilt dilapidated farmhouses for the peasants who worked the estate lands on the *mezzadria* system, built schools, laid roads and sewers and pipelines to bring water from springs in the hills, and veritably made the desert bloom. It was a lifetime commitment. The whole was run under a centuries-old system which had both the benefits and defects of paternalism further entrenched by the fascist regime whose basic principle was to halt the flight from country to town by giving grants of assistance to the more backward agricultural regions. La Foce directly benefited from this.

When her young son Gianni died in 1933, Iris Origo sought some impersonal work which would absorb at least a part of her thoughts. She turned to writing, a practice of her youth, and chose as subject Italy's finest lyric poet but most lugubrious figure, Giacomo Leopardi. He, a self-taught prodigy afflicted by physical deformity from a spinal disease, lived from 1798 to 1837. Leopardi belonged to a closed provincial society of rural nobility and was, as Origo put it, "made to my hand," for no full-length study of him existed in English and his background was one with which she herself was familiar. But what a depressing subject! With his sense of deep personal alienation and bereavement toward life, Leopardi is the poet of soul-torment. It may have been just that quality that attracted her at that low point of her life.

Leopardi was born in the region of the Marches near the Adriatic coast and arrived in Pisa on Italy's opposite shore in 1825, some five years after Byron, the Shelleys, and the Leigh Hunts had all been domiciled together there, leading Origo to speculate on whether a friendship might have been possible had the English poets and the Italian poet happened to meet. But no, she concluded, Leopardi would never have attempted a rapport with such an eccentric English crew: "For here lies one of the most profound differences between the Latin and the Anglo Saxon nature, and one of the greatest barriers to their mutual understanding: the sense of what is due to the conventions and to decorum. Genius, in Latin peoples, is seldom linked up with oddity."[14] Revealing the disparity between cultures had a constant appeal for Origo in her writing of lives, for it reflected her own transcultural background, with its English and American heritages and Italian daily life and education. She was admirably equipped—perhaps uniquely so—to interpret the light of one culture to another. *Ogni tempo ha la sua luce*, each time has its own light, was her friend Elsa Dallolio's favorite dictum.

Santayana's foreword to her biography of Leopardi makes clear that in that first book, despite her youth, Marchesa Origo had rendered a learned picture of Leopardi. Equipped with her "perfect knowledge of Italy and Italians," she had not, however, surrendered "the English point of view" as her perspective for bringing out the Italian poet's depth and tone. Her multicultural background brought considerable success to her first publishing venture and gave her a future reputation as a masterly writer in English about things Italian.

Iris Origo never made writing the central, polarizing fact of her life as, in a sense, did Grazia Deledda when she set herself the goal of bringing her native Sardinia into literature and was rewarded for accomplishing it with the Nobel Prize for Literature in 1926. Important as writing was to Origo (and she did produce ten books), she was not as intrinsically bound to it as was the more reclusive and socially inactive Deledda. Origo did garner successes from all three of her countries: she received Italy's Isabella d'Este medal for her essays and historical studies; *Images and Shadows* was nominated for the National Book Award in the United States, where she also received honorary degrees from Wheaton and Smith Colleges; and in England she was an invited lecturer at Cambridge and a fellow of the Royal Society of Literature.

But she did not go in for self-promotion; she had an innate personal reserve that made pushing herself forward unthinkable; and her inherited financial security removed her from the need of aggressively keeping her books in the public eye, or even in print. She had the privileged way of writing of a Lady Wortley Montagu. Origo's daughter, Donata, is quoted as saying, "She wrote in bed with the door closed. We knew better than to intrude. Of course we had maids, so it didn't matter."[15]

Through being a familiar and titled figure in Tuscan society, with connections to people of importance throughout Italy, Iris also had easy, sometimes unique access to material, such as some background material to her book *Allegra* (the story of Lord Byron's natural daughter who died at age five in the Italian convent where he had placed her), and also to the cache of Byron's hitherto unpublished letters in Italian which became the basis for *The Last Attachment: The Story of Byron and Countess Guiccioli*.

Iris Origo's account of herself as a writer is rather cursorily set out in Part Two of her memoir as the last hurdle in a progression: first came reading and learning, then growing up and coming out, and, finally, writing. Granted that writing is a solitary, private act about which there are few vivid details to relate as there are in the descriptions of her estate life, still, Origo seems too off-hand and self-deprecating about her writing skills, calling herself more of an industrious, versatile, "sedulous ape" than an imaginative artist. Like many other women, she wrote piecemeal in the bits of time between her other duties: "I have written in trains and planes, during illnesses, in an air-raid shelter, in a nursery . . . at least getting on with the book." The brief chapter on "Writing" quotes all and sundry, including Virginia Woolf, on the art of biography but little of what made Iris Origo write and how she practiced it. She leaves no clues, no information as to the steps by which she brought her books to publication nor any accounting of monies made. How, for instance, did she approach her first publisher, Oxford University Press? Was the manuscript completed and simply sent off? Did she write a proposal? Did she have an introduction through her highly placed connections in England or her mother's past connection with the press? Did she have a literary agent? Did she, on her own, decide to write to Leonard and Virginia Woolf's Hogarth Press offering the manuscript of *Allegra*, which they were to publish in 1935, the same year her *Leopardi* came out with Oxford? The story of how she debuted as a writer is never clear. That most crucial part of writing—how one emerges from the solitude of the act to the public reception of one's work—is never addressed. It just seemed to happen for Iris Origo, as if a fairy godmother waved a wand and all the trials of a struggling writer were waived. The same wall of reticence remains about her personal life as about her career. For one so well immersed in "the small change of daily life" of her subjects, Origo is decidedly stingy in sharing the details of her own daily life at home with husband and children, their thoughts on the fascist regime. The aristocratic veil of privacy is rarely lifted.

Virginia Woolf, who told all in her voluminous correspondence and in her *Diaries* (methodically noting how much money her writing brought in and what it bought), left a tantalizing vignette of Marchesa Origo's June 25, 1935, visit to Tavistock Square to discuss with Leonard Woolf Hogarth Press's upcoming October publication of *Allegra*. As Iris was about to leave, Virginia called downstairs "Bring her up for tea, Leonard."[16] And so began the acquaintance between the star-struck thirty-two year old Iris Origo and the fifty-two-year-old renowned English novelist and critic who described her guest as: "young, tremulous, nervous—very— stammers a little—but honest eyed; very blue eyed. . . . Anyhow she's clean & picks her feet up."[17]

On another occasion, Virginia Woolf, clearly charmed, notes: "up in the drawing room, Origo (her name is Iris) sat down on purpose I think by me, & oh dear was it for this I got so free & easy?—she has read my book, & was of course full of stumbling enthusiasm; so I made a rush, I talked about writing, spilling out ideas, of a kind. She lives near Siena, in perfect country; they talk of the seasons; harvest; vintage; share with peasants; have a great vintage feast off goose. And we talked about biography & fiction.

". . . Then the door opened & in came Leo Myers like a du Maurier drawing."

A few days later Virginia is writing to her sister Vanessa, "I've fallen in love with a charming Marchesa Origo, Sybil Scott's daughter, who has an Italian farm near Siena . . . and she's asked us to stay. But then Leo Myers is in love with her, and he looks like a duke of a sort, so well got up, so what chance have I?"[18]

Iris Origo was at this time, to judge by the drawing of her done by Augustus John, an attractive, wide-browed young woman with a look of bemusement playing over her long, oval face. Her very blue eyes are deep-set, imparting a serene, focused gaze, and her neck is aristocratically swan-like. Though in her adolescence she despaired of herself as plain, she clearly is not. She was appealing enough to have caught the attention of King Edward VIII during his short reign before he abdicated to marry Mrs. Simpson and become the Duke of Windsor. Again, Virginia Woolf: "I am told on the very best authority that the new King is a cheap second rate little bounder; whose only points are that he keeps two mistresses and won't marry and make a home; and that he likes dropping into tea with the wives of miners. But this is from Iris Origo who danced with him several times."[19]

This gives interesting shading to the picture of the serious-minded Iris, and one is relieved to know of something flighty and sharp-witted in her nature. For nowhere in Iris Origo's memoir is there mention of dancing with the King, nor of encountering the novelist Leopold Hamilton Myers (1881–1944), who was married to an American woman from Colorado Springs, but smitten with Iris. She was familiar with Myers's work, for in *War in Val D'Orcia* she quotes approvingly a passage from his book *The Pool of Vishnu* about people acting instinctively to help their fellows, for it is only the structure of organized society that makes for the mean second-thoughts of self-protective egoism. Though Iris and Myers did, in fact, come together briefly, she never mentions it in the account of her life. There are things that Iris Origo simply does not tell.

As an accomplished biographer, Origo knows the sleight of hand of her trade: "to select too carefully, to make the points too sharp, is usually to fake the picture"; she knows about "the ingenious transposition or abbreviation of quotations, the slight juggling with dates, the rejection of the inconvenient incident or of the remark that is uncharacteristic or merely flat."[20]

Using, it can be imagined, the same approach with her own story, the portrait Iris Origo has drawn of herself is of a thoughtful, dedicated, somewhat shy, scholarly woman of balance and tact, who is her husband's partner on the estate, a woman dedicated to her home, family, and land; a woman inspired by poetry and classical learning, honest, intelligent, and quite unsuited by her own admission to the vapidness of society. Nevertheless, the keen eye of Virginia Woolf saw also the cosmopolitan, well-dressed young woman come to London from the farm near Siena when she wrote of Iris: "I like her Bird of Paradise flight through the gay world. A long green feather in her hat suggests the image."[21]

Though Origo demurs, perhaps the lady demurs too much: she did have access to the glittering world of international society, she did keep a lavish apartment in Palazzo Orsini in the heart of Rome, she could come and go between Italy and England and New York and know all the best people, have the connections that got her books noticed, and in turn have the perfect place in Italy to which to invite them all. Even so, she was not vapid, nor pretentiously snobbish in the way, say, of the Berensons with their "one of us" criterion or their open expressions of snobbery, as when Mary Berenson writes her family that "Miss Stein came, fat beyond the limits of imagination, and brought an awful Jewess, dressed in a window-curtain. . . . She was called Toklas."

Iris Origo compared her character to that of her English grandfather and was undoubtedly solid in a way that few of her background were, while still harboring an unsuspected lighter side. She revered Virginia Woolf and admired many of the other notable writers of the Bloomsbury group, especially Lytton Strachey, whose *Eminent Victorians* changed biography and greatly influenced Origo's own approach. Both she and Woolf were curious, sensitive, intelligent women who had not been allowed a university education, a lack they regretted all their lives; they both had aristocratic connections, but Iris had something even more— American wealth; they both looked with fascination at lives, and it can be certain that given her wide reading habits, Iris Origo must have been acquainted with Virginia Woolf's essays scrutinizing lives later collected in the *Common Reader* volumes. Could this have been Iris Origo's invitation to write lives? She says as much in her chapter on writing from her autobiography: "Leopardi . . . was an almost ideal subject for a biography in the thirties, especially for a generation whose taste had been formed by Strachey and Maurois, by Harold Nicolson and Virginia Woolf."

Iris Origo published only one other book with the Woolfs' Hogarth Press, *Tribune of Rome: A Biography of Cola di Rienzo*, the fourteenth-century Roman visionary and patriot. This came out in 1938, the same year that Virginia Woolf sold her half interest in the press and it may be that Virginia's withdrawal had some influence on Origo's decision to publish elsewhere from that time on.

When Iris Origo, the accomplished biographer of other lives, came to write her own life at age sixty-eight after years of writing about other people, she had a very keen grasp that one cannot ever disclose the whole of a life, not even one's own. She likes Virginia Woolf's image of biography: it's the past with all its inhabitants miraculously sealed up in a magic tank—"all we have to do is to look and soon the little figures . . . will begin to move and to speak." She is good at listening to other voices—never (almost to a fault) interrupting to superimpose her own views, thoughts, corrections, addenda. Does this come from the isolated childhood when she was invited down from the schoolroom to lunch silently but observantly with her mother and guests—Edith Wharton, Logan Pearsall Smith, George Santayana, the Berensons, or whatever other assembly of wits? Or being taken to I Tatti to hear B. B. pontificate and improvise on endless subjects? Or being a child among grownups who is meant to be seen, not heard, but also retains what she has heard? Origo's remarkable aptitude for the patient reconstruction of lives may have come from just such early background.

Some biographers tell too much—day-by-day minutiae of the most inclusive and tedious kind, as if a pileup of facts about what was done, eaten, worn, performed, and said can constitute all of a life. The seven- or eight-hundred-page tomes called "monumental, definitive" (though ponderous might be the better term) have become the style of this half of the century as compared to Lytton Strachey's stringent rendering of a personality with a minimum of names and events. Selection is necessary, Origo knows: *Le secret d'ennuyer est celui de tout dire.* She is not her mother the compulsive talker, neither in her life nor in her writing. If anything, she is too spare: her portraits are clean, not over-stuffed. They leave, perhaps intentionally, something to the imagination. For she knows all too well the power the biographer has to shape an image by overusing as well as by suppressing information.

What she gives at her best, in her portraits, are lessons in life itself. She has a reflective grasp of her material: she sees into things and plucks out the very kernel of some universal truth. Not a maximalist, she is very much one who sees directly to the point, brushing aside the superfluous. The understanding and compassion with which she writes of Bernard Berenson in her introduction to his *Sunset and Twilight*, the diary of his last eleven years of life from age eighty-two to ninety-three, despite the fact that in her girlhood he was so menacing a figure to her, is a relevant instance of her effort to see the person without prejudice or distorting lens. She approached the subject of Berenson by asking: What remains of a life conditioned to being sheltered and protected both physically and metaphorically from any discomfort; what had filtered through the ever-finer sieve of his consciousness?

She scrutinizes his daily record and finds the dominant themes of his life: an enjoyment of beauty rendered ever sharper by age; an unquenchable intellectual curiosity; an unflinching self-awareness; the warmth of his personal relationships and the need for strong human affection. She reviews who B. B. was, "this last true humanist of Western Europe," and what his legend is. She finds that by 1949 (as was apparent also to Berenson), the values he created at I Tatti are as remote as those of classical Athens or eighteenth-century Versailles. After his period of youth and ascension, there was the period of achieved success and legend-shaping. The third and last period was that of his late-age rediscovery of his true, unadorned Jewish persona, an identity he had previously rejected.

Origo bathed him in a benevolent light; but Alan Moorehead, who had a deep attachment to Berenson and would also have liked to write his life, saw him not only benevolently but also with a judiciousness that included his less marvelous traits: i.e., his inability to see merit in any modern art, his fulminations against those not of his level, his snobbish obsession with being an Englishman, his disparagement of democratic institutions, his questionable attributions to art works from which he profited handsomely. Did Origo's overcompensation for her early dislike of Berenson keep her from seeing the same?

Origo's detachment from the political reality of two decades of fascism in Italy is founded on a complex network of divided loyalty, ambiguity, willed apathy, and withdrawal. She took the line of least resistance. The contact she did have with the regime was to its most appealing and constructive side: the assistance fascism gave to land reclamation, which directly benefited La Foce. Naively, perhaps, land-owning nobles became the paternal benefactors of the lesser beings who worked their lands without questioning the engrained system of dependency. The Origos' purchase and development of the La Foce estate coincided with the entrenchment of the fascist regime's basic principle to halt the flight from country to town by giving grants of assistance to agricultural regions. The English colony in Florence was, for the most part, outspoken against Mussolini, and Bernard Berenson was horrified by Lady Sybil's going "native" during the years of the regime and speaking of *fascismo* with deepest sympathy. It was clearly a time of confusion and conflicted feelings.

Virginia Woolf, in a 1936 diary entry, gives us a glimpse of Iris Origo's feelings in that period after Mussolini's invasion of Abyssinia, when sanctions were imposed against Italy by the League of Nations: "Origo rather contorted: says Italy is blind red hot devoted patriotic: has thrown her wedding ring into the cauldron too."[22] To raise money for the prosecution of the war, Il Duce appealed to the patriotism of Italian women by inviting them to donate their gold wedding rings. Ceremonies were held at war memorials throughout Italy on December 18, 1935, when, led by the Queen, women threw their gold bands into cauldrons and received steel ones in exchange.

This was a period of intense ambivalence for Iris Origo—attachments to the Anglo-American family background and the mother culture weighed against those to the Italy of her childhood and education and now of her husband and new family. She thought she had made a choice with marriage to start a new life—"to identify myself with the work of our farm and with my husband's interests, and to become, if I could, a rather different kind of person."[23] But how difficult it all became—fascism, after all, had helped them reclaim and farm land for the benefit not only of themselves but of all the peasant families at La Foce. And yet, nearby friends like Bernard Berenson and Harold Acton were all vehement in their opposition to the invasion of Abyssinia, and in England her counterparts had formed an Association of Writers for Intellectual Liberty who held public meetings in defense of freedom vs. fascism.

Standing by her husband's side in the courtyard before their villa where a crowd of their farmers and household servants were summoned on June 7, 1940, to hear Il Duce's broadcast of Italy's entry into war against the countries of her heritage, Iris felt the split in herself. At the end of Mussolini's speech, Antonio said "*Viva l'Italia*" and she, seven months pregnant, was left facing the problem of divided loyalties and how best to keep her equanimity; she decided outwardly she would obey the laws of her husband's country. But inwardly? It was then that she determined to write a diary account to record as fully as possible what was going on and to help clear her mind and help her preserve a thread of serenity and hope for the future. It was part of her nature, she pointed out, to take the path of least resistance: "inexperience, shyness, and my own interests so often led me . . . to leave things as they were."

Having dual cultures wasn't all riches; Iris Origo found it was also conflicted allegiances. *A Need to Testify*, published in 1984 when she was eighty-two, contains portraits of four valiant friends united in the anti-fascist movement. Does it represent a need on Origo's part, almost forty years after World War II, to reclaim her position and identify herself with those who did take a stand against fascism? The reviewer in London's *New Statesman* detected a certain suppression, a tendency to tell half a story, to avoid spilling the beans. In her very last book, *Un'Amica: Ritratto di Elsa Dallolio*, published in Florence in 1988 only months before her death, she wrote that she had succeeded in working for the Italian

Red Cross with her friend Elsa's help "despite my Anglo-American origins and my anti-fascist views." But were such views ever voiced other than inwardly?

In Kilkenny, in her long-ago childhood, was the delight of idyllic country days ever blemished by that overlay of unreality that seemed to attach to members of the Anglo-Irish gentry? Origo blandly recounts the Cuffe family history in Ireland as going back to the English invasion under Cromwell without noting the hate, to this day, that is borne against that most detested figure in Irish history. Cromwell rewarded his soldiers (among them her ancestor Joseph Cuffe) for having subjugated Ireland and reduced the people to servitude by giving them huge grants of land and installing them as the ruling class. Granted, that Iris Origo's own grandfather was a decent, caring person—still, as in William Trevor's story, "The News from Ireland," these decent people seem totally oblivious to their being viewed as intruders in a country not theirs, to being resented and wished away. Iris Origo recounts being taken on his rounds of the cottagers on his estate by her grandfather, Lord Desart, who insisted that she be friendly, not shy, with the ill women in the poor cottages where they called. She remembers, as the family filled their little church each Sunday, being "a very small Protestant community in a Catholic world."

As she tagged behind her cousins calling for them to wait for her, she feared that the ragged Irish country folk might materialize from a ditch. Ireland was only fifty years or so past the great potato famines, but the history of that troubled country seemed eerily away from the Anglo-Irish overlords. Thus, it came as a shock and a blow when the family home, Desart Court, was burned to the ground in 1922 during the Irish Civil War. It was "sadness itself" and the family returned to England never to see Ireland again, perhaps never realizing that history had made it inevitable.

Nor does Origo show much interest in the social situation of the United States at the time her Cutting grandfather was accumulating his fortune. The staff at the Westbrook estate on Long Island numbered fourteen indoor servants, twenty-one outdoor, and a retinue of stablemen when horses and carriages were kept. Her grandparents traveled in a private luxurious train with personal staff. She does comment on such a way of life in a time of conspicuous consumption among the rich and of turmoil among the poor by noting that her Cutting grandfather was not a robber baron. In fact, she notes, there was a "repudiation of privilege" among her aunts and uncles, especially marked in her father's younger brother Bronson Cutting who became a U.S. senator and was remembered by Groton classmate George Biddle "for his liberal-mindedness, his valiant fight against reaction and his deep intelligence."²⁴ Origo's father, despite his sickness, always insisted at working at something. Finally, after World War II, the last of that Cutting generation, Iris's aunt Olivia, convinced old Mrs. Cutting to give the Westbrook estate and a million dollar maintenance endowment to the state as a nature preserve for the public. It is a splendid place to visit, a great Tudor-style mansion set on extensive grounds filled with large old-growth specimen trees and facing the sparkling waters of the bay.

Iris Origo's reticence about too deep a probing into painful political truths showed itself as she lived through the years of fascism in Italy, seemingly accommodating it even when sniffing disdainfully at some of the excesses which offended her sensibilities—the crudeness of the virility cult, the ugliness of the strutting black shirts. As she puts it, she reluctantly accepted events in which she could play no part. She is not "La Pasionaria," it is not until events overwhelm her when the war comes literally to her front door that she became more open about her feelings and loyalties, and heroic in her efforts to help the victims.

Iris Origo's ordered country life was to plummet into disarray: seven years after the death of Gianni, a daughter, Benedetta, was born on August 1, 1940, just after Italy had declared war on the Allies. Iris Origo worked two years with the Italian Red Cross in Rome, where she dealt with British prisoners of war. In 1942, expecting another child, she gave up her trips to Rome and stayed at La Foce where she began her war diary. On June 9, 1943, she thus recorded the birth of Donata in a Rome clinic: "During the long night before her birth I heard from the next room through my own pain, the groans for morphine of a young airman whose leg had been amputated."[25]

The diary is full of dramatic episodes and became the widely acclaimed book *War in Val D'Orcia*, which was published in 1947 and has been reissued over the years. Dennis Mack Smith, the renowned English historian of modern Italy, wrote in his fore-word to a reissue that when he came upon it by chance, "my immediate impression was reading a minor masterpiece." Origo's diary is intense, factual, full of the small change of daily living (the same fine detailing that was to inform and bring to life her study of fourteenth-century Franceso di Marco Datini in *The Merchant of Prato*), the suspense of being caught between the Allied campaign and the German occupation, and, above all, the attempt to bring coherence and sense to the events that were overwhelming the lives of her family and their dependents.

It is a riveting story. The diary narrates the mounting tension as the war in Italy crept ever closer to Tuscany and La Foce; in contrast to the dire and tragic outward events that impinged on the lives of the peasant families on the estate as well as on the *padroni* in the villa, there are the revealing moments of a still-privileged way of life—the references to the butler, tea-time going on as usual, Antonio's punctiliousness on matters of national honor, and with it all the trips back and forth to Rome, Florence,

Siena as if they were immune to wartime restrictions and inconveniences.

Although the outcome is known in advance, the story has a dramatic suspense that compels and grips as the Allies draw nearer, the Germans dig in, and the Origos and all their dependents (including twenty-three refugee children from other parts of Italy whom they've taken in) are caught in the crossfire. War and homelessness and grief and the loss of what one has worked so hard for are parts of the story and Iris Origo's straightforward narration is just right for the telling. During all the uncertainty, a scribbled note was smuggled across the Alps somehow by a partisan—one sentence to tell Origo that her mother, having been prevailed upon to leave Villa Medici just days before Italy entered the war, had died in Switzerland in December 1942.

All that was good in the paternal system between noble and retainer came to the fore as the Origos protected and succored their dependents. They may have been naive before events turned so drastic, seemingly knowing nothing of the repressive aspects of the regime including the racial laws against Jews, but once caught in the crisis it was they who looked out for the families on the estate, provided food and clothing, sheltered partisans, tended the wounded. Only later did the Origos recognize the extent to which they had been cut off by a "barrier of privilege" from the kind of person who might have told them of the dark side of fascism, its cruelties and oppressions.

In the struggle to survive, there was no time for introspection about where loyalties lay—the focus was entirely on how to cope day by day, the most fervent wish being that the horror of war should be over and done with and their lives get back to normal. But as the events mounted with the line of battle inexorably drawing closer to La Foce, and the news of Italian troops defecting reached them along with that of partisans fighting the Germans, there came a point when Iris Origo finally speaks of the "whole wretched structure of fascism" collapsing before their eyes. She no longer kept up a detachment from political reality.

The approaching battle was the greatest test of Iris Origo's diverse national background and divided loyalties; the most intense period was concentrated in the years 1943 and 1944, the period of her war diary, when civil war and foreign invasion made their remote corner of Tuscany a no-man's land between the entrenched Germans and the advancing Allies and the battle was literally at her doorstep. By 1943, in addition to her own infant and toddler, Iris Origo found herself having to hold together the whole rural community that made up La Foce plus the refugee children from the bombed cities of Turin and Genoa whom she had taken in, making over the nursery school to house them. She was assailed by conflicting armies and ideologies: she had bonds both to her country of origin and to her country of adoption though they were at war with each other. Ideology became of no concern—succor was given where it was needed.

What was paramount was the day-to-day survival of her family and of the non-combatant villagers and rural people around her who found themselves in the midst of battle for reasons they did not understand—as had been the case from the time of the wars between rival city-states which had in the end rendered the area so desolate and abandoned. In her war diary, Origo recorded a people, a world, and a now-past way of life that is usually left undocumented; history focuses on leaders, battles, and great national interests and leaves untold the story of ordinary lives.

There were refugees to be housed, food to be concealed and doled out; improvisation and self-reliance was the order of the day. People had to learn to make their own soap, to spin and weave the local wool, make shoe-leather out of skins, even learn to convert motor vehicles to run on charcoal. The Origos constantly ran the risk of betrayal as they sent food to the partisans in their woods, helped escaped prisoners on their way, nursed the wounded and dying. "It is odd," Iris Origo writes, "how used one can become to uncertainty for the future, to a complete planlessness, even in one's most private mind. What we shall do and be, and whether we shall, in a few months' time, have any home or possessions, or indeed our lives, is so clearly dependent on events outside our own control as to be almost restful."[26]

At the end of June 1944, the Germans put the Origos out of their home. With a band of refugee children and their own two small daughters they straggled on foot under the hot sun for twelve kilometers down a targeted country road to reach Montepulciano and find refuge in the home of the mayor. Devoid of possessions (except for the change of underwear and eau de cologne that she managed to take with her), Iris Origo relates her feelings of being joined to the common lot of humanity. The dichotomy between her personal good fortune and what most people experience will continue to haunt her: when the anti-fascist writer Ignazio Silone (returned to Italy after years in exile) once offered to bring her a nun for help in the matter of some religious research, Origo responded that she would be uncomfortable receiving the Sister in her Rome apartment "with its unmistakable atmosphere of luxury."[27] To which Silone replied, "No one is satisfied with his own station in life."

When the war ended, Iris and her family left the devastated area around La Foce for the United States and passed some months with her Cutting relatives on the Long Island estate where all was still bucolic and serene. In the fall of 1945, she was back in Italy and stopped in Rome to pay an unannounced visit on George Santayana, who had retired during the war years to a convent of English sisters on Via San Stefano Rotondo. In a letter to a friend, he describes Origo's arrival which was doubly welcome for not being, he says wryly, a visit of veneration with offerings of sweets or jam as if he were an idol or the village elder. Iris Origo had come to report that she and her family had weathered the war, and she brought him pictures of her two little daughters, born during those difficult years. The old philosopher, remembering his melancholy prophecy of years past when Origo's small son had died, rejoiced for her and admitted to his correspondent that, happily, he was not much of a prophet after all for Iris Origo had clearly not gone adrift to wreck on the reefs of El Dorado.

Still, things would never be again what they had been in the prewar world. Back in the carefree times of 1930 when Edith Wharton arrived on one of her frequent visits to I Tatti, Berenson would wander off with her and Nicky Mariano to make a round of visits in Tuscany. They called at La Foce at a bucolic time when the Origos still had their son Gianni and were creating a paradisiacal estate in what had once been barren and forsaken land. Iris Origo had gotten over her shyness with B. B. and was on her way to becoming one of his most perceptive friends.

In May of 1947, Bernard Berenson again lunched at La Foce with Iris and Antonio Origo and this time he recorded: "In the desert of the badlands [they] have created a palace with every up-to-date luxury, and gardens of real beauty. All so willed and so little of it the flowering of the earth's energies on the spot. I wonder how long it will survive its creator."

The Origos had to wonder, too. Different from other proprietors of vast holdings, Iris and Antonio had ideals and social concerns when they arrived, newlyweds, in a wild district where 80 percent of the people were illiterate. During their lifetimes they had seen rural society change, develop, and prosper. Their attempt to reclaim a corner of Tuscany was Utopian, but it is today remembered, studied, and has become legendary in those parts.[28]

Nevertheless, the postwar reaction to decades of fascism made the peasants dissatisfied with the ancient *mezzadria* system of farming the lands of the owner in return for only half of what their labor produced. That system of half-to-the-peasant-half-to-the-landlord had been rooted in Tuscan practice since the Middle

Ages, Origo explains; at its best the division of labor and owner-ship emancipated the Tuscan peasant centuries in advance of the rest of Italy and Europe. It made him superior in many ways and sharper in intelligence. It made him a free man, not a serf, and instilled qualities of foresightedness. But the system was anti-quated for the postwar era; it no longer satisfied the peasant. At war's end the Origos returned to rebuild La Foce only to find that after all the money and effort and hope poured into the land, those who worked it resented them as symbols of the old system.

In the modern era, Tuscan farmers wanted their own lands and responsibilities rather than a benevolent paternalism which kept them in passive dependency. After little more than twenty-five years at La Foce, the idealized compact between landowner and peasant came to an end. Nothing, however, was to be regretted by Iris Origo as she philosophically summarized this period in her autobiography. She had approached—even attained—Henry James's ideal of virtue as he contemplated the lives that could be lived in the beautiful villas around Florence; i.e., achieving in a noble landscape contentment and concentration: "A beautiful occupation in that beautiful position, what could possibly be better?"[29]

Antonio Origo began a modernization program for farming the estate and became the mayor of Chianciano while Iris returned to her writing. In 1966, when the great flood devastated Florence, she was among those who helped with the recovery and wrote about those dramatic days in her preface to a portfolio of flood drawings by Florentine artist Luciano Guarnieri. Some thirty years after the end of World War II, she was awarded the Order of the British Empire for her work with escaped British POWs. The honor was given to her in 1977, the year after Antonio Origo died.

Following the publication of her war diaries, Origo's next work was the biography of Lord Byron and his Italian mistress, Count-ess Teresa Guiccioli. She had successfully prevailed upon Count

Carlo Gamba, Guiccioli's great-nephew, to give her his cache of Teresa's unpublished letters from the English poet, and this despite the fact that they had been refused to several other biographers including André Maurois.

Here again, in Origo's obtaining the Guiccioli papers, there is an intriguing crossing at the distance of almost a century of literary personalities. In 1887, when Henry James was in Florence, he one day met the Countess Gamba who had married a nephew of Byron's last mistress, Teresa Guiccioli. She told Henry James that the Gambas had a great many of Byron's letters, which she found shocking and unprintable and that she herself had burnt one of them. When it was mentioned that it was the Countess's duty to English literature to make the Byron documents public, she responded in anger. "*Elle se fiche bien* of the English public," James wrote in his notebook.[30]

Iris Origo had already written a book about Byron's daughter Allegra, and she recounts how the present Count Gamba, descendant of that irate Countess who didn't give a fig about burning Byron's letter, entrusted the whole little chest of Teresa's letters, Byronic relics, and unpublished memoir to her, the Marchesa Origo, when she called on him.[31] *Noblesse oblige*, to be sure, but even she was astounded.

Origo's is a new portrait of Byron—he's shown in an Italian setting and as seen through contemporary Italian eyes. As Origo was able to do with Leopardi or San Bernardino through her perfect knowledge of Italy and Italians, she does even more so for Byron since her identification with the English lord trying to fit into provincial Italian society was so entwined with her own experience. She could see him in twin vision, through English eyes and her acquired Italian habits. And for the first time she presents Byron's Italian love letters to Teresa along with their translation.

The important emphasis in Origo's study is on Byron's Italianization and his still frequent feelings of foreignness: "Each of them in turn—Byron in Ravenna, Teresa in the English circle in Pisa—had to conform, for the other's sake, to the ways of a bewildering and alien society." Where Byron had previously been shown as the "English Milord in Italy," a foreigner playing a part, he was, in Ravenna, "inoculated into a family." That Bryon had become so Italianized was what shocked and disconcerted the Leigh Hunts and Mary Shelley so much. And yet the fact is that he always remained an Englishman, constantly preoccupied with English opinion of him, always eager for the smallest scrap of news from England. "Lord Byron, inglese," he signed the visitor's book in the Armenian monastery at Venice. At the same time he claims in a poem to Teresa, "My blood is all meridian."[32] That mix of allegiances would be familiar territory to Iris Origo.

Byron's part in the secret Carboneria revolutionary movement in the Ravenna period had been rather slighted since his biographers tended to emphasize the sexual liaison rather than his political activities. "Only think, a free Italy! Why, 'tis the very poetry of politics," Byron wrote in a letter.[33] His Italian venture was prelude to the Greek one where he risked his poet's laurels for those of a man of action. Never could he rid himself of the nagging conviction that the only true criterion of fame and success, the only true achievement, lay in the opinion of Englishmen at home who would esteem more the man of action than the writer of verses ("The successful are always judged favourably in our country," he told Lady Blessington). Before he departed for Greece in 1823, Byron's own notes on the Carboneria secret society were entrusted to an Italian named Mengaldo, but burned by the same Mengaldo rather than being sent on to England.

It is impossible to agree with Origo's estimate of Byron's Italian correspondence as indulging in a "wholly un-Byronic conventionality of sentiment." His Italian usage is, on the contrary, quite an achievement. But Origo muses that he may have been overplaying the Cavalier Servente role. "It is," she says, "to English ears, curiously formal." Declaring that the writer of the Italian letters is an unfamiliar Byron, the result of a partial change of personality, is indeed strange from the woman who had so perceptively observed in her youth that she was not the same person when she spoke Italian as she was speaking in English. She has Italian ears, too, and knows from her own experience how different languages form differing expressions and attitudes.

Iris was too dutiful a child, too primly brought up, too cautious to attempt the flights of fancy that made her idolized Virginia Woolf such a powerful novelist. *Allegra*, written at the beginning of her career, was quite bare of the notes, bibliographic apparatus, and mountain of research which would characterize her later work. She progressively made herself a brilliant researcher and an empathetic observer of life.

Iris Origo's portrait of fourteenth-century Francesco Datini in *The Merchant of Prato*, called by Barbara Tuchman "one of the great biographical works of the twentieth century" is based on 150,000 letters, 500 account books and ledgers and other documents willed to his city of Prato, all written in medieval hand and in need of transcription. Origo elevated this mass of material from dullness and obscurity to a palpable, engrossing story of a hard-driving fourteenth-century merchant and his sharp-tongued wife along with a supporting cast of characters.

Origo's secretary described her working methods: "We'd pull papers out from everywhere. She had huge *armadios* full of papers. . . . Her books were enormous, unbelievable pieces of work. . . . There were so many facts to check . . . notes, so many notes, transcriptions. But she wanted to do everything herself. Datini's letters were all transcribed and spread out everywhere."[34] Origo bridged a gap of six hundred and fifty years to bring forth not only a personality as sharply delineated as a present-day businessman's, but also his times and environs in a work of extraordinary and everlasting interest on a level, according to Tuchman, with Plutarch's *Lives*. The rise of Francesco Datini from orphaned son of a poor tavern owner making his way through the risks and hazards of medieval trade to become a rich and prominent merchant-banker is the equivalent success story of today's self-made millionaires. The most amazing part of Datini's story, however, is that it continues to this day: he left the bulk of his fortune in trust to the commune of Prato instructing the trustees to give out the interest on it each year to the poor of the city. And to this day, from the year of his death in 1410, his bequest is still being distributed in Prato.

Iris Origo's exposure to triple cultural influences had been enriching but had also, especially in childhood, subjected her to feelings of being insecurely rooted. As a writer, this became most manifest in her lack of confidence to write in her own voice until her wartime diary, *War in Val D'Orcia* (not originally meant for publication), was published in 1947 and became one of her most highly regarded works.

Though she chose to write mainly of Italian subjects and made her life an Italian one, Iris Origo was an author in English. The one exception was *Un'Amica*, written in Italian as a tribute to Elsa Dallolio, the close friend of Iris's middle years. Elsa was not only a close collaborator who had read Origo's books line by line in manuscript yet refused recognition in the acknowledgments, but someone who was also, says Origo (to the end ungenerous to her parent), "the mother I never had."

Iris Origo's writing is temperate and civilized, the voice of cultivation and restraint; she is the gifted teller of others' stories and mistress of the visual detail. She uses unparalleled skill and artistry in weaving archival research into compelling narrative. And in telling those stories of past beings, she has also given us her own. As she would later say, we sometimes come closer to people of the past than to our own contemporaries, and that is what makes the art of biography irresistible.

Though a shadow of regret for persons lost and things undone does pass over the harmonious whole of her recounting, in the end the doubts which touched her are dispelled: she was blessed in life by birth, wealth, talent, and education. She never regretted her choice of life; she felt that she and Antonio were singularly fortunate in having had the work and life they wanted: hers was a life of fulfillment, very humanely expressed in the legacy of her writings. She was successful, publicly, in working out a completed composite identity.

In the end, after trials, after triumph, she earned the title she would most have aspired to—not that of nobility, authorship, or honorary degree but of a guide who understood and empathized with life and could impart her wisdom to others. She became acclaimed both in the English-speaking world and in Italy for her consummate art as a biographer-historian, and her style seems to me the very essence of her patrician background and wide learning. Reasoned, controlled, understated, and elegant, Origo's prose and empathy earned her a lovely accolade from Italian critic Geno Pampaloni. In his preface to her last work, *Un'Amica*, he said of Iris Origo that her supreme gift was that she became through her interpretive biographies the poet of the conduct and lessons of life.

From the road, cypresses hid Villa La Foce from my view. However, a road sign on the road reading Azienda Agricola and leading to a courtyard where the estate office is located and where olive oil is sold indicated that it was still a working and productive farm. The villa itself began as a sixteenth-century stage-stop on the road to Siena and belonged originally to the Ospedale della Scala of Siena, whose coat of arms can still be seen on the facade along with the Origo stem. The hitching posts for the horses are still there, and a sense of the past conjoins with a future that continues with the farming, the splendid summer concerts organized by Benedetta Origo in the environs of La Foce, and the great care that is still given the gardens.

Once on the grounds, one can go beyond a small strand of maples to where it opens into a beautiful plantation of beech trees set down in the Napoleonic era, one of the rare exemplars in Italy of a wholly conserved forest. Or, from the villa one can follow, as I did, a path through the woods below the garden on a southern slope to the cemetery. I was thinking, as I walked, of the words of a formidable Roman matron, a relic of past times, with whom I had conversed in Rome. She had known Iris Origo and said of her, "A hard person, the Anglo-Saxon type, but good looking and elegant . . . still, why did she have to write all those books? and always pushing them! She was too closed. Why couldn't she be a nice old woman, just a grandmother?"

I came out of the woods to a roadway bright with clumps of hollyhock, genista, honeysuckle. Opposite a landmark giant oak stands the small churchyard spread out before Pinsent's elegant chapel of travertine, the whole encircled by cypresses. It had been built in 1933 when Gianni died and was laid to rest there. The perfume of pines scents the air and the flame-like frame of tall cypresses shields the calm of the place that also holds the graves of some of those who were killed nearby during the war. There, alongside the chapel, were buried Antonio Origo in 1976, and then Iris Origo in 1988.

I entered the little cemetery and walked toward the modest headstones near the tiny chapel. The inscription on Iris Origo's stone belied all the judgmental words of the Roman matron who had berated her for "writing all those books." Only her name and dates are recorded, plus the simple line "Wife of Antonio for 52 Years."

I had come to the end of my search for the six American women whom I had started out to find in their Italian context.

On the night before I was to fly to Rome my sleep was uneasy. The trip was to visit my daughter Susi and her family and to take in some of the sites associated with the women about whom I was writing. It was years since I had lived in Rome and I dreamt I had to get a train and couldn't find Stazione Termini. This seemed significant: would I have the same feelings that I had voiced in *Umbria*, a long-ago poetry collection in which I recorded my first revelation of Italy? Would I recover old bearings and find my landmarks in the country where I had studied, married, and resided and where my middle daughter and her family now live? Would I be able to carry on conversations in Italian with friends not seen in years?

Once there, I got both the language and my sense of direction back *in toto* and was able once again to navigate the admirable bus lines of Rome. But an unnerving sign of the times was the answer a newsstand vendor offered when I asked where to find the #57 bus stop. Giving me the straight-armed fascist salute he said, "In Piazza Venezia, where the Duce used to be." I wondered, had the reappearance of then Prime Minister Silvio Berlusconi on the political scene emboldened neo-fascism. Had prosperity brought back the old bravado?

Consumerism has adopted English as its language of choice: a supermarket calls itself "Shopping Paradise"; a sign on an apartment building announced an "Open House"—a new concept for Rome real estate. The facades of major buildings were bright with their original umber tones, decades of soot and grime having been blasted off the church of the Gesù, Sant'Andrea delle Valle, Teatro Argentina, the Ministero Grazia e Giustizia, and others throughout the city's center. It started in 1994 for the World Cup events, and was completed for the Holy Year of 2000. Political graffiti on walls, however, still flourished in Italian and some I spotted translated into "Berlusconi thief" and "Down with Packed Buses." A poster that referred to a minister under indictment for the political scandal of the day, read: "Craxi begs, along with a passport, give me back my balls."

I marveled at the new traffic lights and a beginning of ramps for those in wheelchairs. Then I wondered that the Romans hadn't risen in protest over the loss of precious parking spaces because of the presence of trash dumpsters in residential streets. Actually, the dumpster provides an ingenious system, neat and practical: each householder is responsible for taking out his own refuse and the neighborhood's collective trash is carted off by a garbage truck that pulls alongside and attaches to the dumpster, lifts and empties it, then returns it to the street. It spells the end of the picturesque *spazzini*, those ancient, stooped men in gray tunics who once wheeled their trash cans through the streets, as silent as ghosts as they swept away with their long-handled twig brooms. In Italo Calvino's posthumous collection, *The Road to San Giovanni*, there is a piece called "La Poubelle Agrée" (about putting out garbage when he lived in Paris) in which he recalled his first trip to the United States and a visit to us in Croton-on-Hudson where Antonio entertained him with the then inconceivable (for an Italian man) rite of putting out the garbage. Calvino's piece described the same rite come to Europe.

In Rome, I visited Constance Fenimore Woolson's gravesite in the Protestant Cemetery on the centenary of her death in Venice. The cemetery has remained a wonderfully peaceful oasis in the midst of the city's bustle and clamor, a miraculously walled-off spot of serenity. That the site is so protected is due in part to Woolson's niece, Clare Benedict, whose words on her aunt, chiseled into the wall next to the entrance, are explanatory: "As a protection to the sacred and historic place which she loved so dearly and where she now rests, this wall was raised to its present height."

In Rome's historic center, walking through Piazza Capo di Ferro where I once rented work-space, I was pleased to see a new sign identifying the corner building opposite the Trattoria della Quercia as Palazzo Ossoli, Secolo XVI. How many times I had rounded the corner past that handsome building without knowing it as the home of Giovanni Ossoli, Margaret Fuller's young lover. It was a place where she, as an American, a Protestant, and a revolutionary, could never have set foot according to the strict dictates of Giovanni's father and brothers who were part of the papal aristocracy opposed to the unification of Italy.

Not far off was Palazzo Orsini where I was to meet Iris Origo's daughter, Benedetta. The palace had once been the residence of the Duchess of Sermoneta, Marguerite Caetani's sister-in-law, Vittoria Colonna Caetani, and it occupies one of Rome's most spectacular sites, overlooking two superb ancient remains, the Portico of Ottavia and the Theatre of Marcellus. The imposing approach, through gates still surmounted by the rampant bear that is the Orsini device, goes up a long drive bordered with classical asphodel and acanthus, past a fountain surmounted by an obelisk, to the grand entrance. When Palazzo Orsini was divided into luxury apartments, Iris Origo made one her Rome residence, and it is now the home of her daughter.

An elevator took me up to a glorious sun-lit corridor leading into a handsome sitting room dominated by a grand piano. Benedetta Origo's interests and talent, rather than literary as were her mother's, are in music. She is the organizing force behind the successful and exquisite chamber music concerts known as

Incontri in Terra di Siena. Founded in 1989 in memory of Antonio and Iris Origo, the series feature international musicians who gather in the countryside around La Foce where the couple lived and worked for fifty years. Each summer, performances are held in some of the most beautiful surroundings imaginable—courtyards of old castles, at the beautiful country homes and gardens of the Val D'Orcia in Tuscany, a still relatively unspoiled part of the Tuscan region as compared to the foreigners' Chiantishire.

Benedetta Origo, tall, elegant, lithe, and impeccably turned out in simple black pants, open white shirt, belt, sandals, and drop earrings, has tawny blond hair, wears no make-up, and is not only an extremely attractive mother of four, but also a grandmother. She looked very much like pictures I've seen of young Iris Origo, though she claimed her sister Donata has an even greater resemblance to their mother. Over coffee brought by a maid, we spoke of Iris Origo. Benedetta recalled that her mother had wonderful mental focus for her books but was always, in daily life, misplacing things. Benedetta was cordial, but bemused. After all, what more could I possibly want to know, she asked—it's all in her mother's books. Yes, perhaps, but I told her I'd really like to see La Foce if that were possible. With great kindness and dispatch, she telephoned her estate manager at La Foce to arrange my visit there and so we parted.

Palazzo Caetani still stands solidly on Via delle Botteghe Oscure, but its neighbor, the Italian Communist Party Headquarters, has been vacated although its official paper, *L'Unità*, which suspended publication in July 2000, has, like the phoenix, once more come back.

Palazzo Caetani is flanked by Via Michelangelo Caetani, a short street of sad memory—it was here that the bullet-ridden body of Prime Minister Aldo Moro was found in the trunk of an abandoned car following his kidnapping by Red Brigade terrorists in the spring of 1978. A wall plaque commemorates Moro as an earlier one does Don Michelangelo Caetani, 1804–1884, Dante scholar, benefactor of his country, and presenter of the decree which established the new nation of Italy in 1870. He was a singular character even for that colorful family. The Roman painter Nino Costa, who participated in the revolution of 1849, wrote an account of that time in which he noted that on June 3, 1849, when the Garibaldi legions came through the San Pancrazio Gate for the battle of the Janiculum, *"Don Michelangelo Caetani arrivava fra noi che en amateur veniva a godersi la battaglia."*[1] (Don Michelangelo Caetani arrived among us to enjoy the battle as spectator.) The street, short as it is, also holds Palazzo Mattei where the Center for American Studies is located and whose library I used to frequent when I lived in Rome. And beneath the street, amazing excavations, initiated in 1980, are still uncovering layers of the ancient city, with some remains now visible in the handsome new Crypta Balbo Museum across the street from Palazzo Caetani.

From the late 1970s, on my return trips I was reminded constantly that things were no longer what they were when I lived in Rome. Crack vials littered certain areas and McDonald's and the punk look had come to the center of Rome close to the Spanish Steps. Access to banks had to be made through entrance-exit cages with security devices and lockers for depositing metal objects with armed guards inside. One no longer strolled out at night, a past great pleasure of the city.

I made a day trip out of the city to Rieti to retrace Margaret Fuller's life there in the summer of 1848 as she awaited the birth of her child. The seventy-five kilometer trip that took Fuller all day from Rome was an hour and a half bus ride by way of the ancient Via Salaria into a countryside filled with fields of grain, hummocks of hay, and hills of *genestra,* that golden broom plant which fills the eyes like dots of sunshine. This was the land of the ancient Sabine tribes, but papal territory in Fuller's time.

The same area, tree-covered, mountainous, and with few signs of habitation, attracted another American woman in the post-World War II period. Following the lively days in Paris of the 1920s when her husband Harry was still alive and they ran the avant-garde Black Sun Press, Caresse Crosby founded a One World colony in Cyprus and relocated it to the partially restored ancient castle-fortress of Rocca Sinisbaldo in a hamlet in the Sabine hills not far from Rieti. There she housed her commune of artists and social activists, letting herself be known locally as the Principessa of Rocca Sinisbaldo. A vivid contrast to her predecessor, Margaret Fuller, Caresse Crosby was active and preposterous to the end of her life in 1970.

In Florence, I thought of Mabel Dodge decades earlier declaring after nine years of residence that she'd "done" it; I began to feel the same way, glad at least to have seen Florence much earlier before it became so packed with tourists, hordes of students on field trips, and vendors camped on the Ponte Vecchio. The city had become expensive, crowded and difficult to walk in, crammed with fast-food eateries, endless souvenir stuff made by rote, and more rude impatience than was ever common even to Florentines.

I was there to visit Villa Medici with Cristina Anzilotti, director of the Sarah Lawrence college program in Florence. She is the daughter of an American mother and Professor Rolando Anzilotti, the Italian translator of Robert Lowell's poetry. We found Villa Medici though Iris Origo's memoir gives no impression that her childhood home was so close to town—that, in fact, from the back door or service entrance she might (if she were so allowed) have walked up to the main piazza for an ice cream, store browsing, or just to mingle in the evening promenade that is so much a part of small town Italian life. From that back door, it would also have been easy access across the narrow cobbled street to the main entrance of Villa Le Balze, once home of Charles Strong and his wife, a Rockefeller.

We, in fact, entered Villa Medici not by the great and imposing front gates through a landscaped terrace bordered with blooming lemon trees and banks of roses to the main loggia, but through that street door into a tiny kitchen where an old woman was making pasta. The original kitchen had been on a lower floor, off a kitchen garden, and probably much more spacious than the present one, and more suited to the elaborate and endless meals that had to come in steady profusion for Sybil Cutting's household and guests. The front approach would have brought us to a severe facade in the Tuscan manner, the whole roofed over with the typical red tiles of the region. From there and from other look-outs on the descending terraces, the view is westward with the great cupola of Florence's Duomo emerging grandly from the surrounding city. Still, Villa Medici seemed to me a place of past glory.

Not so the Origo country place, La Foce. In a beautiful and uncluttered landscape, it is still a working and productive estate where olive oil is sold from the farm office. At a crossroads on the road to Montepulciano there is a sign for the Ambulatorio Gianni Origo, a small clinic named for Iris's deceased son. Across the road, the Casa dei Bambini, a former school where children from war-ravaged cities were housed, is now occupied by the estate manager. These were the landmarks I knew from Iris Origo's memoir and war diary.

Her gardens at La Foce are still beautifully tended, and a huge new swimming pool put in by Benedetta Origo fronts the *limonaia* where the lemon trees are wintered. Everything was under the care of Alfiero, the estate manager, who has been at La Foce since 1966 and remembers La Marchesa, as he referred to Iris Origo. The walls of his office were lined with posters from Benedetta's musical festivals.

Alfiero walked us over the grounds and pointed out the first modest garden beds with fountain that Iris laid out—and what had flourished from that modest beginning as her American grandmother supplied gifts of money. Eventually, a conduit for water from the hills was built to nourish the extensive gardens and orchards. An absolutely gigantic wisteria, supported by a wall, provided shade under its huge, tenacious branches for little sitting alcoves. Double-petaled peonies were bursting into bloom; a whole avenue of the famous Banksia roses from Villa Medici festooned themselves like fragrant draperies. In the distance was a view of the twisting road up Monte Amiata, one of the most photographed scenes in Italy, Alfiero told us, featured on all panoramic calendars.

From Florence, if we had gone south on Viale Poggio Imperiale, Cristina and I would have come to Mabel Dodge's Villa Curonia; overlooking the city in the opposite direction from Fiesole was Villa Brichieri, where Constance Woolson spent a happy time of her life when she was so briefly landlady to her hero Henry James. Today the villa is Hotel Bellosguardo and the site is still as fine as Woolson described, with its romantic aviary, vine-covered arches, and sweeping view of the city from the grass terrace stretching before the handsome facade. Curiously, a doorman came toward us on the lawn saying it was a private place. It's a hotel, I replied. Yes, but very tranquil, he said incongruously and incorrectly over the noise of a roistering party going on at the adjacent property. Possibly noting his own contradictions, he then said that possibly if we came back the next morning. . . . We did not.

From the site of Constance Woolson's happy days, I went north to Venice where she had leased Palazzo Semitecolo for a long sojourn. Her place was not far from my *pensione* in a charming area near Campo Sant'Agnese with its grand baroque church of the Gesuati and the Accademia art collection. I thought of Woolson in those locales: of her becoming expert at guiding her own gondola and exploring every nook and cranny in Venice, every island in the lagoon, or taking long walks on the Lido with her dog Otello. Her last residence was on the Grand Canal quite close to the one-floor Palazzo Venier dei Leoni, called in Venetian dialect *Maifinío* ("never finished") because money ran out before it was completed. It became the home of another famed American woman, Peggy Guggenheim, who settled there, established an important art collection, and left it to Venice as an overseas wing of the Guggenheim Museum built by her uncle Solomon in New York.

And I thought of Peggy, made an honorary citizen of Venice and called by the grateful city "the last *dogaressa*," and in Gore Vidal's fanciful words, "the last of Henry James's transatlantic heroines."[2] She was a character, though perhaps not one Henry James had in mind; she slept in a bed made of silver since brass had become scarce since the war, and the cerulean blue wall of her bedroom was hung with thousands of earrings. It was said that at night she removed for safe-keeping from vandals the erect penis in the Marino Marini sculpture that stands at the Grand Canal entrance of her palazzo, replacing it the next morning. Bombastic, always with a retinue, she said of Venice that no other place gave her the sense of liberty that it did and that one should only wear fantastic clothing in such a place. And that she did; garbed in long gold-shot tunics and wearing miniature Alexander Calder mobile-earrings. She had a marble throne in a garden pavilion that was modeled after one in a Palladian villa, and there she sat cuddling her pups, a succession of fourteen in the thirty years she lived in Venice. They are interred against the garden wall under a tablet that reads, "Here lie my Beloved Babies." Adjacent another tablet reads, "Here rests Peggy Guggenheim, 1898–1979." Nearby is a planter of daisies, *margherite* in Italian, to recall her given name of Marguerite. She was certainly a legendary personality, made even more so by Mary McCarthy's depiction of her as the sexually predatory character Polly Grabbe in the story "Il Cicerone."

From the Hotel Gritti I looked across the Grand Canal to Constance Woolson's Palazzo Semitecolo; almost facing it across the canal was Mrs. Bronson's palace where Henry James found it the bliss of a summer evening to hang over the balcony smoking a cigarette and watching the water traffic. What would he have made of the gondolier I watched go by talking into a cellular phone cradled on his shoulder while he plied the waters?

The legions of American women who had come to Italy and made it part of their lives made me think of my own Italian interlude. I shared with them the gift of having been able to live and work there, and of having been able to participate in Italian life during a period that was an extraordinarily creative moment for Italian arts. The women's stories reinforced my own gratitude for the Italian interval in my life.

When I first arrived in Italy in 1948, it was still an agricultural country and I was in time to see sheep being herded out of Rome's Piazza del Popolo through the great portal and down Via Flaminia. By the booming sixties, farmers were abandoning the land for the cities; Piazza del Popolo had become a huge, outdoor parking garage. And I had to ask myself, had I really seen a shepherd and his sheep there? I ask myself now, were those sheep an illusion, the imagined metaphor of loss, of a pastoral Italy gone forever? The Arcadian question again. Thankfully, the Piazza is once again traffic-free and restored to the people for whom it is named. And a wonderful confirmation of my original memory is in Eugene Walter's memoir, *Milking the Moon*. Arriving in Rome in the early 1950s, he wrote of having witnessed "early in the morning, flocks of sheep crossing the town, driven by their shepherds to the Doria parks on the Janiculum Hill." Eugene left

Rome when it had become a never-ending traffic jam and political street demonstrations an almost daily occurrence.

We all have the sense of having got there too late or, worse, to have seen what we loved from the past disappear: William Dean Howells in late nineteenth-century Venice lamented the passing of the Corpus Christi ritual of thirty years earlier; Henry James in Rome, after Italy's unification, missed the daily passage through town of the pontiff and deplored the horse-cab stands at Giotto's tower in Florence; D. H. Lawrence was furious in the second decade of the twentieth century at northern Italy's new paved roads. Even official British Army World War II reports lament the damage inflicted by Germans retreating from Florence in 1945 in an almost personal way: "The heart of the old city round the Ponte Vecchio is gone . . . the whole of the famous view looking up the river to the Ponte Vecchio, with the medieval houses is lost forever, twelve palaces destroyed, the most characteristic remains of medieval Florence from Piazza del Pesce to the Loggia del Mercato Nuovo—all have gone."[3]

Decades after my first delicious encounter with Florence, I could regret the loss of a quiet walker's town. For a while there was an unspeakable surge of traffic in those narrow streets made even more impassable with the presence of overflowing garbage dumpsters. I found the seediness of Palazzo Strozzi's display area for a major exhibit of paintings as well as the squalid state of its public restrooms signs of some inexplicable weariness.

It all changes and we all regret it—except for the Italians who swell with pride as their country has passed from an agricultural society of the picturesque peasant with oxen and burro to become a major industrial nation of the world. *Pace* Lawrence, the country is now veined with super highways connecting remote regions everywhere; construction cranes are omnipresent against the once-tranquil landscapes. There is nothing to do about the invasion of the new barbarians: Starbucks has embarked on bringing "actual coffee" to the land of the refined *espresso*. The world has shrunk and everything, everyplace, seems Americanized, not only in Italy.

But perhaps we're all wrong. Perhaps, in Tancredi's words to the Prince in Lampedusa's *The Leopard*, "If we want everything to stay as it is, it all had to change." That, then, is Italy's lesson: ongoing change—and, hopefully, renewal, with each new phase building on the previous.

Henry James had seen how the traveler to Italy became more civilized just by being there: "People who had never before shown knowledge, taste or sensibility, had here quite knocked under."[4] In a country where the fabric of multiple pasts is so richly woven together, sensations, impressions, are multiplied; the fruits of nature and of human endeavor seem more bountiful in Italy than elsewhere and inevitably enrich those who seek and then absorb them. Postwar twentieth-century Italy had the image of *dolce vita* to join to its others—Arcadian Italy, the romance Italy of gothic menace, and the sunny Italy of Longfellow.[5] And they are all constructs of Italy for the imagination, a rich complexity reflected in the many views of it by artists and writers.

Perhaps the greatest gift Italy offers is not only its past and its lesson of continual renovation, but also, as a *New York Times* columnist recently editorialized, the evidence of civilization it imparts in the values of humanity, culture, beauty, . . . and mostly, I would add, in its gift of knowing how to live: *saper vivere.*[6]

Prologue

1. Virgil, *Aeneid*, 4.361.
2. Kazin, *New York Jew*, 157–58.
3. Chalfant, *Both Sides of the Ocean*, 155–56.
4. Adams, *The Education of Henry Adams*, 85.
5. Origo, *Images and Shadows*, 256.
6. Fisher, *A Gentle Journalist Abroad*, 24.
7. Ward, *John Keats: The Making of a Poet*, 401–2. Severn's devotion to Keats was recognized after his death in 1879 when his body was reinterred alongside Keats's grave in Rome.
8. Richards, *Julia Ward Howe, 1819–1910*, 2: 3.
9. Staël, *Corinne, or Italy*, 176.
10. Chanler, *Roman Spring*, 304.
11. Howe, *Reminiscences*, 120.
12. Hawthorne, *Notebooks*, 14: 64.
13. Ibid., 905–6.
14. Vance, *American's Rome*, 2:262.
15. Cheever, Journals.
16. Hawthorne, *Notebooks*, 54.
17. James, *William Wetmore Story and His Friends*, 1:124.

1. Margaret Fuller

Quotes of Margaret Fuller are from her *Memoirs and Letters*.

1. Maria Cropsey, Letter of 10 December 1847. Newington-Cropsey Foundation Library.
2. Thomas Hicks, Letter of 2 August 2 1850. Houghton Library manuscript collection.
3. Woolf, *The Diary of Virginia Woolf*, 1: 23.
4. Chevigny, *Between Women*, 369.
5. Chevigny, *The Woman and the Myth*, 19.

6. Greeley, *Recollections of a Busy Life*, 191.

7. Bowen, ed., *The Young Lady's Book*, 28.

8. The impressions of Fuller are from Frederic Henry Hedge who met her while he was a student at Harvard. Chevigny, *The Woman and the Myth*, 30.

9. Ibid., 29, n. 19.

10. Morse, *Life and Letters of Oliver W. Holmes*, 1: 258.

11. Holmes, *Elsie Venner*, 101.

12. Lawrence, *Studies in Classic American Literature*, 89.

13. James, *William Wetmore Story*, 1: 130.

14. Chevigny, *The Woman and the Myth*, 162.

15. Ibid., 32.

16. Ibid., 335.

17. Brooks, *Flowering of New England*, 47.

18. Fuller, *Literature and Art*, 2: 130–31.

19. Chevigny, *The Woman and the Myth*, 515.

20. Ibid., 301.

21. Fuller, *Those Sad but Glorious Days*, 1.

22. James, *William Wetmore Story*, 1: 130.

23. Although there is no tangible certificate documenting a marriage between Margaret and Ossoli, the testimony of their closest family and friends and that of Lewis Cass Jr., the United States chargé d'affaires in Rome, ratifies it, as well as Fuller's own instructions that she be addressed as Margaret Ossoli or Marchioness Ossoli. Henry James records that William and Emelyn Story, while traveling in Venice the autumn of 1849, received "a letter from Margaret Fuller declaring her marriage to Ossoli." Ibid., 190.

24. Anthony, *Margaret Fuller*, 208.

25. Emerson, *Journals*, 249.

26. Fuller, *Journal*, 119.

27. Fuller took the expression "City of the Soul" regarding Rome from Byron's "Childe Harold's Pilgrimage."

2. Emily Dickinson

1. Sewall, *The Life of Emily Dickinson*, 49.

2. Miller, *Salem is My Dwelling Place*, 424.

3. Gelpi, "Seeing New Englandly," 41.

4. Weiss, "Beethoven's Hair Tells All!" 114.

5. Chevigny, *The Woman and the Myth*, 70–1.

6. Ibid., 203.

7. Dickinson, *Selected Letters*, 2: 376.

8. Dickinson, *Complete Poems*, poem 405.

9. Simpson, "Historic Houses: Emily Dickinson," 102.

10. Dickinson, *Complete Poems*, poem 1705.

11. Gelpi, "Seeing New Englandly," 40.

12. Ibid., 161.

13. Rich, *Vesuvius at Home*, 176.

14. Patterson, *The Riddle of Emily Dickinson*, 146.

15. Capps, *Emily Dickinson's Reading*, 106–7.

16. Before seeing Porter's note, I had quoted Dickinson's poem 80 in my *Introduction to The Dream Book* (New York: Schocken, 1985), 33.

17. Hughes, ed., *A Choice of Emily Dickinson's Verse*, 11.

18. Rich, "Vesuvius at Home," 167.

19. Ibid., 171.

20. Dickinson, *Complete Poems*, poem 994.

3. Constance Fenimore Woolson

1. Pattee, *Development of the American Short Story*, 251.

2. Benedict, *Constance Fenimore Woolson*, 44.

3. Harper, *The House of Harper*, 226.

4. Woolson, *The Front Yard*, 93.

5. Cooper, *Letters and Journals*, 2: 371.

6. Woolson, *The Front Yard*, 148.

7. Benedict, *Constance Fenimore Woolson*, 184–85.

8. Edel, *Henry James*, 2: 415.

9. James, *Letters*, 532.

10. Woolson, *The Front Yard*, 91.

11. James, *Letters*, 536.

12. Strouse, *Alice James*, 307.

13. Ibid., 259.

14. Edel, introduction, *Partial Portraits*, v; Edel, *Henry James*, 2: 409.

15. Strouse, *Alice James*, 312–13.

16. Henry James is quoted in Miller, *Robert Browning,*, 276.

17. James, *Letters*, 3: 553.

18. Ibid., 561.

19. Benedict, *Constance Fenimore Woolson*, 411.

20. James, *Letters*, 457.

21. Ibid., 420.

22. Ibid., 461, n. 3.

4. Mabel Dodge Luhan

Except where otherwise noted, quotes of Mabel Dodge Luhan are from her four-volume *Intimate Memoirs*.

1. Watson, *Strange Bedfellows*, 85.

2. Hahn, *Mabel*, 167.

3. Ibid., 111–12.

4. Frazer, *Mabel Dodge Luhan*, 48.

5. Watson, *Strange Bedfellows*, 131.

6. Draper, *Music at Midnight*, 10.

7. Secrest, *Being B. B.: A Biography*, 282.

8. Blanche, *Portraits of a Lifetime*, 95.

9. Davidson, *Between Sittings*, 82.

10. Luhan, *Lorenzo in Taos*, 15.

11. Secrest, *Being B. B.*, 282.

12. Stein, *The Autobiography of Alice B. Toklas*, 115.

13. Simon, *The Biography of Alice B. Toklas*, 106.

14. Toklas, *What Is Remembered*, 76–7.

15. Davidson, *Between Sittings*, 85.

16. Toklas, *What Is Remembered*, 75.

17. Skinner, *Dithers and Jitters*, 4–5.

18. Lueders, *Carl Van Vechten and the Twenties*, 20.

19. Douglas, *Margaret Sanger*, 26.

20. Eastman, *Enjoyment of Living*, 537.

21. Ibid., 523.

22. Stein, *Journeys into the Self*, 119.

23. Sterne, *Shadow and Light*, 134.

24. Luhan, *Lorenzo in Taos*, 15–16.

25. Meyers, *D. H. Lawrence and the Experience of Italy*, 1.

26. Lawrence, *Phoenix*, 160.

27. Carswell, *The Savage Pilgrimage*, 180.

28. Rudnick, *Mabel Dodge Luhan*, 210.

29. Letter of Bennett Cerf to Mabel Dodge Luhan, uncatalogued collection, ZaMs Luhan, Box Collier-Dd, Beinecke Library, Yale University.

30. Carswell, *The Savage Pilgrimage*, 255.

31. Sterne, *Shadow and Light*, 236.

32. Horgan, *Tracings*, 83.

33. Cowley, *Think Back on Us*, 123–26.

34. Hahn, *Mabel*, 213–14.

35. Rudnick, *Mabel Dodge Luhan*, 314.

36. Ibid., xv.

5. *Marguerite Caetani*

Quotes of Marguerite Caetani are from correspondence in the Eugene Walter Collection of the Harry Ransome Humanities Research Collection, University of Texas at Austin, and the Katherine Chapin Biddle papers at Georgetown University.

1. *New York Times*, 7 January 1941, 14.

2. Bolton, *Under Gemini*, 79–80.

3. *New York Times*, 9 November 1922, 18.

4. Origo, "Marguerite Caetani," 81.

5. Chapin, *Musical Chairs*, 27.

6. Stanley, *Under Italian Skies*, 196–97.

7. Note from Prince Roffredo Caetani to the director of the Boston Philharmonic, Houghton Library, Harvard.

8. *New York Herald*, 17 November 1911.

9. From Denis Mack Smith's *Italy: A Modern History* (1969), 102: "Of all the Roman nobility, the Duke of Sermoneta alone had been a confessed liberal before 1870. From then onward there was to be a gradual process of conversion."

10. Beach, *Shakespeare & Company*, 143.

11. Joyce quotes are from his *Letters*, 3: 99, 106–8, 110.

12. Donaldson, *Archibald MacLeish, An American Life*, 147.

13. Beach, *Shakespeare & Company*, 124.

14. Stock, *Life of Ezra Pound*, 262–63.

15. Katherine Chapin Biddle's papers, Georgetown University Library, Washington, D.C.

16. Rennell Rodd, *Social and Diplomatic Memories, 1902–1919*, 8.

17. Origo, "Marguerite Caetani," 84.

18. Heymann, *Ezra Pound*, 317.

19. *New York Times*, 21 December 1922, 2.

20. Reich, *Christian Science Monitor*, 1 July 1950, 8.

21. Colonna, *Sparkle, Distant Worlds*, 147.

22. Colonna, *Things Past*, 271–72.

23. Merrill, *A Different Person*, 106.

24. Author's telephone conversation with Eugene Walter.

25. On Columbus Day, 1942, Biddle ordered released the Italian nationals living in the United States from virtually all the restrictions imposed on "enemy aliens."

26. Obituary of Roffredo Caetani, *Il Tempo*, 18 April 1961.

27. Origo, "Marguerite Caetani," 85.

28. Biddle, *In Brief Authority*, 262.

29. Carpenter, *A Serious Character*, 790–91.

30. Chester, *Head of a Sad Angel: Stories 1953–1966*, 305. Chester's novel *The Exquisite Corpse* was published in 1967. He died in Jerusalem under mysterious circumstances in 1971 at the age of forty-two.

31. Matthews, *Great Tom*, 172.

32. Roethke, *Selected Letters*, 178.

6. Iris Origo

1. Mignani, *The Medicean Villas by Giusto Utens*, 13.

2. Origo, *Images*, 113.

3. Origo, *A Measure of Love*, 7.

4. Santayana, *Persons and Places*, 397.

5. Ibid.

6. Moorehead, *The Villa Diana*, 108.

7. Wharton, *A Backward Glance*, 137.

8. Beevor, *A Tuscan Childhood*, 145.

9. Berenson, *A Self-Portrait*, 204.

10. Origo, "The Homecoming."

11. Acton, *Memoirs of an Aesthete*, 9.

12. Origo, *Images*, 150.

13. Origo, *War in Val D'Orcia*, 7.

14. Origo, *Leopardi*, 135–36.

15. Wilde-Menozzi, "Iris Origo," 489.

16. Origo, *Images*, 176.

17. Woolf, *Diary*, 4: 327.

18. Woolf, *Letters of Virginia Woolf*, 5: 412. The following year, 1936, Woolf describes Iris as "the daughter of Lady Sybil Lubbock."

19. Woolf, *Letters*, 6: 10–11.

20. Origo, *A Measure of Love*, 9.

21. Woolf, *Diary*, 5: 8.

22. Ibid., 5.

23. Origo, *Images*, 173.

24. Biddle, *An American Artist's Story*, 59.

25. Origo, *War*, 39.

26. Ibid., 140.

27. Origo, *A Need to Testify*, 234.

28. Benedetta Origo, *La Foce*, 6, 21.

29. Cole, ed. *Florence*, 194.

30. Edel, *Henry James*, 337.

31. Origo, *The Last Attachment*, Introduction.

32. Ibid., 62.

33. Lord Byron, *Letters & Journals*, 5: 205.

34. Wilde-Mengozzi, "Iris Origo," 488.

Afterword

1. Costa, Journal.

2. Guggenheim, *Out of This Century*, xii.

3. Cole, *Florence*, 263.

4. James, *William Wetmore Story*, 2: 209–10.

5. "The sunny Italy of Longfellow" is from a Longfellow quote: "Italy has always been, and always will be, the land of the sun, and the land of song." In Tuttleton and Lombardo, eds., *The Sweetest Impression of Life*, 2.

6. The columnist is Anthony Lewis, whose piece "A Civilized Society" appeared in the *New York Times*, 8 September 2001, A13.

Acton, Harold. *Memoirs of an Aesthete*. New York: Viking Press, 1971.

Adams, Henry. *The Education of Henry Adams*. Boston: Houghton Mifflin, 1918.

Anthony, Katharine. *Margaret Fuller: A Psychological Biography*. New York: Harcourt Brace, 1921.

Barolini, Helen. *Introduction to The Dream Book*. New York: Schocken, 1985.

Beach, Sylvia. *Shakespeare and Company*. New York: Harcourt Brace, 1959.

Beevor, Kinta. *A Tuscan Childhood*. New York: Pantheon, 1993.

Benedict, Clare. *Constance Fenimore Woolson* and *Voices out of the Past*. Parts 2 and 3 of *Five Generations*. London: Ellis, 1929–30.

Berenson, Bernard. *Sunset and Twilight*. New York: Harcourt Brace, 1963.

Berenson, Mary. *A Self-Portrait from Her Diaries and Letters*. Edited by Barbara Strachey and Jayne Samuels. New York: Norton, 1983.

Biddle, Francis. *A Casual Past*. Garden City, N.Y.: Doubleday, 1961.

———. *In Brief Authority*. Garden City, N.Y.: Doubleday, 1962.

Biddle, George. *An American Artist's Story*. Boston: Little, Brown, 1939.

Blanche, Jacques-Emile. *Portraits of a Lifetime*. New York: Coward-McCann, 1938.

Bolton, Isabel. *Under Gemini: A Memoir*. New York: Harcourt Brace, 1969.

Brooks, Van Wyck. *Dream of Arcadia: American Writers and Artists in Italy, 1760–1915*. New York: Dutton, 1958.

———. *Flowering of New England*. New York: Dutton, 1936.

Byron, Lord. *Letters and Journals*. Edited by Rowland E. Prothero. 6 vols. New York: Scribner, 1922–24.

Caetani, Marguerite, ed. *An Anthology of New Italian Writers*. New York: New Directions, 1950.

Caetani, Marguerite, and Giorgio Bassani, eds. *Botteghe Oscure* 1–25. Rome, 1948–62.

Capps, Jack L. *Emily Dickinson's Reading*. Cambridge, Mass.: Harvard University Press, 1966.

Carpenter, Humphrey. *A Serious Character: The Life of Ezra Pound*. Boston: Houghton Mifflin, 1988.

Carswell, Catherine. *The Savage Pilgrimage: A Narrative of D. H. Lawrence*. New York: Harcourt Brace, 1932.

Chalfant, Edward. *Both Sides of the Ocean*. New York: Anchor Books, 1982.

Chanler, Margaret Terry. *Roman Spring*. Boston: Little, Brown, 1934.

Chapin, Katherine Garrison. *The Other Journey*. Minneapolis: University of Minnesota Press, 1959.

Chapin, Miles. "My Ninfa." *Garden Design*, August/September 1995.

Chapin, Schuyler. *Musical Chairs: A Life in the Arts*. New York: Putnam, 1977.

Cheever, John. "Journals (Part II)." *New Yorker*, August 13, 1990, passim.

Chester, Alfred. *Head of a Sad Angel: Stories 1953–1966*. Edited by Edward Field. Santa Rosa, Calif.: Black Sparrow Press, 1990.

Chevigny, Bell Gale. *The Woman and the Myth: Margaret Fuller's Life and Writings*. Old Westbury, N.Y.: Feminist Press, 1976.

———. "Daughters Writing." In *Between Women*. Boston: Beacon Press, 1984.

Cole, Toby, ed. *Florence: A Traveler's Anthology*. Westport, Conn.: Lawrence Hill, 1981.

Colonna, Vittoria. *Things Past*. London: Hutchinson, 1929.

———. *Sparkle, Distant Worlds*. London: Hutchinson, 1947.

Commerce: Cahiers Trimestriels. Kraus reprint, 1969.

Cooper, James Fenimore. *Letters and Journals*. Edited by James F. Beard. Cambridge, Mass.: Belknap Press, 1960–68.

Costa, Nino. Journal. Library, Center for American Studies, Rome.

Cowley, Malcolm. *Think Back on Us: A Contemporary Chronicle of the 1930s*. Carbondale: Southern Illinois University Press, 1972.

Crunden, Robert. *From Self to Society, 1919–1941*. Englewood Cliffs, N.J.: Prentice-Hall, 1972.

Davidson, Jo. *Between Sittings*. New York: Dial Press, 1951.

Deiss, Joseph Jay. *The Roman Years of Margaret Fuller*. New York: Crowell, 1969.

Dickinson, Emily. *Complete Poems*. Edited by Thomas H. Johnson. Boston: Little, Brown, 1960.

———. *Selected Letters*. Edited by Thomas H. Johnson. Cambridge, Mass.: Belknap Press, 1971.

Donaldson, Scott. *Archibald MacLeish: An American Life*. With R. H. Winnick. Boston: Houghton Mifflin, 1992.

Douglas, Emily Taft. *Margaret Sanger*. New York: Holt, Rinehart and Winston, 1969.

Draper, Muriel. *Music at Midnight*. New York: Harper, 1929.

Eastman, Max. *Enjoyment of Living*. New York: Harper, 1948.

Edel, Leon. *Henry James*. 5 vols. Philadelphia: J. B. Lippincott, 1953.

———. "Introduction" to *Partial Portraits* by Henry James. Ann Arbor: University of Michigan Press, 1970.

Emerson, Ralph Waldo. *Journals*. Boston: Houghton Mifflin, 1910.

Everett, Patricia R. *A History of Having a Great Many Times Not Continued to Be Friends: Correspondence between Mabel Dodge and Gertrude Stein, 1911–1934*. Albuquerque: University of New Mexico Press, 1996.

Fisher, Estelle. *A Gentle Journalist Abroad: The Papers of Anne Hampton Brewster*. Philadelphia: Free Library of Philadelphia, 1947.

Frazer, Winifred L. *Mabel Dodge Luhan*. Boston: Twayne, 1984.

Fuller, Margaret. *The Letters of Margaret Fuller*. Edited by Robert Hudspeth. Ithaca, N.Y.: Cornell University Press, 1983.

———. *Memoirs of Margaret Fuller Ossoli*. Edited by R. W. Emerson, W. H. Channing, and J. F. Clarke. New York: Burt Franklin, 1972.

———. *My Heart Is a Large Kingdom*. Edited by Robert Hudspeth. Ithaca, N.Y.: Cornell University Press, 2001.

———. *Those Sad but Glorious Days: Dispatches from Europe, 1846–1850*. Edited by Larry J. Reynolds and Susan Belasco Smith. New Haven, Conn.: Yale University Press, 1992.

———. *Journal, June–October 1844*. Proceedings of the Massachusetts Historical Society, v. 102, Boston, 1990.

———. *Woman in the Nineteenth Century*. New York: Jewett, 1845.

———. *Papers on Literature and Art*. New York: Wiley and Putnam, 1846.

Garrett, George, ed. *Botteghe Oscure Reader*. Middletown, Conn.: Wesleyan University Press, 1974.

Gelpi, Alfred. "Seeing New Englandly." In *Emily Dickinson*. Modern Critical Views Series, edited by Harold Bloom. New York: Chelsea House, 1985.

Gide, André. *Journals: 1889–1949.* 4 vols. New York: Knopf, 1947–51.

Greeley, Horace. *Recollections of a Busy Life.* New York: J. B. Ford, 1869.

Guggenheim, Peggy. *Out of this Century.* New York: Universe Books, 1979.

Hahn, Emily. *Mabel.* Boston: Houghton Mifflin, 1977.

Hapgood, Hutchens. *A Victorian in the Modern World.* New York: Harcourt Brace, 1939.

Harper, Joseph H. *The House of Harper.* New York: Harper and Brothers, 1912.

Hawthorne, Nathaniel. *The French and Italian Notebooks.* Edited by Thomas Woodson. Columbus: Ohio State University Press, 1980.

Heymann, C. David. *Ezra Pound: The Last Rower; A Political Profile.* New York: Viking Press, 1976.

Holmes, Oliver Wendell. *Elsie Venner: A Romance of Destiny.* Boston: Houghton Mifflin, 1900.

Horgan, Paul. *Tracings: A Book of Partial Portraits.* New York: Farrar, Straus, Giroux, 1993.

Howe, Julia Ward. *Reminiscences.* Boston: Houghton Mifflin, 1916.

Howells, William Dean. *Venetian Life.* Boston: Houghton Mifflin, 1907.

Hughes, Ted, ed. *A Choice of Emily Dickinson's Verse.* London: Faber and Faber, 1968.

James, Henry. *Italian Hours.* New York: Horizon, 1968.

———. *Letters.* Edited by Leon Edel. Cambridge, Mass.: Belknap Press, 1980.

———. *Partial Portraits.* Introduction by Leon Edel. Ann Arbor: Michigan University Press, 1970.

———. *William Wetmore Story and His Friends.* Boston: Houghton Mifflin, 1903.

Johnson, Thomas H. *Emily Dickinson: An Interpretive Biography.* Cambridge, Mass.: Belknap Press, 1955.

Joyce, James. *Letters.* Edited by Richard Ellmann. New York: Viking Press, 1966.

Kazin, Alfred. *New York Jew.* New York: Knopf, 1978.

Lasch, Christopher. *The New Radicalism in America, 1889–1963: The Intellectual as a Social Type.* New York: Knopf, 1965.

Lawrence, D. H. *The Complete Short Stories.* New York: Penguin, 1961.

———. *Letters, 1909–1930.* Edited by Aldous Huxley. Leipzig: Albatross, 1939.

———. *Phoenix: The Posthumous Papers of D. H. Lawrence*. Edited by Edward McDonald. New York: Viking, 1968.

———. *Studies in Classic American Literature*. New York: Penguin Books, 1977.

———. *Twilight in Italy*. New York: Viking Press, 1958.

Lueders, Edward. *Carl Van Vechten and the Twenties*. Albuquerque: University of New Mexico Press, 1955.

Luhan, Mabel Dodge. *Intimate Memories*. 4 vols. New York: Harcourt Brace, 1933–37.

———. *Lorenzo in Taos*. New York: Knopf, 1932.

———. *Winter in Taos*. New York: Harcourt, Brace, 1935.

MacLeish, Archibald. *Letters of Archibald MacLeish*. Boston: Houghton Mifflin, 1983.

Matthews, T. S. *Great Tom*. New York: Harper and Row, 1974.

Mellow, James. *Charmed Circle: Gertrude Stein and Company*. New York: Praeger, 1974.

Merrill, James. *A Different Person*. New York: Knopf, 1993.

Meyers, Jeffrey. *D. H. Lawrence and the Experience of Italy*. Philadelphia: University of Pennsylvania Press, 1990.

Mignani, Daniela. *The Medicean Villas by Giusto Utens*. Florence: Arnaud, 1991.

Miller, Betty Bergson. *Robert Browning: A Portrait*. London: J. Murray, 1952.

Miller, Edwin H. *Salem is My Dwelling Place*. Iowa City: University of Iowa Press, 1991.

Moorehead, Alan. *The Villa Diana*. New York: Scribner's, 1951.

Morse, John. *Life and Letters of Oliver W. Holmes*. Boston: Houghton Mifflin, 1896.

Ninfa: una citta, un giardino. Rome: Fondazione Camillo Caetani, 1990.

Origo, Benedetta. *La Foce: A Garden and Landscape in Tuscany*. Philadelphia: University of Pennsylvania Press, 2001.

Origo, Iris. *Images and Shadows: Part of a Life*. New York: Harcourt Brace Jovanovich, 1970.

———. *A Measure of Love*. London: Jonathan Cape, 1957.

———. *A Need to Testify*. London: John Murray, 1984.

———. *The Last Attachment: The Story of Byron and Teresa Guiccioli as Told in Their Unpublished Letters and Other Family Papers*. New York: Scribner, 1949.

————. *Leopardi*. Oxford: Oxford University Press, 1935.

————. *War in Val D'Orcia: An Italian War Diary, 1943–4*. London: John Murray, 1984.

————. "Marguerite Caetani." *Atlantic Monthly*, February, 1965.

————. *Un'Amica*. Florence: Passigli Editori, 1988.

————. "The Homecoming." *New Statesman and Nation*, Feb. 16, 1957.

————. "The Long Pilgrimage." *Cornhill Magazine*, spring, 1960.

Pattee, Fred Lewis. *Development of the American Short Story*. New York: Bilbo and Tannen, 1975.

Patterson, Rebecca. *The Riddle of Emily Dickinson*. Boston: Houghton Mifflin, 1951.

Prezzolini, Giuseppe. *Come gli americani scoprirono l'Italia*. Bologna: Massimiliano Boni editore, 1971.

Quaranta, Emanuela. "La Signora di Ninfa." *L'Illustrazione Italiana*, July, 1956.

Quest-Ritson, Charles. *The English Garden Abroad*. New York: Viking, 1992.

Quinn, Arthur Hobson. *American Fiction: An Historical and Critical Survey*. New York: Appleton, 1964.

Reich, Willi. "Sunny Isle." *Christian Science Monitor*, 1 July 1950.

Rennell Rodd, Sir James. *Social and Diplomatic Memories, 1902–1919*. London: Edward Arnold, 1925.

Rich, Adrienne. "Vesuvius at Home." In *On Lies, Secrets, and Silence: Selected Prose*. New York: Norton, 1979.

Richards, Laura. *Julia Ward Howe, 1819–1910*. Boston: Houghton Mifflin, 1916.

Roethke, Theodore. *Selected Letters*. Seattle: University of Washington Press, 1968.

Rudnick, Lois. *Mabel Dodge Luhan: New Woman, New Worlds*. Albuquerque: University of New Mexico Press, 1984.

Santayana, George. *Persons and Places*. New York: Scribner's, 1963.

Scott, Lady Sybil. *A Book of the Sea*. Oxford: Clarendon Press, 1918.

Secrest, Meryle. *Being B. B.: A Biography*. New York: Holt, Rinehart and Winston, 1979.

Sedgwick, Catharine Maria. *Letters from Abroad to Kindred at Home*. New York: Harper, 1841.

Sewall, Richard. *The Life of Emily Dickinson*. New York: Farrar, Straus, 1974.

Seymour, Miranda. *A Ring of Conspirators: Henry James and His Literary Circle.* Boston: Houghton Mifflin, 1988.

Simon, Linda. *The Biography of Alice B. Toklas.* Garden City, N.Y.: Doubleday, 1977.

Simpson, Jeffrey. "Historic Houses: Emily Dickinson." In *Architectural Digest*, July, 1992.

Skinner, Cornelia Otis. "A Brief Digest of the Intimate Memoirs of Mabel Fudge Hulan." In *Dithers and Jitters.* New York: Dodd, Mead, 1938.

Sontag, Susan. *The Volcano Lover.* Farrar, Straus, Giroux, 1991.

Staël, Germaine de. *Corinne, or Italy.* Translated by Avriel Goldberger. New Brunswick, N.J.: Rutgers University Press, 1987.

Stanley, Arthur. *Under Italian Skies.* London: Gollancz, 1950.

Stebbins, Theodore, et al. *The Lure of Italy: American Artists and the Italian Experience, 1760–1914.* H. N. Abrams, 1992.

Stedman, Edmund Clarence. Papers. Manuscript Collection Library, Columbia University, New York.

Stein, Gertrude. "Mabel Dodge at Villa Curonia." In *Portraits and Prayers.* New York: Random House, 1934.

———. *Autobiography of Alice B. Toklas.* New York: Vintage Books, 1961.

Stein, Leo. *Journeys into the Self.* New York: Crown, 1950.

Sterne, Maurice. *Shadow and Light.* New York: Harcourt Brace, 1965.

Stock, Noel. *Life of Ezra Pound.* New York: Pantheon, 1970.

Strouse, Jean. *Alice James: A Biography.* Boston: Houghton Mifflin, 1980.

Toklas, Alice B. *What is Remembered.* New York: Holt, Rinehart and Winston, 1963.

Torsney, Cheryl B. *Critical Essays on Constance Fenimore Woolson.* Thorndike, Maine: GK Hall, 1992.

Van Vechten, Carl. *Peter Whiffle.* New York: Modern Library, 1929.

———. *Sacred and Profane Memories.* New York: Knopf, 1932.

Vance, William. *American's Rome.* 2 vols. New Haven: Yale University Press, 1989.

Ward, Aileen. *John Keats: The Making of a Poet.* New York: Viking Press, 1963.

Watson, Steven. *Strange Bedfellows: The First American Avant-Garde.* New York: Abbeville Press, 1991.

Weimer, Joan Myers. "Woman Artists as Exile in the Fiction of Constance Fenimore Woolson," *Legacy* 3 (fall 1986).

Weiss, Philip "Beethoven's Hair Tells All!" *New York Times Magazine*, November 29, 1998.

Wharton, Edith. *A Backward Glance*. New York: Scribner, 1964.

Whitaker, John T. *We Cannot Escape History*. New York: Macmillan, 1943.

Wilde-Menozzi, Wallis. "Iris Origo," *Southwest Review* (fall 1990).

Woolf, Virginia. *The Diary of Virginia Woolf*. 5 vols. Edited by Anne Olivier Bell. New York: Harcourt Brace Jovanovich, 1977–84.

———. *Letters of Virginia Woolf*. Edited by Nigel Nicolson. New York: Harcourt Brace Jovanovich, 1975–80.

Woolson, Constance. *The Front Yard and Other Italian Stories*. Freeport, N.Y.: Books for Libraries Press, 1969.

Wright, Nathalia. *American Novelists in Italy*. Philadelphia: University of Pennsylvania Press, 1965.

Wynne, George. *Early Americans in Rome*. Rome: DARCO Press, 1966.

The Young Lady's Book: A Manual of Elegant Recreations, Exercises, and Pursuits. Edited by Abel Bowen. 7th ed. Boston: 1840.